The 758th Tank Battalion
in World War II

The 758th Tank Battalion in World War II

The U.S. Army's First All African American Tank Unit

JOE WILSON, JR.

Foreword by William Holley
Foreword by Matt Hewitt
Afterword by Joseph E. Wilson, Sr.

McFarland & Company, Inc., Publishers
Jefferson, North Carolina

Excerpts from *The Invisible Soldier* by Mary Penick Motley,
copyright © 1975, Wayne State University Press.
Used with permission of Wayne State University Press.

LIBRARY OF CONGRESS CATALOGUING-IN-PUBLICATION DATA

Names: Wilson, Joe, 1955– author.
Title: The 758th Tank Battalion in World War II : the U.S. Army's first all
African American tank unit / Joe Wilson, Jr. ; foreword by William Holley;
afterword by Joseph E. Wilson, Sr.
Other titles: U.S. Army's first all African American tank unit
Description: Jefferson, North Carolina : McFarland & Company, Inc.,
Publishers, 2018 | Includes bibliographical references and index.
Identifiers: LCCN 2017054088 | ISBN 9781476669991 (softcover : acid free paper) ∞
Subjects: LCSH: United States. Army. Tank Battalion, 758th
(1941–1945)—History. | United States. Army—African American troops—
History—20th century. | World War, 1939–1945—Campaigns—Italy. |
World War, 1939–1945—Tank warfare.
Classification: LCC D769.306 758th .W55 2018 | DDC 940.54/1273—dc23
LC record available at https://lccn.loc.gov/2017054088

BRITISH LIBRARY CATALOGUING DATA ARE AVAILABLE

ISBN (print) 978-1-4766-6999-1
ISBN (ebook) 978-1-4766-2944-5

Front cover photograph: Soldiers on a tank at Camp Claiborne, 1942
(National Archives and Records Administration); insignias, left to right:
Fifth Army, 92nd Infantry Division, 442nd Regimental Combat Team,
758th Tank Battalion, 758th Tank Battalion unit crest; back cover insignias,
left to right: 64th Tank Battalion, 3rd Infantry Division, 24th Infantry Division

Printed in the United States of America

*McFarland & Company, Inc., Publishers
Box 611, Jefferson, North Carolina 28640
www.mcfarlandpub.com*

Acknowledgments

This book would not have been possible without the cooperation and effort of the many dedicated people who contributed their hard-earned knowledge, precious photographs, and rare documents. Many have departed this world, leaving their stories and photographs behind. To those who contributed to this effort, I wish to express my sincere gratitude and acknowledge with great honor and respect for their endowment to future generations.

I make *no* apologies for any seeming inaccuracies in the combat stories! They are as the eyewitnesses told them and in the confusion and danger of battle, things happen for which there is no obvious explanation—"the fog of war."

As I reflect with pride on the research, planning, and actual writing of this book, my gratitude goes out to all who so willingly gave encouragement and inspiration. This will be a memory I'll forever cherish. I therefore hope that when you yourselves pick up this phenomenal book (because you made it this way) you know that I am saying a warm personal thanks to all of you. Over the years the notes for special mention grew and grew. I wanted to mention you all personally but the fear of leaving someone out and the volume of pages it would take prevented it. Please know that your kindness is etched in my heart and mind forever.

Thank you all.

Table of Contents

Foreword

by First Sergeant William Holley
(Field Artillery), USA (Ret.)

I have to give my friend Joe Wilson, Jr., a very hearty *"Well done!"* for including a part of the Combined Arms Team that I have not seen in any of the military history books, war movies, or plays about military events. The Combined Arms Team consists of Infantry, Armor, and Artillery. All too often when you read about a battle and its participants, that particular work centers on the Infantry or Armor. The third participant in those battles is the Field Artillery. No matter how well the battle is going or how fast the Infantry or Armor, or both, advance, they make it a point not to outrun their artillery support. Whenever the Infantry and Armor advance, their supporting artillery units advance as well. Many civilians believe that Field Artillery is way behind the lines. Not true! If the enemy breaks through the infantry, the next line they encounter is the supporting field artillery units.

During the Battle of the Bulge, the enemy broke through on a wide front. As a result of that breakthrough many field artillery units became the front line. Members of one of the field artillery units near Malmedy were murdered along with the infantrymen who were captured by the Germans.

To give you some idea of just how important artillery is, consider this: All infantry and armor regiments are commanded by a full colonel. The division artillery (DIVARTY) commander is a brigadier general. All major commands above division have their own artillery units that are used whenever the divisions have more artillery targets than they have artillery pieces to engage.

The missions of field artillery units are as follows:

- At division level each infantry/armor regiment has an artillery battalion that directly supports them in all of their operations. This mission is called direct support and it is assigned to the artillery unit by the DIVARTY commander.
- DIVARTY has an additional artillery battalion that backs up the direct support battalions, and its mission is direct support reinforcing.

- The artillery units located at corps level reinforce the units at division level, and their mission is general support of the corps and reinforcing the division artillery units of the division is assigned to the corps.
- Each corps is assigned to a field army and the field army has artillery units that back up the corps artillery units. Their unit mission is general support of the field army and ensures that there are enough artillery units available at all times to support the maneuver units (infantry/armor).
- Artillery units are never placed in reserve. Whenever an infantry or armor unit goes into reserve, their supporting artillery unit is usually given the mission of direct support reinforcing until their regular unit goes back into action.

This book on the 758th Tank Battalion (an all-black unit, as was the 92nd Infantry Division) discusses the use of artillery during the period it was attached to the U.S. 92nd Infantry Division in Italy during World War II. This unit was the first of three "Negro" (colored) armored units activated and shipped overseas to Europe and Italy. The 758th Tank Battalion was attached to the 92nd Infantry Division. This was the only all-black division that remained intact after it arrived in the theater.

Prejudice and racial stereotyping was the order of the day in this division from the top down. Although the racial policy totally demoralized the men of the 758th Tank Battalion, the unit performed its assigned missions in an outstanding manner. The 758th's Assault Gun Platoon provided support to the famous 100th Infantry Battalion of the 442nd Regimental Combat Team (Nisei) in its push on Mt. Belvedere near Seravezza.

On April 5, 1945, elements of the 758th Tank Battalion supported the 370th Infantry Regiment for its final offensive action in Italy. They advanced north to take the mountain town of Massa. Stiff enemy resistance and mountainous terrain slowed the pace. After several weeks of fighting, the regiment reached its objective.

During World War II the United States had two million Negro troops under arms, and thanks to authors like Joe Wilson their story is being told. There were many other Negro combat units activated during the war. A good

First Sergeant William Holley, USA (Ret).

2

number of those units were deactivated when they arrived overseas and their personnel were converted to service troops and assigned to transportation and quartermaster units. There was a large number of "Negro" field artillery units activated and shipped overseas as well but these units remained intact and provided support to white combat units. At the end of the war the "Negro" units were deactivated while they were still overseas and their personnel returned to the States as individual soldiers. The white units remained intact and returned to the States to participate in victory parades down Broadway in New York City.

In my case, I'm an artilleryman who was qualified in cannons as well as rockets and missiles. I worked with cannons in Vietnam and free-flight rockets in other artillery units.

Foreword

by Captain Matt Hewett (Armor Branch), USA (Ret.)

I was once a soldier.

While stationed in Germany in the early 1980s never did I see the overt racism that existed in the 1940s. That's not to say it did not exist, but much progress had been made by the time I served. In my days, we said that there was no black or white. We felt we all bled army green. In combat arms, as a Tanker, you have to trust those on your left and right. In the tight confines of a tank, there is no room for anything but teamwork and trust. I knew vaguely of the 1st Battalion, 64th Armor Regiment history, that our unit had descended from a black unit in World War II, but had no idea of the full story behind those names and unit identifications.

This book is the third of Joe Wilson's works on the three black tank battalions of World War II. An Army brat, Joe's dad served with distinction, duly noted in *761st "Black Panther" Tank Battalion in World War II*, continued with the *784th Tank Battalion in World War II* and now the *758th Battalion in World War II*. The experiences of all three units were similar, but each unit fully earned its own book. All are rich in details provided by years of research—literally spanning almost two full decades, four times the duration of the war itself. Because black units were so poorly covered by the press, achievements overlooked by white officers, the records have been lost, scattered and in some cases, destroyed. Many historians who had access to far more material have done less than Joe. But with patience, diligence, assistance from the veterans themselves, these three books are a much needed addition to the history of the U.S. Army in general, and the Armor forces in particular.

It is essential to remember these heroes to give us the courage to carry on in the never ending fight for freedom, for liberty, for civil rights and equality. It is essential to remember these heroes and what they learned the hard way, that freedom is never free. It must be fought for, not only in times of war, but in times of peace. Not only in times of hardship, but in times of prosperity. They continued the struggle for freedom long after the war was officially over. But there is never true peace or prosperity when there remains hunger, a lack of opportunity or a lack of hope.

These men trained hard, because an ounce of sweat in training prevents a gallon of blood in battle. They learned to trust each other and be alert at all times, for the cost of failure meant the loss of a brother. It is incumbent upon all of us to continue that same sense of vigilance, of diligence and activism to fight the never ending presence of evil. It was evil that began World War II. We won that war, but have we remembered the lessons? That evil never is truly defeated? It can be beaten down, but it always lurks in the shadows, ready to emerge when it can. Evil has many shapes, wears many uniforms—Nazi, Imperial Japanese, or KKK hoods and robes.

We can never cease to be vigilant against racism and hatred, for they always look for opportunities to strike. It's up to us to follow in the footsteps of the men of the 761st, the 784th and 758th Tank Battalions who fought and died for us. It's up to us to do as they did, fight for a better nation, fight for a better future, to fight for our children. They did what all great leaders do—they set the example, faced their fears, went forward one step at a time to accomplish what no one thought they could do. Except, of course themselves. For they knew what they could do, they trusted in each other. It's up to us now to carry that forward. To do any less would dishonor these brave souls.

It has been a honor and privilege to meet Joe Wilson, Jr., to learn from him, to read about these men in his books. His efforts have spanned many years, taken him all over the country and are reflected in the moving tribute to the black warriors of the independent tank battalions. His own service in the 82nd Airborne Division gives him a soldier's perspective on the sacrifices of those who serve. The 758th tank Battalion was later redesignated the 64th Armored Regiment, the unit insignia a black elephant against a white shield. "The Tuskers" have changed unit designations a few times in their history, but I have a much greater affection and respect for the 1/64 Armor insignia I proudly wore.

The 758th origins are well told here. The unit history continued into the Cold War and beyond, but those are stories for another book, another time. It is with great pride to be part of that lineage and privilege to be allowed to make a contribution towards Joe's efforts.

We Pierce!

Preface

In 1941 the U.S. Army activated the 758th Tank Battalion, the first all-black tank battalion. This took years of protests and a lot of political clout to bring about because African Americans had to fight for the right to fight. Segregation and discrimination had reached critical levels, and the *Pittsburgh Courier* called for the "Double V Campaign," which appealed for victory abroad against the forces of global domination and victory at home against racism.

Two other all-black tank battalions joined the 5th Tank Group: the 761st in 1942 and the 784th in 1943. The 758th fought the Nazis and the Fascists in northern Italy from the beautiful beaches of the Ligurian Sea through the Po Valley and up into the rugged Apennine Mountains. They breached the Gothic Line with the 92nd "Buffalo" Infantry Division. After the war they deactivated, but unlike their sister battalions—the 761st and the 784th—they were reborn in the 64th Tank Battalion, keeping their distinguished unit insignia, a black rampant elephant head with white tusks and the scrolled motto of "We Pierce." Again reborn, this time as the 64th Armored Regiment, they comprised four separate battalions—the 1/64th, 2/64th, 3/64th, and 4/64th. The ancestral 758th Tank Battalion established in 1941 began with the rudimentary Stuart light tank and advanced to the Sherman medium tank, the Pershing medium/heavy tank, and then the Patton main battle tank. The battalion now operates the ultra-modern Abrams main battle tank. Over the unit's existence it has gone from the meek 37-millimeter cannon to a technically advanced 120-millimeter main gun augmented by a thermal viewer, an inter-vehicle tracker, a guided missile system, and other high-tech devices.

This unit fought racial discrimination up until it became integrated in 1953. Although discrimination continued after that at the individual level, the unit overcame it. It is ironic that these men entered the Korean War to fight for democracy as a segregated unit. However, they returned to the United States fully integrated.

1

The Shadow of Coming War

The aftermath of World War I combined with the Great Depression destroyed the fragile German economy and democratic government. In 1933 Adolf Hitler took power with his National Socialist German Workers Party (Nazi), a racist, right-wing, nationalistic, anti-democratic, and anti–Semitic mass movement. The Nazis immediately strengthened Germany's armed forces and sought to overturn the Versailles Treaty, recover German territory lost in peace settlements, and "liberate" German-speaking minorities from surrounding countries. This set the stage for Germany's second attempt at world conquest. Hitler assumed dictatorial powers and proclaimed the Third Reich—the third German empire. In respect to the first empire, *Heiliges Römisches Reich* (962–1806), and the second empire, *Deutsches Reich* (1871–1918), Hitler proclaimed a thousand-year empire and gained popular support.

In Hitler's autobiography, *Mein Kampf* (My Struggle), first published in 1925, he outlined his political ideology and future plans for Germany, akin to America's Manifest Destiny. He clearly intended to invade the Soviet Union, asserting that the German people needed *Lebensraum* (living space). He viewed the Soviet Union and East European people as *Untermenschen* (subhumans) ruled by conspiring Jews. Accordingly, he would liquidate, deport, or enslave the non–Aryan populations and repopulate the land with the Nordic "master race" of German people. Hitler relied on diplomatic bluff to overcome any German shortcomings. He shrewdly secured triumphs without war and in 1935 fiddled the confidence of Italian Fascist dictator Benito Mussolini into a Rome-Berlin alliance (the Axis Powers).

Meanwhile, in the Far East, the island nation of Japan—Asia's only industrial power—longed for the expansive lands and natural resources of China and Southeast Asia. Japan's sense of entitlement rested in their religious, self-righteous uniqueness as an emperor nation of *shinsei* (divine nature) and their industrial superpower status. In 1931, Japan invaded Manchuria and established a puppet government and in 1936 established a similar puppet government in Mongolia. In 1937 Japan invaded China, launching a conflict against Mao Zedong's Communists and Chiang Kai-shek's Nationalists, who were already engaged in a civil war. Japanese atrocities, known as the Asian Holocaust, took place in Asian and Pacific countries during their occupation.

Then on September 27, 1940, Japan signed a pact with Nazi Germany and Fascist Italy and joined the Axis powers.

The United States, which was in the midst of the Great Depression, remained largely indifferent to the international crisis. Isolationist views in Congress led to the Neutrality Act of 1937 which made it unlawful to trade with belligerent nations. America's policy focused on continental security, the navy being the first line of defense, followed by powerful coastal defense batteries. This allowed the underfunded army populated with hard-nosed, long-serving "lifers" to begin mobilizing for war. Innovative thinking and preparation took place in this intra-war period. Experiments with armored and mechanized vehicles, air-ground coordination, and aerial transport of troops took place despite limited resources. The army developed an interest in amphibious warfare and related techniques being pioneered by the Marine Corps. The signal corps became a leader in radio communications, and American artillery developed sophisticated fire direction and control techniques. Additionally, war plans for various contingencies had been drawn up including industrial and manpower mobilization plans. Colonel George C. Marshall, assistant commandant of the Infantry School, groomed a number of young officers, reflective of himself, for leadership positions.

On March 12, 1938, German troops marched into Austria and brought it into the Third Reich. Then Hitler announced that the "oppression" of ethnic Germans living in Czechoslovakia would no longer be tolerated. England and France met with Hitler, formed the Munich Pact and compelled Czechoslovakia to relinquish its border regions to Germany to secure "peace in our time." It seemed as if Hitler had signed the Munich Pact in disappearing ink, because in March 1939 he seized the rest of Czechoslovakia. From there he turned his attention to Poland. Hitler and Soviet dictator Josef Stalin signed a secret mutual nonaggression pact in August 1939. Then German forces overran western Poland while Soviet troops entered from the east on September 1, 1939. World War II began in earnest.

The years between World War I and World War II ushered in the broadened use of tanks. Military commanders such as Britain's Sir Basil Hart and Sir J.F.C. Fuller, France's Charles de Gaulle, the United States' George Patton, and Germany's Oswald Lutz and Heinz Guderian advocated the use and development of armored warfare. They believed armored vehicles held the key to breaking the trench warfare stalemates experienced in World War I. However, the Germans took this farther with their *blitzkrieg*, amassing tanks in division-size units, with infantry, artillery, engineers, and other supporting units, all of them advancing in unison.

In April 1940 the German blitzkrieg struck Norway and Denmark and then in May Germany invaded the Netherlands, Belgium, and Luxembourg. Late in the same month they circumvented the Maginot Line and entered France. Their columns blitzed to the English Channel, cutting off British and French troops in northern France and Belgium. The French army, plagued by low morale and a divided command, fell apart. British troops escaped only with their lives during their evacuation at Dunkirk and left most of their equipment behind. The Germans captured Paris on

June 14 and the politically divided French government importuned the Nazis for an armistice. The success of the German blitzkrieg forced the rest of the world to rethink their doctrine and restructure their armies.

While the Nazis occupied northern France and established a pro–Nazi puppet government in the south, Hitler turned the planes of his *Luftwaffe* against British airfields and cities to pave a way for invasion. From July to October 1940, while German landing barges and invasion forces waited on the Channel, the Royal Air Force, greatly outnumbered, drove the Luftwaffe from the daytime skies. At sea the British navy, with increasing American cooperation, fought desperately to keep the English Channel closed and the North Atlantic open. Britain's determination forced Hitler to abandon his plans to invade England.

In February 1941, Hitler sent troops to North Africa and the Balkans and routed the British in Greece. German paratroopers seized the island of Crete. Then in June, against the advice of his generals, Hitler turned against his supposed ally, the Soviet Union. Operation Barbarossa, launched on an 1,800-mile front from the Arctic Circle to the Black Sea, blitzed deep into the Soviet Union. This operation would fulfill Hitler's ideological aspiration to conquer Soviet territory as outlined in *Mein Kampf*. Suffering tremendous losses, Soviet forces withdrew deep into their expansive land. The Nazis expected a quick victory but the severe winter weather stopped them thirty miles outside of Moscow.

The Germans withstood winter counterattacks and resumed their offensive the following spring. The Soviets faced the bulk of the German forces and casualties ran into the millions. The Nazis committed wholesale atrocities—mistreatment of prisoners, enslavement of civilians, and, in the case of Jews and undesirable races, outright genocide. German troops were deeply indoctrinated with racist ideology. Nazi propaganda portrayed their war against the Soviet Union as being twofold, first as an ideological war between German National Socialism and Jewish Bolshevism and second as a race war between the Nordic Aryans and the *Untermenschen*. Not to be outdone in atrocities, the Soviets carried out mass summary executions of prisoners and civilians.

In the United States preparations for war moved slowly, as the army remained hard pressed to carry out its mission of defending the continental United States. George C. Marshall, now a general, took over as chief of staff in 1939. President Franklin D. Roosevelt (FDR) launched a limited preparedness campaign, and military leaders drafted new war plans. The focus of military policy changed from continental to hemispheric defense. With the outbreak of war in Europe and Asia, FDR had proclaimed a limited national emergency and authorized increased military spending. Congress amended the Neutrality Act to permit munitions sales to the French and British. The army concentrated on equipping its forces and in 1940 held the first army and corps-size maneuvers. Lieutenant General Lesley J. McNair, chief of the Army Ground Forces and an ardent advocate of mobile warfare, pushed the development of armored and airborne divisions. He directed the restructuring of existing organizations, from the World War I "square" division based on four infantry regiments into a lighter, more maneuverable "triangular" division with three infantry regiments.

The rapid defeat of France, with Britain on the brink of collapse, dramatically accelerated defense preparations. Congress repealed some provisions of the Neutrality Act and passed the Lend-Lease Act, which gave FDR authority to sell, transfer, or lease war goods to countries whose defense he deemed vital to the defense of the United States. FDR proclaimed the United States as the "Arsenal of Democracy." A few weeks later Congress passed the Selective Service and Training Act, establishing the draft.

On December 7, 1941, while German armies froze before Moscow, Japan suddenly attacked United States Armed Forces in the Pacific and forced a stunned America into the deadliest war known to history. The December 7 bolt-from-the-blue attack on Pearl Harbor is burned into the American consciousness. But just hours after that early-morning attack, across the international dateline, thus making it December 8, Japanese planes bombed American bases and the city of Manila in the Philippines. Days later, in keeping with the Axis pact, Hitler declared war against the United States.

Early in 1942 British and American leaders recommitted to their priority of the European Theater. The British preferred to strike the Nazis in the Mediterranean, acknowledging the eventual necessity to invade France. Prime Minister Winston Churchill suggested an Anglo-American landing in North Africa to bring the French Foreign Legions into the war against the Italians. FDR directed General Marshall to plan and carry out an amphibious landing on the coast of North Africa before the end of 1942. General Marshall selected Lieutenant General Dwight D. Eisenhower (Ike) to command the North African invasion. While Ike monitored operations from Gibraltar, American forces convoyed from the United States to the coast of French Morocco. Due to France's military disorder, confusion took over and the French Foreign Legionnaires fought against Allied forces. Negotiations soon led to a ceasefire, and the French Legionnaires joined the Allied forces.

The Allies secured a stronghold in Morocco and Algeria as their troops reached strategic positions in neighboring Tunisia, while the German and Italian Forces reeled back to Libya. Cognizant to this threat, the Germans deployed troops into Tunisia by air and sea, brushing aside weak French forces there. Axis air power based in Sicily, Sardinia, and Italy pounded the advancing Allied columns before torrential rains turned the countryside into a quagmire that resulted in a stalemate. As the weather cleared, the U.S. II Corps, commanded by Major General George Smith Patton, Jr., attacked in coordination with Britain's Field Marshall Montgomery. They squeezed Axis forces into Tunisia as British armored units entered Tunis. Days later the last Axis Powers in Africa capitulated.

The next objective was Sicily. This Allied invasion, code named Operation Husky, consisted of a large-scale amphibious and airborne assault. The Sicilian Campaign, launched on the night of July 9, 1943, ended on August 17. Strategically, Operation Husky drove Axis air, land, and naval forces from the island and opened the Mediterranean Sea lanes, thus clearing the way for the invasion of Italy. As a result, Italian dictator Benito Mussolini (*Il Duce*) fell from power. On July 25, 1943, Il Duce was voted out of power by his own Grand Council and arrested upon leaving a meeting with King Vittorio Emanuele, who told him the war was lost. The Italian government held Mussolini captive at the Campo Imperatore Hotel, a resort high in the Apennine Mountains. The Germans intercepted messages and determined his location, then Hitler personally ordered an airborne operation to rescue his friend.

On September 12, 1943, Lieutenant Colonel Otto Skorzeny, with his elite team of twenty-six *Waffen* SS commandos, accompanied by eighty-two *Fallschirmjagers,* landed on the mountain peak in a dozen gliders. They caught the well-armed carabinieri (military police) off guard. General Fernando Soleti of the carabinieri, who flew with this mission, ordered them to stand down or be executed for treason. Skorzeny formally greeted Mussolini: "Duce, the Führer has sent me to set you free!" Mussolini replied, "I knew that my friend would not forsake me!"[1]

This high-risk operation provided a rare propaganda opportunity that the Germans and Fascist Italians took full advantage of. Mussolini was made leader of the Italian Social Republic, the German puppet government in the German-occupied section of Italy. At this news, the Germans swiftly disarmed the Italian army and took over its defensive positions. A British fleet sailed into Taranto Harbor and disembarked troops, and the U.S. Fifth Army landed on the beaches near Salerno on September 9, 1943. Counterattacks by German armor threatened the beaches, but on September 16 American and British forces linked up. Two weeks later American troops entered Naples, the largest Italian city south of Rome. Allied plans called for a continued advance to tie down German troops and prevent their transfer to France or the Russian Front. As the Allies advanced up the mountainous terrain, they confronted a series of heavily fortified defensive positions. This, coupled with delaying tactics, made the campaign in Italy one endless siege. The brilliant tactics employed by the German commander in Italy, Field Marshal Albert Kesselring, exacted a high price for every Allied advance.

In October 1943, moving north from Naples, the Allies forced a crossing of the Volturno River and advanced to the Winter Line, a defensive position along the mountains near Casino. Repeated attempts over the next six months failed to breech it. In January 1944 an amphibious assault at Anzio failed to outflank it. Kesselring had time to call in reserves, including artillery that brought Allied-held ground under intense bombardment. The Allies dug in and their advance turned into another siege.

Meanwhile, an attempt to cross the Rapido River, timed to coincide with the Anzio landing, became a "murderous blunder."[2] In a diversionary attack, these men followed orders and attempted the impossible. Less than half of them returned; the rest were killed, captured, wounded, or missing in action. "There were bodies everywhere, mostly parts, arms, legs, some decapitated, bodies with hardly any clothes left on.... And there was always that spine-chilling cry for 'medic.' But there weren't any left," remembered Private First Class Bill Hartung of the 36th Infantry Division.[3] Sergeant Billy Kirby, 36th Infantry Division, recalled, "[B]oats [were] being hit all around me and guys [were] falling out and swimming. I never knew whether they made it or not. I had never seen so many bodies of our own guys. Just about everybody was hit.

I didn't have a single good friend who wasn't killed or wounded."[4] And Captain Zerk Robertson, 36th Infantry Division, said, "I had 184 men.... [F]orty-eight hours later, I had 17. If that's not mass murder, I don't know what is."[5]

Lieutenant General Mark Clark, the commander of the U.S. Fifth Army, with disregard for the intelligence provided, had arrogantly ordered the attack in the face of objections by subordinate staff officers. Despite this blunder, Clark received a promotion to four-star general and became commander of all Allied Ground Forces in Italy, which were renamed the 15th Army Group. Following the war, the incompetent Clark escaped accountability with the help of cronies. He dodged the congressional hearing in 1946 in which survivors of the 36th Infantry Division testified and urged Congress to correct a military system riddled with cronyism that elevated the inept Clark and other "good-ole-boys" to high leadership positions. Nevertheless, the secretary of war publicly exonerated Clark of all culpability, concluding that the river crossing, "was a necessary one and General Clark exercised sound judgment in planning and in ordering it."

Meanwhile, Allied efforts to blast a path through the Italian Winter Line mountain defenses seemed pointless until the constant air bombardment took its toll. In May 1944 a succession of coordinated attacks by the U.S. Fifth Army and British Eighth Army finally forced the Germans to retreat to another defensive line. Then, on June 4, 1944, two days prior to the D-Day invasion of Normandy, France, the Allied forces entered Rome. The D-Day invasion rendered the Italian campaign a secondary theater but the intense fighting continued. In August the Allies smacked into another defensive line—the Gothic Line in the northern Apennine Mountains. This became another siege, as appreciable headway could not be made.

The 92nd Infantry Division landed piecemeal in Italy between August and November 1944, the 758th Tank Battalion arriving in December. Rumors in Naples of the arrival of the Buffalo Division preceded them. As thousands of black soldiers disembarked from the crowded troopships they presented an awe-inspiring scene. Armed with basic infantry weapons and full field packs, wearing the circular buffalo shoulder patch, they fell sharply into unit formations. As they turned and moved away, every man in step to the soulful cadence, they marched to a rumble. Then a low chatter from the spectators broke out into cheers that lasted until the last Buffalo infantrymen marched out of visual range.

2

The Double V Campaign

Only by confronting the racist reality on the home front can we truly begin to understand what the black soldier experienced in World War II. What you've started to read may be disturbing. The personal accounts and images ahead will allow you to go through a portion of what these gallant soldiers of color experienced at home and abroad. The racist doctrine of "separate but equal" became official law in 1896. The United States Supreme Court ruled in *Plessey vs. Ferguson*, a landmark decision that upheld the constitutionality of state segregation laws. This remained customary doctrine until its repudiation in 1954 by the Supreme Court's *Brown vs. Board of Education* majority ruling.

The Wall Street crash of 1929 triggered the Great Depression. The initial crash occurred over several days—"Black Thursday," "Black Monday," and "Black Tuesday," with Tuesday being the most devastating—and set off a wave of suicides in the financial districts. The exact causes of the Great Depression are widely contended. Some debated sources include overproduction, weak banking, over-financing, Prohibition, and the government's hands-off approach to the economy. Clearly these and other, lesser-known, causes combined to contribute to it.

Many homeless men and women rode railcars as hobos, and a large number were killed or injured jumping trains. Among the riders were the future Supreme Court justice William O. Douglas (1898–1980), renowned writer Louis L'Amour (1908–1988), and famous folk singer Woody Guthrie (1912–1967). The problems of the Great Depression affected all Americans. No group was harder hit than African Americans. By 1932, approximately half of all African Americans were out of work. In the North, whites called for blacks to be fired from jobs as long as there were whites out of work. In the South, racial violence escalated, with a sharp increase in lynching. Although most African Americans traditionally voted Republican, the election of President Franklin D. Roosevelt (FDR) began to change voting patterns. FDR entertained African American visitors at the White House and had a number of black advisers. Many African Americans felt a sense of belonging and excitement over FDR's approach to change and direct engagement of Great Depression issues.

Three young African American men from Chicago, Willie Topps, Thomas "Tee

Jay" Mann, and John Weston, entered the military around the same time. Willie Topps came of age during the Great Depression and tells his story as follows:

I was born in 1919. The Great Depression came in 1929. I was living out in the country then. My father had been gored by a bull and he was pretty much helpless. He lived with my aunt and he gave us children to her to manage. I was the baby of the family. There were three other boys and me and one sister. Well you heard that saying, "mean as a junkyard dog?" That's what my aunt was! If anyone saw me do something, no matter how minor, they told her and she would promise me a whipping. Well, on Saturday night when things quieted down and nobody was going to the field the next day, it was whipping time. I would get into that old galvanized tub and get me a bath and I would go to bed and be just as quiet as a mouse in a cheese factory hoping that she would forget but she never did. And by the time I would think she forgot she would call my name: "You, Willie! Come here, boy!" She had us to bring her the switch earlier in the day. And she always had to have 3 that she would braid like a woman braids her hair. Her favorite was a peach tree switch. Those didn't break, they wrapped around you. She would say, "Pull those rags off, boy. I bought you those." Then she said, "Sister so-and-so said she saw you doing so-and-so." Then she would take a sip of coffee before giving me eight or ten licks. Then she would go to the next thing she said someone told her I did. By the time she finished I had a darn good whipping. That was the reason, when I became 14 years old, I ran away.

I rode the Southern Pacific Railroad. My first stop was Tyler, Texas, and the next stop was Yuma, Arizona. There I dug sugar beets and stayed there about 3 weeks. Then I moved on to California where I picked oranges, lemons, and grapes. We only made about 25 to 50 cents a day. If you got 50 cents, you had a full day's pay.

We hoboed, rode the freight trains. Back then the firemen carried something like a pick handle and the conductor on the crate stand carried a rifle. And we would be in the car and one would be coming from the front and the other from the rear. And we had to put that freight down no matter how fast it was going—jump. They would wait until they got into Texas where they had a lot of prickly pears—cactus. And we put that freight train down and had to jump sometimes 50–60 feet into prickly pear thorns. We had to pick them out and would be as sore as you could be. Then we would run over to the hobo jungle. It would be under a bridge and we all gathered there. They were mostly white but they had one or two of us among the group. Everything we had we shared. Sometimes someone brought a pie or cake that they stole from someone's window, corn stolen from someone's field, maybe even a pig stolen from someone's barnyard. We killed, dressed, and cooked it. We had our coffee, sardine cans, whatever you had. After the food was done, everyone would share it. We didn't go hungry.

Then we left that hobo jungle and caught the next train coming through. We tried to catch them at an incline where they slowed down enough for you to catch on to the boxcar. This train hauled vegetables, fruits, and so forth and had ice. So at one end of the boxcar it was cool and comfortable. There I made the mistake of going to sleep in Mississippi not far from Greenwood. The sheriff caught me that night and locked me up. The next day, this guy named Douglas Walker, he had a big plantation, he came to get me. I was to work my fine off for riding the freight train. He introduced me to all of his family. He had two boys and two girls. One boy was named Elmer and the other Douglas after him. One of the girls was named Elizabeth after her mother and the other was named Dorothy. After the introduction he said, "Now, I whip all my Nigger's asses to let them know who is the boss. So you come with me to the lot. You clean out the lot. Clean out the stalls. You clean out the troughs and put in fresh feed and water in them. Put down hay and everything so that when field hands come in all they had to do was turn the mules loose and everything would be ready for them." So that was supposed to be my job.

So that evening he said, "You are going to live with my foreman. He will look after you. His name is Lee." He was a tall black guy, about 6 foot, 3 inches, heavy set. So that evening

Douglas Walker went with me and showed me what I had to do down at the lot. He said, "Now, I whip my nigger's ass." When I turned, he had this whip in his hands and I had that pitchfork in mine because I had already started cleaning out the stalls. So I told him that if he draws that whip to hit me, I will put this fork through him. He turned blood red and looked at me. He had false teeth. He clicked his old teeth and pulled his britches up and he went home.

So later on when the field hands came in around five o'clock in the evening, Lee says to me, "You new, boy?" I said, "Yes, sir!" He said, "My name is Lee. I am the foreman. And you will stay in my home. So put down everything, you come with me." His wife had cooked dinner. He had two children, a boy and a girl. After dinner we went out on the porch, he and I. Back then they had those old shotgun houses. You go to the front and you can look clear out to the back. While sitting on the front stoop, he says to me, "Boy! Mr. Walker's going to kill you." "Why?" "Didn't you threaten him?" I said, "He threatened to whip me with a whip and I told him I wasn't taking anymore whippings. I had been whipped enough by my aunt." Then Lee said, "Boy! He's going to kill you." That's when I got up off of that stoop, walked through the house, down the back steps, and down through the cotton fields. They haven't seen me from that day since.

From there I went through Greenwood, the same town I had been taken in. I walked through it and caught a train the next day. It made every stop. It was a passenger train. I was riding what we called the blinds—on a passenger train it was between the cars. It has a bellows that opens and closes like an accordion. So this elderly lady came through and she called me: "Boy! You are going to get killed out there. You come with me." She had a bunch of children, six or seven. Between the two seats back then they could be folded together to form something like a wigwam. She took her bags out from under there and put me in there and put bags in front of me. And the other bags, she must have put them on top. That's the way I came into Chicago.

When the train stopped at the 11th Street Station she called me out of there and I went out with them. At the station I saw a black guy cleaning up around 11th Street. I said, "Sir?" He said, "Yes!" I asked, "Where do black people live around here?" He said, "Go west of here to State Street. When you leave the station go straight—don't turn. Wabash and State are the streets where we live." So when I got to Wabash, I turned south because I asked another man where we live around here. He said, "Well, we live around here and on out up until you get to 63rd Street." So I ended up on 28th Street and Wabash.

Well, I'm standing and a man on a chart with a wagon, he had ice and he had coal on it. I said, "Sir?" He said, "Yeah, boy." I asked if he needed help and he said, "Yes." And I said, "Thank you!" I worked with him that day and at the end of that day he gave me a quarter. He said, "Now there's a restaurant across the street."

The first meal I had was sauerkraut, pigs feet, and corn bread. That was 15 cents for dinner. I worked with that gentleman for about three weeks. Each evening after working with him I searched the telephone books for the bureau of vital statistics. When I finally found my brother I called. They said they had a Clyde Topps registered at 4511 Vincents Avenue. So they gave me the telephone number and I called. His wife answered and asked, "Who is this?" I said, "This is Willie Topps, Clyde's brother." She said, "Where are you?" I told her and she said, "Stay there and I will be right there." She got into a jitney and came to pick me up and took me out and I met my brother for the first time. He was the oldest boy.

I roomed with him and I had to pay him rent. I got a job, but the first job I got I had to buy. It cost me $18.50. So once you finished paying that $18.50 off, they usually lay you off. I think I worked there four or five weeks. We rode a bicycle making deliveries. One boy rode the bike for twelve hours and I rode for twelve hours. The boss called me in about the 3rd or 4th day. He said, "Willie." I said, "Yes Sir!" His name was Kurtz. He said, "If you turn your money in from your bottle deposits to me, come the end of the week, I will pay you and you will have a bigger check." Well I was only making $3.50 per week so I said, "Yes Sir!" So that's what I did, I turned my money in to him. Well, come that Saturday, I got the $3.50.

17

Come the next week, I got the same thing. Come the next Saturday, I got $3.50. So from that point on, when someone gave me a bottle, I took it and separated it from the house bottles. Back then you got two cents for a Coke bottle, a Pepsi bottle. The quart bottle you got a nickel. The half-gallon bottle you got a dime. So that's what I did, I kept that money separate. So at the end of the day I turned in the house bottles. That went on for about a month. Then he had me arrested! He said I was stealing his money. So I went to court and right around from the courthouse on 46th and Indiana, was a youth advocate. She came to my trial. When I told the judge what had happened, the judge told this Jew, "I should sentence you if you do that boy like that again!" The judge then told me to go on about my business. So I left and naturally I had no job anymore.

The next job I got was at a lead foundry. My brother worked on the other side of the railroad tracks on 59th Street. He worked in a blue stone factory. He came by one Saturday and said, "Bill. Billy Boy. Let's go fishing tomorrow." I said, "I'm sorry, I have to clean the flues tomorrow." He said, "You've been cleaning the flues ever since you've been there. Boy, you will get lead poisoning!" I said, "Well, I committed myself and I've got to do it! I've got to be a man of my word." So I worked that Saturday and again the next weekend. And then the next Saturday, he had my name on the board again. So then the foreman called me. He said, "Willie?" I said, "Yes, sir!" He said, "You will work again tomorrow." I asked, "What will I do?" He said, "Clean the flues." I said, "No, I won't. I've been cleaning the flues ever since I've been here. And I am quite sure you have more men than just me. I know I need a job bad but I am not taking a chance on getting lead poisoning." He said, "If you don't clean the flues you got no job." I left there.

That following Monday I spoke to a gentleman who lived near me. He was the son of an undertaker. He says, "Topps! Go out to the stockyard and they will possibly put you on if they need any help. When you go, take your work clothes." So I thanked him and went there. It was something like a big coliseum, men waiting there to be called. The foreman came through and he picked out five of us. He said, "You, you, you, you! Do you want to work? Come with me." So I grabbed my bag and went on and worked that day. He assigned me to a job beef lugging. It was the hindquarter or forequarter of the cow or bull. It weighed about 170 pounds if it's the hindquarter and about 230 pounds if it's the forequarter. That's what I had to carry. I was about 5 foot 8 and I weighed about 175 pounds. I worked with a crew of five and we would rotate, every man would get a chance to hook and unhook and every man would carry. We didn't have a union then, what we did was piecework. We got paid approximately 42 cents per hour. The first week I worked there I came out with 32 dollars and I thought I was a millionaire. I worked there until I went into the army. I lived like a king. I went downtown Chicago and got me a Kuppenheimer suit, a Chesterfield overcoat, Netherton shoes, Arrow Point shirt and tie, Stetson hat. Oh, I was sharp! I would go out on the town. At that time I was solo. I didn't know a damned thing about courting. I went to the Regal to see either Duke Ellington or Count Basie, I don't exactly remember. Two young ladies were sitting down in the front and I sat right by them. And about half way through the performance, I asked if I could take them home. And they said, "Oh, yes!" Well I didn't know where they lived. I lived on the south side and they lived on the west side. Well, the west-side black people didn't get along with the south-side black people. But I didn't know that. So I am sharp, I go there to see them home, and I'm getting out. I'm going to catch the streetcar back when a little gang over there saw me. They said, "There is a south side nigger! Let's go get him." They took off after me and I outran the streetcar and caught another one. I didn't go back to the west side until I left the service.

Those were the days I tell you, good ole days. They were ruff, no ifs and or buts about it. I had finished high school according to the South. Black people, when you got a 12th grade education, you can file for a teaching position. I had finished 9th grade and I was considered a high school graduate. I went to Du Sable High School that had just opened in Chicago. I went for one semester. In the army I got my GED and with that I was issued a high school diploma from Du Sable.[1]

The second young man from Chicago, T.J. Mann, graduated from Wendell Phillips High School in 1938. He attended Southern University in Baton Rouge, Louisiana, before family finances ran out. "I never had a real job," he said. "I worked at a theater as a doorman and in the summer as a lifeguard at Chicago Lake. I didn't want to go into the army. They drafted me and I had to go. I was inducted in 1941 and went up to Fort Custer, Michigan, all of us from the northern areas. The ninety of us, after we took the exam, they picked top guys. We left Fort Custer and went to Fort Knox, Kentucky. When we got there we were told that we would be a part of a black tank outfit, a new unit. We formed the 758th Tank Battalion."[2]

The third young man from Chicago, John Weston, recalls the following: "I went to Willard Grammar School and graduated from Hyde Park High in Chicago. Then I knocked around with different jobs and things before I got called in on the first draft in 1940. I finished my eighteen-month training and I was supposed to come home in 1941. This was right before Pearl Harbor. I had turned in my equipment and was waiting in the orderly room while they cut my orders, and then over the radio came—Pearl Harbor got bombed. So they turned us around and I had to go back. I was trapped in the service."[3]

Meanwhile, another young man, William H. Smith from Pittsburgh, Pennsylvania, who was coming of age during the Great Depression, had a completely dissimilar experience:

> The Depression didn't affect me at all because my father kept a job. He was a detective in Pittsburgh and he worked every day. We didn't have any grief at all about food or clothing because he made good money. He was a detective and he was Gus Greenlee's bodyguard. There were four of us kids and we dressed well and we all had an allowance.
>
> I was around six or seven years old and my mother tried to teach me how to play piano. My father tried to teach me how to play the guitar. And I didn't like either one of them. My grandmother wanted me on violin. I took that for a while and then I saw this trombone in front of the band. I used to sit in front of my house and watch the bands go by. The trombone excited me and made me want to be in music. From a child up I always appreciated music. There was a neighbor who played the trombone with the Elks band. I used to sit on his door step and listen to him rehearse so when I went to junior high the first thing I picked up was the trombone. Earl Hines, Louie Armstrong, Duke Ellington, and Roy Eldridge are the ones that really got me interested in music and I wanted to be in a band.
>
> When I first got started, there was a talent show on KUV in Pittsburgh called the *Candy Kids*. Lee and Dorothy Matthews ran it. Dorothy accepted me into the band and I played from then on for radio bands. From there I went to Billy Eckstein's band and stayed with him for four years. I left Billy's band and put together a six-piece combo of my own, the Billy Smith Band. We played different nightclubs around and in Pittsburgh. I was the youngest guy in the band, about fourteen or fifteen years old. They didn't allow too many people to come and ask me questions or anything of that sort, they kept people away from me. That was good too but I learned a lot from it.
>
> I was getting a dollar a night and that was big money for me. People who came in would leave tips and the owner saw that. He didn't want me to quit, so he started paying me five dollars. I told my Daddy that he didn't have to give me any money anymore because I had five dollars. And then I felt big buying my own clothes. In the 1930s, five dollars would last me a long time because I would spend a nickel here and a dime there. A Baby Ruth chocolate bar was a nickel, a soda was 5 cents. I will tell you, the biggest money I made was in Boston, Massachusetts. When I went up there with a band and played in a pit orchestra

where we played along with the movie and made $73 for that one week. I wanted to go back but the police had been there and said, "He is too small, too young to work here so get him out of here." That was around 1934/35.

I was working nightclubs and the night when Prohibition ended and beer came back, I was on the job playing and I wanted some of that beer so bad. I was about fourteen or fifteen years old but I still wanted some of that beer. The drinking age was twenty-one.

I would go to different band rehearsals. When I heard a band was there I would sit in with them. And a lot of times I got hired that way. They would say, "Look fella, you can play, you got a job." I played for Roy Eldridge and the Eldridge Brothers for about six months and then I had to go back and finish school. I was about 17 or 18 years old. I met Earl Hines, Duke Ellington, Cab Calloway and his sister Jean Calloway, who had a band of her own. But the best of them were pick-up bands. At clubs if they needed a band they would see the different musicians on the street and call on them. No rehearsal at all, we just played. During this time the gangsters were fighting each other, killing up each other. The Opie brothers from New York came to Pittsburgh and killed people and it went back and forth, gang wars and stuff like that.

There were places where they didn't want blacks in. But every other place you could go, you see the colored people had their own places of business and so forth. So we didn't suffer too much there. We had our own theaters, our own ball clubs—like the Pittsburgh Crawfords were all black, the Negro National League. Gus Greenlee was the owner. He built a stadium for them. They played a lot of the white teams and beat them. They were good. They had a pitcher there named Satchel Page, remember him? He was their ace pitcher. Satchel and I were good friends. I would go to the games and sit up there and holler and eat peanuts, I had a ball!

Whites would come to the clubs, but the trouble was, whites would come to the black clubs but the blacks couldn't go to the white clubs. They always wanted to come to the black clubs because they said we had better music. I know that every night when I would sit up in the band, I would see white folks coming in and getting choice tables and stuff like that.

Before I got drafted I got out of the band and was doing work as a laborer. I got tired of that and I went back to the band and [they] wouldn't take me back right away, so I tried to enlist in the 10th Cavalry. The 9th and 10th cavalries were all black. They had horses and I wanted to ride one of them horses. But they wouldn't accept me because they had met their quota. But then three years later, here comes Uncle Sam. I was 24 then and got drafted and stayed in the army three years. I wanted to go into special services where they entertained the troops, but they put me in a tank outfit, but once in a while I would sit in with the band.[4]

Meanwhile, by December 1941 Hitler had conquered and held control of more than 330 million people, from the Mediterranean to the outskirts of Moscow. The Nazis had murdered Jews routinely since 1933, but in July 1941 Reichsmarschall Hermann Göring called for the "final solution." Special killing units called *Einsatzgruppen* began rounding up Jews and other "undesirable" human beings for extermination.

In North Africa, forces of Italian Fascist dictator Benito Mussolini invaded Ethiopia and indiscriminately used poisonous gas. Ethiopian Emperor Haile Selassie called the attack a "refinement of barbarism." In Libya an army of British, Australian, and Indian soldiers defeated the Italians and took more than 40,000 prisoners. Several months later the desert winds shifted as Germany's Afrika Korps, commanded by Field Marshal Erwin Rommel, came to Mussolini's aid.

In the North Atlantic Ocean, packs of German U-boats prowled the depths, hoping to cut England's vital supply artery with North America. In Asia, the Japanese Army swept through most of China, bringing millions of people under its brutal rule. The Chinese, ravaged by a 15-year civil war between Mao Zedong's Communists and Chiang Kai-Shek's Nationalists could not defend against the Japanese onslaught.

In America, the daily newspapers reported death and destruction around the world. These reports touched many Americans, who nevertheless felt safe and isolated from the world's problems. Military preparedness and the building of FDR's "Arsenal of Democracy" created a national prosperity on such an unprecedented scale that it ended the Great Depression. This brought steady paychecks to more Americans than in the preceding years. Life became good for many Americans who had never known anything other than poverty as the military ranks swelled with enlistees and draftees during the nation's first peacetime draft and the government encouraged the public to invest in America's security by purchasing defense bonds. During this national prosperity a wave of disillusionment swept through America's black communities. African Americans wanted their slice of the national pie of prosperity. Unfortunately, 75 percent of defense contractors refused to hire African Americans in any capacity, 15 percent offered only menial labor positions, and skilled labor was institutionally excluded. Many craft unions under the jurisdiction of the American Federation of Labor (AFL) barred African Americans from admission to their local chapters.

A. Philip Randolph, head of the Brotherhood of Sleeping Car Porters, along with other African American leaders, called for an exercise of First Amendment rights by marching on Washington. The march, scheduled for July 1, 1941, was against employment discrimination and segregation in the national defense program. Randolph pledged 100,000 Negroes would participate. On June 25 FDR called Randolph and other African American leaders to the White House for an urgent meeting. The president urged the civil rights leaders to call off the march, characterizing it as a "bad and unintelligent" tactic. Randolph urged FDR to issue an executive order with enough teeth to compel the defense industry to give all citizens equal employment opportunities. Later that day the president issued Executive Order 8802 forbidding racial and religious discrimination in defense industries and government training programs. Randolph called off the march.

On July 19 FDR established the Fair Employment Practices Committee to monitor discrimination in defense industries. This committee, along with Executive Order 8802, was initially hailed as the most significant executive action since the Emancipation Proclamation. But disappointment followed when discrimination continued due to the committee's bureaucratic inefficiencies and stiff opposition from southern states.

Despite treatment as second-class citizens, segregation in the armed forces, and being shut out of most munitions jobs, African Americans embraced World War II with the same patriotic fervor as the rest of the nation. Women knitted socks and sweaters for the troops. Victory gardens sprang up in every vacant lot. Volunteers collected metal and worked as air-raid wardens. World-renowned entertainers put on benefits to raise money. And young and middle-aged men unhesitatingly enlisted in the armed forces.

With the American economy on the rise for the first time in 12 years, the debate over isolation versus intervention in the war intensified. On December 7, 1941, the debate ended when Japan attacked United States forces in the Pacific. Early that Sunday morning, Pearl Harbor, on the Hawaiian Island of Oahu, came under attack without warning. Mess Attendant Doris "Dorie" Miller, from Waco, Texas, was aboard the USS *West Virginia* when the general alarm sounded. Miller, aged 22, a former high school running back and the current heavyweight boxing champion of his ship, went immediately to his battle station. He found it destroyed. Despite intense strafing, bombings, and fire-swept decks, he aided in the removal of the ship's gravely wounded captain from the bridge to a safer location. Although Miller had no weapons training, he manned an antiaircraft machine gun and fired on Japanese Zeros. He was instrumental in blasting several Japanese planes out of the sky. Subsequently, public pressure forced the navy to recognize Miller's heroic achievement. The Navy reluctantly issued Miller a letter of commendation, one of the lowest forms of recognition. After more public pressure, FDR ordered Miller's commendation upgraded to the Navy Cross, second only to the Medal of Honor. African Americans had their first war hero.

The right-wing propaganda floating around the ship claimed that Dorie Miller was the ship's bully. In an attempt to discredit his heroism, they said that he shot American planes out of the sky despite the obvious fact that the attacking Japanese aircraft destroyed the American airfields first. They didn't want American warplanes to engage them or chase them back to their carriers.

Taken by surprise at Pearl Harbor, the United States suffered the loss of 18 ships sunk or seriously damaged; 347 aircraft destroyed or disabled; Hickam, Wheeler, Ford Island, Kaneohe, and Ewa airfields in flames; 2,403 Americans dead and another 1,178 wounded. To inflict this terrible pain, the Japanese sacrificed fewer than 1,000 men, 29 planes, and five midget submarines. On December 8

Army recruit Thomas J. Mann in 1941 (courtesy Thomas J. Mann).

William Harold Smith is playing the trombone, far right, second row. "Smith played with Billy Eckstine's Big Band and a few other famous Big Bands during the late 1930s through early 1940s," according to his daughter Ms. Delores Williams (courtesy William H. Smith).

FDR asked and received from Congress a declaration of war against the Imperial Japanese Empire. Days later Hitler and Mussolini declared war on the United States of America. A stunned America found itself in World War II.

Dorie Miller and his mother went on national tour for the War Department. They traveled mainly to black communities, where they encouraged enlistment, sold war bonds, and supported the war effort. Nearly two years later Miller found himself still a mess man, this time aboard the escort carrier USS *Liscome Bay*. Early Thanksgiving morning 1943, Miller's new ship rolled over and sank minutes after being struck by two Japanese torpedoes near the Gilbert Islands. Mrs. Henrietta Miller was heartbroken from the news that her son had been trapped inside the burning ship. Dorie Miller was reported missing in action and was never heard from again.

Filled with a patriotic zeal, African Americans sought to participate in the crusade to crush the oppression imposed on the world by the racist Axis powers of Japan, Germany, and Italy. Willie Topps' response was typical of the time: "I was in Chicago lying down on the sofa in front of the radio listening to *The Shadow*. Then it got interrupted by the news that the Japanese just bombed Pearl Harbor. That stunned me. I became angry. I wanted to volunteer immediately. Shortly thereafter I became a regular army volunteer." But allowed to participate only under the same humiliating discrimination that had been their plight since inception the black soldiers found their assignments menial, such as digging ditches, driving garbage trucks, sweeping out warehouses, and slinging bedpans in hospitals.

With the hopes of the world resting with America, FDR challenged the nation with these words: "We are in the war. We are in it all the way. Every single man, woman, and child is a partner in the most tremendous undertaking of our American history. We must share together the bad news, the good news, the defeats, the victories, the changing fortunes of war." A few hours after the attack, December 7th/8th with respect to the date line, African Americans had another war hero. Private First Class (PFC) Robert H. Brooks died during the Japanese attack near Fort Stotsenburg, Philippine Islands. Attempts to honor him revealed his well-kept secret: He was an African American in a segregated all-white army unit. Fellow Kentuckians in the 192nd Tank Battalion didn't know that PFC Brooks was black, and the army didn't find out until officers decided to name a parade ground at Fort Knox in his honor as the first member of the U.S. Armored Force killed in action during World War II. PFC Brooks, from Sadieville, Kentucky, was killed in the initial Japanese bombing of Clark Airfield. He apparently died within minutes after the first bombs fell, said Kenneth Hourigan, who served with Brooks in the Philippines. Hourigan pointed out that no one suspected Brooks was black and Hourigan learned the truth only when he returned home after the war.

The 192nd Tank Battalion had been on full alert since the attack on Pearl Harbor. The Japanese bombers arrived over Clark Airfield in the Philippines around 1230 hours, and strategically dropped bombs. As the explosions shook the ground, fire and smoke enveloped the area. The Japanese planes strafed and then took off back to their carriers in the China Sea. The 192nd suffered one dead, PFC Brooks. Sadieville resident Sam Wood, who grew up with Brooks, said he was sure Brooks never tried to pass for white. However, "His complexion was light; from his looks you could easily think he was white."[5] W.T. Warring, then cashier at the Farmer's Deposit Bank of Sadieville, was the man the army contacted regarding this ceremony. Warring mentioned Brooks' parents as ordinary black tenant farmers. The army representative called back and said, "Did you say they were black? This might change things a little."[6] But this did not change a thing. The dedication went on as planned for December 23, 1941.

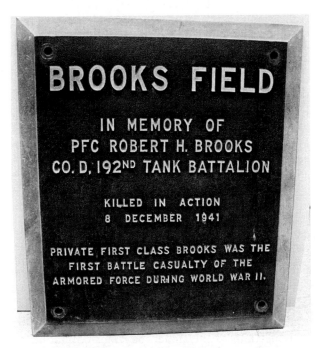

The original Brooks Field marker was located at the northwest corner of Brooks Field right across the street from the commanding general's quarters. It was removed in 2011 with the dedication of the new one at the parade stand (courtesy Matthew Rector, Historic Preservation Specialist, Fort Knox, Kentucky).

The chief of the Armored Force, Major General Jacob L. Devers, sent a letter to the parents of PFC Brooks dated December 22, 1941: "My dear Mr. and Mrs. Brooks: It is with the deepest regret that I have learned of the death of your son, Robert, who gave his life in defense of his country, December 8, 1941, in a battle near Fort Stotsenburg, Philippine Islands. With appreciation of your suffering, my sincere sympathy goes out to you. Robert was the first battle casualty of the Armored Force and because of this and his excellent record, I have directed that the main parade ground at Fort Knox be named Brooks Field in honor of your son. The dedication of Brooks Field will take place at 11:00 Tuesday morning, December 23, and I am sending this letter to you by special messenger in the hope that you may attend this ceremony."[7] This scandal sent shock waves throughout Fort Knox and Major General Devers directly addressed it: "For the preservation of America, the soldiers and sailors guarding our outposts are giving their lives. In death there is no grade or rank. And in this, the greatest democracy the world has known neither riches nor poverty neither creed nor *race* draws a line of demarcation in this hour of national crisis."[8] During the ceremony, while Major General Devers and the leadership of Fort Knox stood at attention, Colonel F.A. Macon's voice rang out across the parade ground: "General Order Number 43: With the concurrence of the post commander, the main parade ground, Fort Knox, Kentucky, is designated 'Brooks Field' in honor of the late Private First Class Robert H. Brooks, Company D, 192nd Tank Battalion."[9] The bigoted officers opposed to this stood at attention and kept their mouths shut. The War Department continued fighting to limit or keep African Americans out of the Armored Force and other branches. This was an extremely rare defeat they suffered. Finally, three volleys of rifle fire pierced the thin cold air followed by the haunting bugle sound of Taps. The ceremony ended without the parents of PFC Brooks in attendance. The flag went back up the flagpole and the soldiers marched away. The Armored Force had just honored its dead and returned to the work of avenging this black soldier's sacrifice.

Private Thomas J. Mann, 758th Tank Battalion, sums up: "One very interesting thing, they named a field, Brooks Field while we were there. The day they were going to dedicate it, those folks wanted to back out, they didn't want to name it. Brooks must have had a white father and a black mother. Well, they named the parade field at Fort Knox, Brooks Field."[10]

Before and during this period of mobilization for war, the Office of the U.S. Army Ground Forces in Washington debated whether or not to use African American soldiers in armored units. The power structure in Washington fostered the attitude that African Americans did not have the brains, the quickness, or the stamina to fight in a war, referring to their experiences from World War I. The commander of the 367th Infantry Regiment, 92nd Division, stated, "As fighting troops, the Negro must be rated as second class material, this primarily due to his inferior intelligence and lack of mental and moral qualities."[11] The commander of the 371st Infantry Regiment, 93rd Division, stated, "In a future war, the main use of the Negro should be in labor organizations." And General George S. Patton, Jr., had his own opinion: "A colored soldier cannot think fast enough to fight in armor." The armed forces embraced these

Major General Jacob Devers leading the Fort Knox leadership in a salute at the Brooks Field dedication ceremony, December 23, 1941 (courtesy Matthew Rector, Historic Preservation Specialist, Fort Knox, Kentucky).

beliefs and recommendations, overlooking the documented fact that African Americans had fought with courage and distinction in every war and conflict ever waged by the nation, from the Revolutionary War through World War I. They especially overlooked the facts that the four separate regiments of the 93rd Infantry Division had served with the French in World War I and that the French government awarded the coveted Croix de Guerre to three of the four regiments and a company of the fourth and the 1st Battalion, 367th Infantry Regiment, 92nd Division.

The traditional Christian-based Southern values were widely accepted and adopted by the army as the basis of policy and procedure regarding African American soldiers. This acceptance resulted in a toxic caste system where mostly incompetent white officers commanded their undesired black subjects. Expressing an anecdote destroying the myth that Southerners were best suited to command African Americans, a Judge Hastie related how a black Christian chaplain had been relegated to bunking in the enlisted men's barracks because his white fellow Christian officers had rebelled at sharing quarters with him.

Humiliation was a way of life for black soldiers. The army never demanded that white communities respect the black man in uniform. Instead, they expected him to be humble and subordinate, accepting of his second-class citizenship. Resentment and bitterness reflected in letters home exemplified the plight of these men. White, and even black, military police (MP) were known for their abuse and violence against black soldiers, which further depressed morale. Add in the hostility and physical attacks by white civilians, and morale fell to the depths of despair and wrath. Lieutenant General Leslie McNair, chief of the U.S. Army Ground Forces and main proponent to allow African Americans into armor, had to fight against this mindset. He never accepted the vehement denial of the fighting qualities of the African American soldier. He believed this nation could ill afford to exclude such a potentially important source of strength.

Out of this spasm of abuse and violence the Negro Press, the National Association for the Advancement of Colored People (NAACP), and the Congress of Racial Equality (CORE) put increasing pressure on the War Department and the Roosevelt administration to allow African Americans to serve on equal footing with their opposite numbers—white soldiers. Ira Lewis of the *Pittsburgh Courier* inspired the "Double *V* Campaign," which called for victory at home and abroad and thus became a rallying cry for racial justice. Labor leader A. Philip Randolph, NAACP activist Walter White, educator Dr. Mary McLeod Bethune, and other civil rights leaders fought along with the Negro press for this victory at home that would mean full civil rights for future generations.

The president's wife, ahead of her time regarding the equality of the races, stood up front with the civil rights leaders and the Negro Press. She, unlike her husband, had a genuine empathy for the plight of African Americans. But, oh, how the establishment hated her. Eleanor Roosevelt began her antiracist struggle in the 1930s. It was she who chastised the Daughters of the American Revolution for their refusal to allow black opera singer Marian Anderson to perform at Constitution Hall. Mrs. Roosevelt then arranged for Anderson to sing at the Lincoln Memorial. In 1934 she assisted Walter White in the struggle to place into law the Costigan-Wagner antilynching bill. She invited African American citizens to the White House as guests and friends. The treatment of African American servicemen was one of her chief concerns, and she was determined that they would receive a chance to fight in this war. She suggested doing "a little educating among our Southern white men and officers."[12]

Secretary of War Henry Stimson had little patience with Eleanor Roosevelt's liberal/progressive views and her desire to advance civil rights as a war raged. To pull the thorn from Stimson's side, Judge William H. Hastie, an African American, was quickly appointed to handle the sticky issue of race relations for the War Department. Along with the appointment of Judge Hastie, Colonel Benjamin Davis, Sr., was nominated for promotion to brigadier general. The War Department committed itself to these appointments in answer to the promises of the 1940 political campaign. However, African Americans still remained in segregated units.

The contrast between Judge Hastie and Brigadier General B.O. Davis, Sr., also an African American, could not have been clearer. The 36-year-old judge was an activist by nature. The 64-year-old general, who had served over 40 years in the U.S. Army, had embraced early in his career the philosophy that for an African American soldier to survive in the military he had to accept his second-class citizenship. Although Davis became the first African American to achieve the star rank, the message he sent to the black soldier was, "You are my color, but not my kind." This floated through the ranks, causing black soldiers to view the token general as self-righteous.

To the War Department's dismay, Judge Hastie lobbied for integration in training centers and combat operations. Secretary Stimson, influenced by the strident traditional racism of the South, resisted. At times, notations with "not to be shown to Judge Hastie" were attached to documents dealing with phases of Negro troop utilization. Hastie often replied, "I wish again to emphasize the fact that the principal usefulness of this office is destroyed if we are not consulted with reference to such matters." After two years of frustration, Judge Hastie resigned in disgust. His assistant Truman Gibson, Jr., succeeded him.

Through this racial turmoil, in March 1941 ninety-eight selected black soldiers from Fort Custer, Michigan, reported to Fort Knox, Kentucky, for armored warfare training with the 78th Tank Battalion. It was the first time in American history that Negroes served in the armored force for specific training in that field. For three months the men trained as the arrival of more enlisted personnel from other army camps joined. One of the 98 was Willie Topps, who later said, "I left Chicago at night and reported at Fort Custer, Michigan. From there I reported to Fort Knox for basic training. We had the forced marches of 20–25 miles. We got our basic training with light tanks. It was like shooting a popgun—the 37 millimeter." John Weston had this to say: "From [Chicago] I went up to Camp Custer, Michigan, for basic and then due to my mechanical aptitude, they sent me down to Fort Knox, Kentucky. This is where we were organized as the 758th, the first black tank outfit.... Just outside of Fort Knox—I think it was Elizabethtown, not sure—we could go through there and stop to buy liquor, but we could not stop there otherwise. We had to go to the next place." On June 1, 1941, the 758th Tank Battalion was activated. The 78th became the 758th. They trained steadily and after three months of intense run-throughs in tank operations, radio mechanics, and related phases of mechanized warfare they departed Fort Knox and moved down to Camp Claiborne, Louisiana.

The War Department activated five tank groups with three tank battalions each. The experimental 5th Tank Group, commanded by Colonel Leroy Nichols, was to be made up of black enlisted men and white officers. With the 758th Tank Battalion in place two more tank battalions would be activated to complete the 5th Tank Group.

3

The Lee Street Riot

"I am not at all glad it happened," said Ollie Stewart, a newspaper correspondent who covered twenty army camps. "But if you will remember my story of Camp Claiborne and Alexandria, Louisiana, you will recall that I tabbed the town a 'Powder Keg.' My surprise is that it took so long to explode."[1]

The army concentrated several key training camps in central Louisiana: Camp Claiborne, Camp Livingston, Camp Beauregard, Camp Polk, several Army airfields, and other smaller installations. Soldiers from these camps flooded Alexandria on weekend passes, with the black troops being restricted to a diminutive section of town. Business owners of Alexandria appreciated the economic boom but the inhabitants resented the presence of soldiers they deemed as "damned Yankees." However, the sight of black soldiers infuriated them to the breaking point. The fact that black soldiers wore the U.S. Army uniform, a symbol of authority, insulted their Dixie culture to the core. They took every opportunity to express their bitterness. The Lee Street disturbance provided the opportunity to shoot and beat black soldiers and a chance to remind Negro civilians that this was still the South.

Conditions in Alexandria culminated in disaster on Saturday night, January 10, 1942. A number of youthful swaggering black soldiers from northern states were exuberant over their idol Joe Louis knocking out Buddy Baer in the first round the previous night. This, coupled with their unfamiliarity with "Jim Crow," prompted them to react to the violent arrest of a black soldier by white MPs in front of the Ritz Theater. Military police backed up by city police engaged the black troops. Troop E of the Louisiana State Police, headquartered at the intersection of Lee Street and Masonic Drive, immediately sprang into action. Soon additional MPs from Camp Livingston and a white vigilante mob swarmed into the melee along the four-block corridor of Lee Street, which was a bustling thoroughfare in the isolated black section of town where brothels and bars hosted nightly fistfights and stabbings. The place was already a nightmare.

The white MPs came mainly from the 32nd Military Police Company. The black troops came from the 367th Infantry Regiment and the 758th Tank Battalion stationed at Camp Claiborne and the 350th Field Artillery Regiment quartered at Camp Livingston. Although clubbed, tear gassed, and fired upon, the black troops fought back using bricks, rocks, bottles, and whatever they could get their hands on. In an hour, Lee Street resembled a war zone. In the end, the beaten soldiers left standing awaited transfer back to camp to be confined to quarters. The bodies of others lay where they had fallen. The injured and wounded were taken to camp hospitals. Several wounded soldiers crawled under nearby houses and died there. Local police answered several calls days later and had the bodies removed.

The army immediately cordoned off this sector of Lee Street and cleaned it up. They refused to provide information other than prepared general statements and denied the press access to those soldiers involved. Despite the army's restricted coverage and conservative newspapers printing denials, word leaked out that twelve black soldiers had been shot and killed. The *Afro-American* newspaper, with correspondents already in the field, covertly interviewed several survivors and witnesses. Following are four press accounts published in the *Afro-American* on January 24, 1942. The first interview is from a soldier tear gassed in a night club, the second is from a civilian on a side street, the third was a gangster soldier, and the fourth describes an MP's getting shot:

First Account:

"For several minutes I looked on stunned, unwilling to believe my eyes. I thought this was more like a movie than real." Thus spoke a lanky Oklahoma soldier [from Camp Livingston] (name withheld for obvious reason), describing to the AFRO how he was first impressed when he went out into the street and found bullets whizzing about his head as military and civilian police opened fire on defenseless soldiers and civilians here Saturday night. "I was standing in a café," he continued. "A bunch of us were laughing and telling jokes—just having a good time, without the slightest thought of trouble. The first commotion in the street did not disturb us at all because it sounded just like another Saturday night quarrel which would die down in a moment. Suddenly there was a mad surge of men and they pushed over tables and chairs, ducking for cover.... I saw a white civil policeman standing in the middle of the floor with a smoking revolver. Another officer yelled: 'Let them have it.' I thought he meant bullets, so I ducked to the floor, but he evidently meant a tear gas bomb because in a second there was a muffled explosion and the room was filled with gas. We pushed and shoved our way to the street. I did not know what was going on out there until I reached the sidewalk" [Unidentified Witness].[2]

Second Account:

"I listened to the commotion for some time. I herded my family together so none would get hurt. When I thought it had died down I cautiously crept on my porch. I got down on my hands and knees when I saw two white MPs coming down the street. They leaped over my ledge and hid when they saw a colored soldier approach. I distinctly heard one of them say, 'Here comes a damn nigger soldier now; let him have it.' They started shooting point blank at him as he fled, with the pair in hot pursuit, pumping their revolvers. I don't know whether they struck him or not" [Unidentified Witness].[3]

Third Account:

"When the riot broke out, we didn't know what it was all about. They just told us that the cops were shooting up the street and as we weren't armed we started to run. One chap said he knew where a car was parked with a pistol in it and we better make it to the car. But as we dashed from the place there were so many people in the street they got in our path and one of my buddies stumbled. As he fell, I saw a policeman open fire and plug him. It was then that one of those strange things happened. My other buddies and I went back and tried to drag him to safety. How we did it I don't know, because bullets were whizzing all around our heads. We got him to the car and we started off driving. We had to cross Lee Street again to reach the road leading to camp. We wondered how we could make it. My buddy told me to take the wheel and keep my head down low while he hung on the side of the car with the revolver. He began to blaze away at the white cops as we passed. I am certain he plugged an MP right in the ear, because I saw his hand fly up in pain. After we were out of danger, it was all I could do to per-suade them not to go back. They wanted to shoot it out.... I told them I was not going to pal around with them anymore because they acted like they had been gangsters at home. They were that tough—but I guess they were just sore, that's all" [Unidentified Witness].[4]

Fourth Account:

"Other cops were clubbing heads for no reason at all. I saw a colored MP standing in the center of the street. His arm band was plainly visible and he was trying to direct us out to safety. 'Get to the bus station,' he yelled, and then he bawled bloody murder as a white MP seemed deliber-ately to shoot him in the foot" [Unidentified Witness].[5]

The police assembled at the main line of resistance, the Ritz Theater, and advanced from there. They set up a reserve line at 10th and Lee streets along the rail-road tracks, the line of demarcation that separated Alexandria by race. There they established barricades and machine-gun positions. PFC Joseph Henry Hairston, 350th Field Artillery Regiment, a medic on a weekend pass from Camp Livingston, takes up the story with the immediacy of a firsthand account:

Before I went to OCS I was stationed in Alexandria [Camp Livingston], Louisiana which is very near the maneuver area and where my wife lived. The black part of town, Lee Street had what was the center part of the black area was one long block about the equivalent of two city blocks long with nothing across it and between. It was just shoulder to shoulder with jukes joints, beer joints, and all this sort of stuff. And on this particular day a couple of soldiers were drunk and the black MPs picked them up to take them into custody. And as they were taking these two black drunk soldiers out legitimately a couple white MPs came along and took control from the black MPs. Now everybody is in the street like maggots. And it didn't bother them that the black MPs had taken a couple of drunks, but they see the white MPs, "why are they here?" So they beat the hell out of the white MPs and chased the white MPs out. The white MPs went back and got reinforcements, more white MPs. Now the crowd is jubilant, they beat the hell out of the more MPs and they leave. Remember I said it was that this is a very long block with cross streets at either end. I saw this happening at the beginning. The good Lord takes care of fools and Joe Hairston. And for some reason or another I had moved away from the center and was at the cross street at the beginning of this very long block. I was standing right at the corner, now coming down the block were the white MPs again with civilian policemen with shot guns. And as they get to the corner where I just happen to be standing there, one white policeman, pushed me in the chest and said, "get out of my way nigger!" He pushed me out and at that time they opened fire point blank into the soldiers. We don't know how many were killed. You won't find a report at least I couldn't find a report, as to how many were killed. When I heard the gunshots I got off the street, I went to the movie that was peanut heaven, you go to the white movie and you go upstairs. I figured if there was shooting around I want to be out of sight. So when I come out of the movie, the MPs immediately got me on the bus and sent me back to the post. We were quarantined for 30 days, we couldn't go to town. But you will never find a report of that incident, let's put it this way, I can't find a report. I know that. Back to BO Davis Jr., his father was a brigadier general. His father was sent to do an investigation. I've never seen the report, I've gone to the archives, and I can't find anything. I know that people were killed, I don't know how many, I saw the fire myself. That was before I was commissioned, it was after that when I went to OSC.[6]

The police stated that they only fired over the soldiers' heads and refused to admit or deny the allegations of killing twelve soldiers. The Louisiana State Police made no statement. Police Chief George C. Gray of the Alexandria Police Department made a brief statement: "We have no statement to make. The whole affair is being handled by the army."[7] There is no direct evidence that anyone from the 758th Tank Battalion participated in this incident. However, many of the men routinely went to Alexandria on weekend pass and that weekend was no exception. Willie Topps commented:

> I was on extra duty. I ran into a problem because I hit a second lieutenant. I was sent to the stockade and then I had 13 weeks of extra duty every evening after retreat. I had to dig a six-by-six trench if the weather wasn't bad. If it was bad, I had to wash all the pots and pans and clean up the mess hall. One day I had to scrub the steps with a toothbrush. However, I know about the riot because we were involved. Fortunately I wasn't there. I was still restricted to the base. Around Camp Claiborne we had Camps Beauregard, Livingston, and Polk all right around Alexandria. I can imagine that it was thousands of soldiers in that area at that particular time.[8]

Brigadier General Benjamin O. Davis, Sr., on tour inspecting southern camps, when approached by the black press stated, "I know nothing of this affair and can make no investigation unless especially requested to do so by the War Department in Washington. The army practice is to leave such matters to the Corps Area headquarters."[9] The army never requested the general's investigative services but they did instruct him to address the black troops at the camps. Corporal Thomas J. Mann, A/758th Tank Battalion, later recalled this event:

> The strangest story in the world came out. B.O. Davis, he was the black general, the only general we had. He came down to Camp Claiborne and they had us all in the theater. The first words out of his mouth: "You're my color but you're not my kind!" We all got up and walked out! We all walked out, the whole unit walked out. I can't remember what happened after that but we would not sit there to listen to B.O. Davis. That's how bad it was. It really was. They were prejudiced. We just didn't tolerate it because the 758th was just about all northern boys. We were out of California, Chicago, Detroit, New York, New Jersey, and places like that. We didn't have many southern boys in our outfit at all. Sometimes when I think about it I think they sent us on purpose because they knew we weren't going to stand for some of the things they did. I'm assuming that we broke it down.[10]

Eleven months later in a strange turn of events, the government uncovered their own cover-up. They unintentionally confirmed the initial eyewitness reports when the U.S. Department of Justice (DOJ) made a key detection. Investigator G. Maynard Smith sent a report to the DOJ chief of Civil Rights, Victor W. Rotnem, dated December 15, 1942. While investigating another high-profile racial murder—a black MP was shot and killed by a white state trooper in Alexandria—he made a reference to the January 10, 1942, incident: "During the course of the trouble someone produced a machine gun and shot at random into the crowd, wounding some twenty-six Negro soldiers and killed twelve."[11]

As 1942 drew to a close, racial violence continued nonstop in Alexandria and around the country. On November 1, Louisiana state trooper Dalton McCollum murdered black military policeman Private Raymond Carr. In this situation black MPs, armed only with nightsticks, had intervened in an argument between two civilians, a man and a woman. When the state troopers arrived the woman said the man had hit her. Carr reported that he did not see a blow struck. That incensed the state troopers, who accused Carr of interfering and then ordered the two black MPs into a car and placed under arrest. Carr and the other MP asserted they were on duty for the United States Army and could not abandon their post. The two troopers left and returned with backup. Carr ran and was chased down and shot in the abdomen by McCollum. When word reached Washington that a military policeman had been blatantly shot and killed by a civilian policeman, Secretary of War Stimson, at the urging of an outraged Undersecretary Patterson, called on Department of Justice to investigate. The case against McCollum was solid, with nine eyewitnesses describing a cold-blooded murder. Additionally, the slowly dying MP made a declaration to two

Lee Street, Alexandria, Louisiana: a Saturday night on the town. Strolling, left to right, are Private Thomas Washington, Private William Rice, and Sergeant Louis Monk of the 761st Tank Battalion (August 1942 *Yank*, "The U.S. Army's Weekly Magazine," courtesy Matthew D. Rector).

hospital nurses. DOJ investigator G. Maynard Smith reported: "The colored witnesses are above average in intelligence, and they make very frank, fair statements about how the crime occurred and are the type that will stand up very well under cross-examination. They are not inclined to be smart-alecks but impress you with the truthfulness of their story."[12]

With few exceptions, no one doubted that a terrible crime had been committed. Despite this, tensions in town ran high to the point that the commander of Camp Beauregard argued against prosecution. The camp commander, Smith reported, "feels that a great wrong has been done and one that deserves punishment no doubt, but he is looking to the future and what might happen without the whole hearted support of the state and municipal police authorities." Secretary of War Stimson argued for a federal prosecution but U.S. Attorney General Francis Biddle recommended the case be turned over to state authorities. Biddle wrote a telegram to Louisiana governor Sam Houston Jones recommending state prosecution of McCollum. McCollum was never prosecuted.

The civilian aide to the secretary or war, Judge William Hastie, and his assistant, Mr. Truman K. Gibson, Jr., were outraged. They wrote Stimson urging that Alexandria be declared off limits to all military personnel and that black MPs be armed with guns to defend themselves "against any interference with the performance of their duty."[13] The letter expounded that it was high time for the army to cease being "unwilling to risk offending the sensibilities of the Negro-hating elements of the South."[14] The letter also proposed that legislation be sought from Congress to make violence against military personnel a federal crime. This letter was in vain.

The War Department became so concerned by the escalating racial turmoil that it formed a special committee to confront these injustices. The underhanded aspect of the War Department's decision to create a special committee was that nobody told Bill Hastie, the War Department's point man on issues concerning African American soldiers. Undersecretary Patterson complained: "The creation of this board, without notice to him or participation by him, has caused him a good deal of uneasiness, and it is one of the factors that has led him to question his usefulness as Special Aide to the Secretary of War on Negro Affairs."[15] Hastie wrote it off as just the latest in a long series of insults. Finally on January 6, 1943, after further incitements and in complete disgust of the War Department's furtive activities, he resigned.

4

Camp Claiborne

Camp Evangeline sprung up in 1930, named for the Evangeline District of the Kisatchie National Forest. In 1939, as mass construction took off, it received the namesake Claiborne after the first governor of Louisiana, William C.C. Claiborne. Construction soon ceased due to an infestation of poisonous snakes. A special crew came in to remove the snakes before construction resumed. Construction crews expanded the camp and the U.S. Army activated it in 1940. During World War II over half a million soldiers went through Camp Claiborne, mainly for basic training and artillery practice. It also served as home to the Engineering Unit Training Command (EUTC) and the Special Service Forces trained there, including Railway Operating units.

Before America entered World War II this camp took part in the Louisiana Maneuvers. Two opposing forces, based around the concept of mass and mobility, "the first with the most," faced each other across the Red River. At that time, the U.S. Army operated primarily as an infantry force supported by artillery, armor, engineers, cavalry, along with supply and service units. Few mechanized units existed, exposing the need to modernize to stay current with Germany's blitzkrieg. During the intense exercises 26 men perished from drowning and vehicle accidents. One died when struck by lightning and one of a heart attack at age 24.

The isolated population surrounding Camp Claiborne resided around bayou swamps in gray weather-beaten shacks that looked much as they did during the Civil War. The people had practically no telephones, electricity, cars, or daily newspapers. Due to wartime rationing and the curtailment of automobile sales, horses and mules outnumbered motorized vehicles. There were two distinct communities: the Cajun Catholic community where dancing, drinking, fishing, and going to Sunday mass was the way of life, and the Southern Baptist community where drinking and dancing were considered mortal sins and going to church on Sundays and Wednesday night prayer meetings was the way of life.

Camp Claiborne, located in Rapides Parish on the west side of U.S. Highway 165 about seventeen miles southwest of Alexandria, rested in snake-infested swamplands. The camp consisted of tents, hutments, and a few permanent structures. The segregated area for black soldiers stood directly east of the sewage plant. A typical unit area had rows of tents with wooden floors and walkways. The headquarters, a square wooden hutment, stood tall in front of the tents. Directly in front of the headquarters hutment sprawled an assembly area. A large tank park, motor pool, and maintenance shed stood to one side and the mess hall, a large square wooden tar paper-encased shack, stood on the other side.

The 758th Tank Battalion arrived at Camp Claiborne in September 1941. Platoon sergeant John Weston, A/758th Tank Battalion, recalled his feelings about the place:

> Don't mention Camp Claiborne! That was one of the biggest mud holes that there ever was. There we built that camp up, every time you batted an eye they put us on extra duty. That is where we built the drainage canal. We practically built Camp Claiborne.... If you go to town you have to stand in line and wait until all the white soldiers got on the bus and any space left is what you would get. There was an engineering outfit down there with us and they got tired of that treatment and they had a riot and all of that came back on us. Then we left and went on the Tennessee maneuvers.[1]

Corporal T.J. Mann, A/758th Tank Battalion, recalled:

> When we got down to Camp Claiborne, Louisiana, it was all prejudiced. You had a black PX and a white PX. We had white sergeants and all of the black sergeants were lance sergeants. Since I could ride a motorcycle, I started riding one. At that time we were getting paid twenty-one dollars a month. Instead of the army delivering it to us, we would block off two blocks in front of the bank and pick up the cash on motorcycles. We had machine guns.... We performed very well and learned about tanks. The first tanks we had started with a diesel. We had to fire up the diesel with a shotgun shell to start the tank. Then we got twin Cadillac engine tanks and those tanks rolled pretty fast. We got a lot of training at night and we always went on maneuvers, we practically stayed on maneuvers that gave us our training.[2]

Sergeant Willie Topps, Service/758th Tank Battalion, said this of the place:

> I reported to Camp Claiborne from Fort Knox. That is where we had a Lieutenant Colonel Nichols as our commanding officer. We had a guy from New York who had sent for his wife out of New Jersey. She came down and he met her in Alexandria and he got her a room. Rooms then were 25 cents a night. On their way to get the room, they met these three white folks. And because they didn't get off the sidewalk for them, they jumped on him and broke his arm. The next morning Lieutenant Colonel Nichols had a meeting. And his saying to us was this: "First you are men! Second you are soldiers! And DAMMIT! If you don't go to the aid of one of your men if he's in trouble, I will court-martial you!"[3]

In early 1942 *Life* magazine visited the 758th Tank Battalion and wrote a motivating article intended for American wartime consumption: "Negroes at War." It came out in their June 15 issue and featured the 758th and other black army units:

> Tank Manned by Three Negro Non-Coms and Technician-Gunner maneuvers under sunny Louisiana Skies. They belong to the 758th (GHQ) Tank Battalion ... an all–Negro crew in a fast new 13-ton U.S. Army tank will probably be a surprise to many U.S. citizens. But this summer it could be duplicated hundreds of times at training camps throughout the country. By next spring it could be duplicated several thousand times. The U.S. Army is getting rid of its old prejudices against the Negro and is putting him where he will do the most good— in the front ranks of its fighting men. At Camp Claiborne, La. ... the white colonel commanding a Negro outfit told LIFE Photographer K. Chester: "I'm a cotton-patch Southerner myself, and I don't call these boys niggers. I call them American soldiers and damned good ones!"

This is bad news for the propagandists of Germany and Japan, who have long nursed a delusion that the 13,000,000 U.S. Negroes were ripe for rebellion and would surely refuse to fight. It is perfectly true that U.S. Negroes have never had a square deal from the U.S. white majority, but they know their lot would be far worse under the racial fanatics of the Axis. Now, when their country needs them, they are glad to work and fight and die alongside their white fellow-citizens. That is the spirit which will someday wipe every trace of racial bigotry off the map of America.[4]

In July 1942 the 758th and 761st Tank battalions received a boost to moral and lowered racial tension with the arrival of their first black officers. The new 90-day wonders came from the Officer Candidate School (OCS), according to Sergeant Willie Topps, Service/758th Tank Battalion: "We got a truck load of second lieutenants. We got Lieutenant English, Lieutenant Bobo, Lieutenant Jenkins, Lieutenant Morgan, and I can't remember them all. But we got an entire 6-by-6 of second lieutenants coming out of Fort Riley. Barbour was highly educated and he was from Chicago, English was from New Orleans, Morgan was from Philadelphia or somewhere. They were appointed to all of the companies and they assumed command as the white first lieutenants got promoted and moved on."[5]

In June 1941 the U.S. Army began conducting maneuvers in Tennessee. Major General George S. Patton, Jr., initiated the war games with the 2nd Armored Division and he outmaneuvered and soundly defeated the opposing force. This gave credence to large-scale armor fighting in response to the blitzkrieg. Patton credited the cavalry doctrine of Civil War Confederate general Nathan Bedford Forrest. As a result, over 850,000 soldiers from twenty-five U.S. Army divisions trained in the Tennessee Maneuver Area between 1941 and 1944. The maneuvers tested the ability of large mechanized units to move long distances and the capability of maintaining vehicles in combat conditions and overcoming tactical problems. In July 1942 the War Department selected Cumberland University in Lebanon, Tennessee, as the headquarters for the Tennessee Maneuvers. According to Platoon Sergeant John Weston, A/758th Tank Battalion:

> We went on the Tennessee maneuvers right after we set the cadre up for the 761st. We went to a staging area. We had our own train and they sent us around the country to different camps to show them how to protect themselves against tanks. They dug trenches and chopped down trees and made barricades. The first place we went to was a place we never did like, Camp Jackson, near Columbia, South Carolina. You talk about prejudice? It was prejudiced right down to the hick. We couldn't come and go through the front gate and we had to use a side gate. One unit had to pitch tents outside of the camp. But they kept us isolated from the other parts of camp. From there we went to Fort Leonard Wood, Missouri. That is where they had the hardest trees in the world. We would go through the forest and when a tank hit a stump it couldn't move.[6]

The 758th Tank Battalion disembarked from the train and road marched to their destination. Headquarters Company took the lead, followed by Companies Able, Baker, and then Charlie. Elements of Service Company and the Medical Detachment pulled up the rear. The light tanks kept twenty-yard intervals and proceeded at a deliberate pace to avoid at all costs engine failure or throwing a track. Sergeant Topps continues:

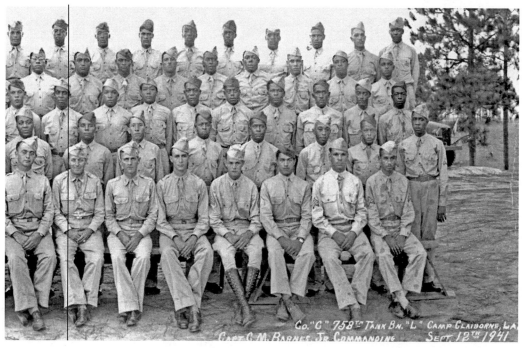

Charlie Company, 758th Tank Battalion, September 12, 1941; one photo, split: left side top, right side bottom (courtesy Rebecca J. Balfour, daughter of Major Frank Hirt Balfour, Jr., seated on first row, top, sixth from left).

We left Camp Claiborne going on maneuvers—we convoyed to Lookout Mountain and Murfreesboro, Tennessee. We went through Camp Gordon, Georgia to Camp Jackson, South Carolina. There we had trucks to take us to Columbia. We had something like a canteen there where the black troops could go. They had music and food. We could dance, eat, and sit and play cards and so forth. Then the chief of police in Columbia decided that he was going to arrest the troops and take the trucks. They put the men in jail and locked the trucks up. I'm not sure who we told—Captain Morgan or Captain English—that night. So the next day we were on the move—departing that area—the entire convoy on the go. As we passed through the city hall area, they unlocked our trucks and turned our men loose. They got us out of Camp Jackson the very next day. Then we motored over Lookout Mountain and to Murfreesboro, Tullahoma, Slayden. We left from there and went briefly to Fort Leonard Wood, Missouri. We had a problem there. We were informed that the mayor said, "I heard that you have some rough niggers. We are not going to tolerate them here." We stayed outside that town a day or two and then we went back to Camp Claiborne.[7]

The 758th Tank Battalion maneuvered through the hills and mountains of middle Tennessee, passing through towns and villages. They had rest periods between phases.

At far right is Corporal Tee Jay Mann on a reconnaissance motorcycle, Headquarters Company, 758th Tank Battalion, Camp Claiborne, Louisiana, April 1942 (courtesy Thomas J. Mann).

The 758th Tank Battalion on maneuvers (National Archives and Records Administration, courtesy *Olde Tanker* and Jeffery Toole, U.S. Army Brotherhood of Tankers).

The phases lasted three to four days with objectives such as crossing the Cumberland River and executing outflanking maneuvers. They saw plenty of action and stayed on the move: "One of our fellows made a mistake and hit a telephone pole with his tank. Well, it just brought out the whole town. It was about two in the morning. One old guy was just looking at us and then at the tanks going back and forth. Finally, he says: 'My God, I didn't know they had niggers in tanks.' He was just so taken back. We thought it was funny. We laughed right at him. He was so ignorant, and we just laughed at ignorance" (Sergeant Allen Thompson, A/758th Tank Battalion).[8]

The 758th Tank Battalion conducted fire and movement tactics against set-up obstacles and maneuvered against the 4th Armored Division. They conducted these war games in hazardous conditions: "The entire outfit went to Tennessee. One of the tanks slipped off the embankment and fell into a river near Columbia, Tennessee. I think they lost that whole crew. We lost one motorcycle. To clear the roads they used motorcycles. This fellow was a master on the motorcycle. The day after we had rain he slipped and fell a couple of times just in front of me. And the next thing I knew they were stopping the whole column. He had gotten killed. He slipped off the motorcycle and fell into the suspension system of one of the tanks" (Sergeant John Weston, A/758th Tank Battalion).[9]

A reconnaissance motorcyclist, Corporal Thomas J. Mann, will pick up this story:

We would ride in front of the tanks. It was recon. But what we worried about was that at night, we used night lights. When it would rain and the fields got muddy, the guys could get in a rut with a motorcycle and get killed. We had a boy killed. I believe his name was Morgan, where a tank ran over him. I used to tell the guys. "Don't ride in front of those doggone tanks!" They would ride with night lights, they had no lights. They were little things they had on the tanks. Then we got rid of the motorcycles before we went overseas.... From there they sent us to Fort Leonard Wood near St. Louis. I was riding a motorcycle so I made it there before a lot of the tanks. The provost martial met us about 10 miles outside of the fort and told our colonel, "We understand you got some bad niggers, we don't tolerate it. So we said—Bubba Lewis, Raymond Mack, and a guy named Theo, we were riding motorcycles—we said, "Hardy, har, har." That's what we said. And the provost martial, they just looked at us. We stayed there for one week and they kept us off the post because we created a lot of problems. From there we went to Camp Jackson, South Carolina, for I don't remember how long. Then they send us to Fort McPherson. That was in Atlanta, Georgia.[10]

This time the 758th Tank Battalion didn't go home to Camp Claiborne but traveled directly to their new duty station, Camp Hood. During their departure, her progeny, the 761st and 784th Tank battalions, continued catching hell on and off Camp Claiborne. Corporal Claude Sharrieff-Frazier, B/784th Tank Battalion, explains:

The 758th Tank Battalion on maneuvers (National Archives and Records Administration, courtesy *Olde Tanker* and Jeffery Toole, U.S. Army Brotherhood of Tankers).

We suffered quite a bit of what today would be called racism. It was outright segregation and discrimination. We had to be very careful when we went into town to avoid problems. It would appear that the MPs, even the black ones, the few that they had, would mistreat us. And being young people, still teenagers, we would stay away from the bars because none of us were into drinking as the older men were. And of course we had a terrible incident at Claiborne. We had a lot of problems when we went into Alexandria. A lot of times we got into fights and the MPs would arrest us and they would beat us. Fortunately for me I never got beat up but there were times where I had to move fast to get out of the way of those crazy MPs. I know we had one big flare-up that is a little vague in my mind. It was bad enough that General B.O. Davis had to come down with a lot of military officials to kind of whip us in line. Because at that time black troops were separated from white troops and they claimed that we had gotten into a lot of fighting and they wanted to arrest us. I am talking about the local law enforcement along with the commander of the post. And of course we resisted—young men didn't take a lot of flak without fighting back. Anyone who looked like they had an injury or whatever, they wanted arrested. But fortunately, the commanding officer of our battalion, Lieutenant Colonel Dalia, refused to turn over any of his men and he was backed up by a general. The compromise was that we had to leave there almost overnight. We packed up our vehicles and put them on flatcars for Camp Hood, Texas.[11]

Willie and Cozetta Topps on their wedding day in Chicago, August 10, 1943. Willie was on leave from Camp Claiborne (courtesy Willie Topps).

The bus situation received some relief while the 758th Tank Battalion was out on maneuvers:

I was with the 784th Tank Battalion that was right across the road from the 761st. We stayed on one side of the road and 761st on the other. Jackie Robinson came from the cavalry, he was a second lieutenant. He transferred, not to my 784th but to [the author's] father's 761st. He came there and we got to know him. That first Saturday we all wanted to go to town on leave. That's when Jackie came out and he addressed the black soldiers at that base. If you were at camp at that period and if you were black and you wanted to go on pass to town, you had the last seat on the bus. It would hold five people. And if you think of all the black people there, a battalion has around seven to eight hundred people. So if you add up just the two tank battalions, it's about fifteen hundred people. And that doesn't include all the other black outfits on base. But anyway, it would take you hours of standing in line to get on a bus. So Jackie Robinson came out there and assessed the situation and saw about a hundred people standing in line. The buses wouldn't take but five blacks at a time. He found a keg or something and stood up on it and he yelled, "Hey—'Colored' soldiers! Listen here!" (We were called "colored" soldiers back then, not "Negro" yet.) He said, "Get out of that line! I have a better plan." He told us all we have to do is call cabs. Back during that time it was about 50 cents to go into town by bus. Jackie just started calling cabs and that was the first time I met him. We split the cab fares. In a cab we wound up paying about 25 cents each for the total fare of about a dollar and a quarter. And with that we felt good about ourselves. It gave us dignity! We no longer had to stand in line with all that pushing and shoving and yelling and fighting. Jackie Robinson had the leadership to restore our self-respect [Corporal James Baldwin, HQ/784th Tank Battalion].[12]

Back on April 1, 1942, the army activated the 761st Tank Battalion at Camp Claiborne. One year later the 784th was activated, thus completing the 5th Tank Group with three battalions. The 758th provided a cadre of officers and enlisted men to both units as graduates from the Armored Force School filled their ranks. "The date that sticks out in my mind is December the 4th, 1942. While I was training a crew on the light tank directing fire on targets, somehow or another, an infantryman or whoever, discharged a round into my right foot causing me to have a split heel and crushed ankle.

Disembarking while on maneuvers with the 758th Tank Battalion (National Archives and Records Administration, courtesy *Olde Tanker* and Jeffery Toole, U.S. Army Brotherhood of Tankers).

It bled profusely! I was taken to the Fort Knox hospital and I spent the next five months there. I got out of there in May 1943. By that time the guys I came in with had moved down to Camp Claiborne to be with the 761st and 784th Tank Battalions," remembered Corporal Claude Sharrieff-Frazier, B/784th Tank Battalion.[13] He continues:

> After being discharged from the hospital, I was given leave that lasted a few weeks. I overstayed my leave in New York. On my way back to Camp Claiborne, I got stopped in Chicago and they checked my papers and found I was AWOL. They held me over for eight or nine days and then sent me on. That is when I got assigned to the 784th Tank Battalion. When I finally arrived at Claiborne, they had just brought in about 300 men—I don't know if they were volunteers but I think they were draftees. They came out of Mississippi. I remember cities like Meridian, Jackson, where a bulk of these young men came from. They were nice guys but a little backward of course. At that time, people like us, so-called Negroes, the title of black folks back then. The Southern kids didn't have much of an education. We had to help them with the basics of signing names and stuff on the payroll sheets for those who were married and wanted to send money back home and so forth.
>
> We had very extensive training in Claiborne for several months. The best that I can remember is that I was rather proficient in tanks from gunner to commander, etc. I participated in a lot of field problems—maneuvers. I was moving along quite well I thought.[14]

"Around that time, Ronald Reagan, he was a captain then, and Dorothy McGuire a movie star, they came to put on a performance. But black men were not allowed to go. So that started trouble there too. We always took our time and took care of our troops. When they started it, we finished it! I am not one to brag, but all of the black tankers, we were good!" said Sergeant Willie Topps. Racial tensions continued boiling over and this news reached the White House. Corporal Thomas J. Mann continues the narrative:

> At Camp Claiborne we had riots. We had a sergeant from New York, his name was Sergeant Turley. He was a First Sergeant. Turley was at the PX and bought some items like cigarettes, shave equipment. He gave the man, if I'm not mistaken, twenty dollars. The man kept five dollars of his money. Turley said, "You didn't give me my change. He and the man had words and Turley grabbed him. The man reached down and got a pick ax handle and split his head. Then word came down to us that Turley got his head split. Then we got our tanks and tore the PX down. Well it was a black PX but we tore it down. And from then on we started having riots—a black soldier get killed one night, a white soldier get killed the next night. It was a humdinger, that Louisiana. I never did go around much because I had gone to school in Louisiana. If you walked down the street with a black girl the MPs and the police would stop you to see if she had a health card. It got bad there, where girls wouldn't go out with the soldiers. That's the way it got. Then we got a couple more soldiers killed and a lot of white soldiers killed. It was a riot, you know, and so what? In fact the guys wanted to go to Alexandria to tear houses down it got so bad.[15]

During this period, local folks, enraged over rumors of white women being raped by black soldiers, roamed the woods surrounding military installations housing black troops. They carried rifles and their kids carried .22 caliber rifles and BB guns. The racial friction at Camp Claiborne caught First Lady Eleanor Roosevelt's attention and she wrote to the army chief of staff requesting an explanation. She attached an excerpt from a letter she received from a white officer at the camp who told her about the racial turmoil there. She received the following response, from General George C. Marshall:

It is unfortunate that the young officer arrived at the Camp when conditions were such that a discouraging impression was obtained by him. A thorough investigation has been made at Camp Claiborne. It was found that some of the personnel were influenced by a Negro soldier who is an ex-criminal and was able to excite a group to acts of violence. He and his immediate followers have been tried by courts martial and sentenced. As a result of our investigation some officers have been found not suited to command colored troops and have been transferred from that station and a new camp commander had been assigned.[16]

The investigators followed the typical government strategy: they rounded up black soldiers and blamed outside agitation. Then the camp's leadership convicted as many black soldiers as possible. The white soldiers were treated as victims and not held accountable. The white officers in command were not held accountable. In extreme circumstances some white officers would be transferred to other units. What was even more interesting, the white officers involved usually received promotions shortly afterward. This strategy was never intended to solve problems. Racial flare-ups continued as small fights grew into larger fights that exploded into riots.

This miserable camp deactivated in 1945 and was returned to the National Forest System, where only relics of the past exist today. Can you believe that this godforsaken hell hole is the birthplace of America's legendary 82nd and 101st Airborne divisions?

5

Camp Hood

The 758th Tank Battalion pulled into Camp Hood, Texas, in September 1943 and joined the Tank Destroyer Center for continued training. They were glad to have the swampy, flat, and densely vegetated terrain of Camp Claiborne behind them. They arrived at Camp Hood experts in extricating tanks from mud and undergrowth, but they never became experts at dealing with racism:

> We arrived late in the day at Camp Hood. We put our tanks, trucks, jeeps, and motorcycles up in the motor pool after we washed them and lined them up. Then we showered and everything and the guys wanted to get themselves a beer and a sandwich. We went to the snack bar and there was nothing there but white. So they wanted to put us out and we weren't going and they got the provost. He came and was going to have us arrested. By that time one of the guys got Lieutenant Colonel Steele. Steele asked the provost, "How long have you been a lieutenant colonel?" He said, "Thirteen years." Steele told him that he stayed a second lieutenant for thirteen years and then dressed him down. We had our problems there [Sergeant Willie Topps].[1]

"For our tank maneuvers we had to go through a field and a little village. Sometimes we would move our tanks off the road and when the camp commander came by he would make us get out of those tanks and walk back to our camp. He said send someone to drive the tank back. They just resented us there. Camp Hood was a tough place for us," said Platoon Sergeant John Weston.[2] The resulting frustration and restrained rage took its toll, according to Sergeant Willie Topps:

> We had a captain out of Alabama, his name was Hall. I asked if he would sign my furlough that evening because there was only one train coming through Temple that evening. He made the statement that he didn't care if my mammy was dead. That set it off. And I committed another bad act. I stomped him. But fortunately, we had a major from Waycross, Georgia—Major Chattem. He heard the whole thing but he wouldn't stop me until I started stomping the man. He stopped me. He first hit my legs and knocked them out from under me. While I was on the ground he began to talk to me. When I got out of the stockade I began to settle down and I got my buck sergeant rating. Later I got my staff sergeant rating. I was in Headquarters Company and from there I was transferred to Service Company. I worked in supply. I ordered supplies, made out the requisitions, took the inventories, and issued out the supplies to each company.[3]

The War Department announced the Camp Hood location in January 1942 and completed the initial construction eight months later. It was named after Confederate general John Bell Hood, commander of the Texas Brigade. The need for wide-open space to test and train tank destroyers arose to counter the German blitzkrieg. Camp Hood's terrain was ideal for tank operations: hills, valleys, woods, open grounds, closed grounds. The men trained as school troops, constantly on maneuvers in the field and at the various tactical and firing centers. They tested their skills against tank destroyers, which generally came in two varieties: those towed from half-tracks and those mounted on specially developed tanks. "Splitting trail" referred to separating the towed antitank gun from the vehicle before firing. Expert crews could "split trail" and be on target in fifteen seconds. During the Army Ground Forces tests to reveal their readiness for combat, they maneuvered against units like the 758th Tank Battalion. As the 758th Tank Battalion continued to train, black officers from the Officer Candidate School (OCS) Armored Force Replacement Training Center, Fort Knox, Kentucky, arrived to replace the departing white officers:

> Once my training was completed I was sent to Camp Hood, Texas to join the 758th Tank Battalion.... The prejudice and discrimination at Camp Hood made Fort Knox seem ultraliberal in its attitude. Camp Hood was frightening and made you wonder if you were still in the same army. Segregation there was so complete I saw outhouses marked white, colored, and Mexican; this was on federal property.... At Fort Knox I had not been segregated from my [OCS] classmates. At Camp Hood they shifted white officers in order to place me in C Company, 3rd Platoon; 3rd Platoon was the ragtag platoon of all the outfits, the end of the line. Black officers were segregated in every respect at Camp Hood. My Captain was an ROTC man from Louisiana. He was an excellent officer and made a point of never referring to the men as, "boys." He was transferred later to command the 784th. I believe then and I believe now that the captain was one of our "lost boundaries" [Second-Lieutenant Harry Duplessis, C/758th Tank Battalion].[4]

The black soldiers at Camp Hood flocked to Belton and Temple on Sundays to partake of the Negro spirituals and companionship compelled by their deep-seated religion and culture. This was originated by enslaved Africans who were imparting their indoctrinated Christian values while describing the hardships of slavery. Slaves were forbidden from speaking their native languages and converted to Christianity because slave owners believed that Christian slaves would be obedient. At any rate, the harmonized choral arrangements uplifted spirits and sustained the black solders through the rigors of racism. "On Sundays we got invited to a church in Temple, Texas, and they treated us royal. The deacons invited us to their homes after service, where we had something to eat and we were treated well," said Sergeant Willie Topps.[5]

The only off-camp areas where the black soldiers could shelter their wives and families stood in the small towns of Belton and Temple, approximately twenty-three miles away. The commanding officer from the 761st Tank Battalion, Lieutenant Colonel Paul Bates, recounts the following: "The worst thing here was the bus situation. The only recreation area they had was off post here in Killeen and very small towns and Belton and Temple. The bus drivers took a vicious pleasure on the last bus at night, which was always full of soldiers. They were always in the back area or standing. Getting about two or three miles from the post and say, 'the bus was overloaded some of you have to get out.' They would make six or eight of them get out and walk back to post. They clearly enjoyed it."[6]

The black soldiers at Camp Hood found a welcoming town in Austin, which stood approximately seventy miles away, said Corporal Claude Sharrieff-Frazier: "It was during training that I got an opportunity to go to Austin, Texas, which was a fine town. It had two black colleges, Tillotson and Huston. At that time they were not joined and being that there were very few guys on any campus, we had a good time with the young ladies since there was nobody around. I guess those young men were in the service like we were. Hood was quite an experience. We trained very hard. I knew a lot of the guys from the 758th and 761st from my training at Fort Knox."[7]

In November 1943, the 758th Tank Battalion relocated to Fort Huachuca, Arizona: "I returned to Fort Knox to study tank maintenance and after Hood I had a vague notion of how the slaves felt on Emancipation Day. When I returned to my unit ten weeks later we had moved to Fort Huachuca, Arizona, and were training with the 92nd Division" [Second-Lieutenant Harry Duplessis, C/758th Tank Battalion].[8]

6

Fort Huachuca

The Indian Wars in the late 1800s produced Fort Huachuca. In February 1877 the commander of the Department of Arizona ordered the 6th Cavalry Regiment to establish a camp in the Huachuca Mountains. From there they could protect settlers and block the Apache escape routes to Mexico. In 1882 the camp became permanent and was designated Fort Huachuca and by 1886 it became the forward command post for the campaign against Geronimo. Following Geronimo's surrender many frontier forts closed, but because of its strategic location Fort Huachuca remained open. In the decades that followed, troops from the post engaged renegade Indians, Mexican bandits, and American outlaws. In 1913 the 10th Cavalry Regiment arrived and in 1933 the 25th Infantry Regiment replaced them.

The name Huachuca comes from the Sobaipuri Indian tribe, who used the word to describe their village at the mountain. It translates to "place of thunder." Thunder, a notable feature during the summer months, occurred frequently along with extreme heat and freezing temperatures all in the same day. Legend has it that the ghosts of Cochise and Geronimo haunt the canyons to remind inhabitants of the land's tragic past.

During World War II, Fort Huachuca's population soared to over 30,000 soldiers as the two black infantry divisions, the 92nd and 93rd, trained there. In October 1943 the 758th Tank Battalion traveled by rail to Fort Huachuca. "In Arkansas we were informed to pull the shades on our coach windows because the hillbillies were shooting on black troop trains. As we traveled, we were side tracked for all the passenger trains. We continuously pulled over to the side. We pulled over into Texarkana for the entire night and pulled off late the next day. Those were the only problems. It was a good experience. I was young and foolish and it didn't take much to set me off back then but I settled down," said Sergeant Willie Topps.[1]

By November, the 758th had procured their tanks and equipment. Intense training that emphasized Infantry-Artillery-Tank (Combined Arms) coordination commenced. Each infantry battalion, supported by artillery, and one light tank company took part. Together they operated in the mountains, crossed streams, and conducted patrols and, according to Sergeant Topps, they "trained with the 92nd Infantry Division. We were right under Geronimo's Peak and the mountain lions would come in

NOTICE OF CHANGE OF ADDRESS

(A sufficient number of these cards will be distributed to each soldier when his mail
address is changed to permit him to send one to each of his regular correspondents.)

Date........**16 November**.............., 194_**3**_

This is to advise you that my correct address now is—

Cpl...........**Orion S. Bennafield**............**32352779**
(Grade)   _(Name)_   _(Army Serial No.)_

Co. "B"........................**758th Tank Battalion (L)**
(Company or comparable unit)   _(Regiment or comparable unit)_

APO No. **XXXXXXXXXX**   c/o Postmaster..**Ft. Huachuca, Arizona**
(Strike out if not applicable)   _(Name of post office)_

Signature...

NOTE.—Newspapers and magazines may need your old address for correct processing.

My old address was........**Co. "B", 758th Tank Battalion (L)**

Camp Hood, Texas

W. D., A. G. O.   Form No. 204
April 8, 1943   16—33987–1   GPO

NOTICE OF CHANGE OF ADDRESS

(A sufficient number of these cards will be distributed to each soldier when his mail
address is changed to permit him to send one to each of his regular correspondents.)

Date............................., 194___

This is to advise you that my correct address now is—

Cpl   Orion S. Bennafield   32352779
(Grade)   _(Name)_   _(Army Serial No.)_

Co "B" 758th Light Tank Bn
(Company or comparable unit)   _(Regiment or comparable unit)_

APO No. **17106**   c/o Postmaster.....**NEW YORK, NEW YORK**
(Strike out if not applicable)   _(Name of post office)_

Signature **Orion S. Bennafield**

NOTE.—Newspapers and magazines may need your old address for correct processing.

My old address was.....758th Light Tank Battalion

Camp Hood, Texas

W. D., A. G. O.   Form No. 204
April 8, 1943   16—33987–1   GPO

Change of address notice for Corporal Orion Bennafield (courtesy George Hardy).

Corporal Orion Bennafield (courtesy George Hardy).

our area every night to raid the garbage."[2] They trained 48 hours each week, traveling miles through arid plains and rugged mountainous terrain. At any hour of the day or night tank crews had to be prepared to move into action; thus tank maintenance was constant, as strong winds whipped up desert dust into high spirals—again the spirit energy of Cochise and Geronimo.

Training conducted in the combined arms doctrine concentrated on welding individual units into a combined entity and maintaining its cohesiveness under battle conditions. Emphasis on combat firing and unit coordination took place. A critique followed each exercise and some had to be repeated in order to attain proficiency. At least one surprise field problem or alert took place each month to keep the men vigilant. This training included 25-mile marches, instruction in the handling of land mines and booby traps, and movement through the infiltration course under machine-gun fire. Combat firing proficiency tests given by Army Ground Forces instructors allowed no low or average scores. "I wasn't at Fort Huachuca very long. Once we got there we had artillery practice. The big thing at Fort Huachuca is that we had to do a 25-mile hike. I went back to school several times and not with the outfit very long. Any time something opened up, my lieutenant sent me back to school at Fort Knox," remembers Platoon Sergeant John Weston.[3]

The 92nd Infantry Division had a World War II slogan, "Deeds Not Words." Its insignia, a circular shoulder patch with a black border and a black buffalo on an olive drab background, symbolically dated back to the Indian wars. The black soldiers of the regular army, the 9th and 10th cavalry and the 24th and 25th Infantry regiments, were known as Buffalo Soldiers by the Indians. Historians disagree on the origins of the sobriquet Buffalo Soldiers. However, according to the Buffalo Soldiers National Museum, it originated with the Cheyenne. In addition to a resemblance to a buffalo—in essence the kinky hair, wide nostrils, full lips, dark skin, and the wearing of buffalo fur coats—when cornered and wounded the men became ferocious fighters "who had fought like a cornered buffalo; who like a buffalo had suffered wound after wound, yet had not died; and who like a buffalo had a thick and shaggy mane of hair,"[4] an allusion to a September 1867 skirmish. Private John Randall, G Troop, 10th Cavalry Regiment, escorted two civilians on a hunting excursion when suddenly they became the hunted. A band of 70 Cheyenne warriors swept down and killed the two civilians and shot Randall's horse out from beneath him. Randall scrambled to safety and returned fire with only his revolver and 17 rounds of ammunition. When help from the nearby camp arrived, the Cheyenne retreated, leaving behind thirteen fallen warriors. Randall suffered a serious gunshot wound to his shoulder and eleven smaller wounds. It is believed that the Cheyenne spread word of this new kind of soldier, comparing him to a cornered buffalo.

Despite the romanticized legends of the Buffalo Soldier, the men took part in the Native Americans' nightmare, which limited their traditional freedoms and confined them to reservations. Records indicate that Buffalo Soldiers did not take part in genocide. However, they, being oppressed themselves and manipulated by a racist government, seemed to willingly oppressed the Native Americans.

The 92nd Infantry Division conducted a ceremony each week. Their mascot, a young buffalo from an Oklahoma herd, was presented to the division by the Department of the Interior. The bison is powerful and peaceful, but when angered it can become dangerous. "There was a brigadier general as the commander of the post. He only had one eye. Every Saturday he had us to march in review. We had a staff sergeant who took care of a buffalo. That was their mascot. If that buffalo stopped to do his business, we had to stop and do it all over again," recalls Sergeant Willie Topps.[5] The 92nd Infantry Division's commanding officer, over objections, named the bison Buffalo Bill after Buffalo Bill Cody. The men objected because Cody, while working for the Kansas Pacific Railroad, shot and killed approximately 4,000 buffalo in eight months, and thus became the illustrious Buffalo Bill.

The army chief of staff, General George C. Marshall, had selected his friend Edward Almond, a fellow Virginia Military Institute schoolmate, to be promoted ahead of his peers, to major general and commander of the 92nd Infantry Division. Almond was not a field commander but a staff officer, whose combat experience amounted to only one month. Almond himself explains why Marshall chose him: "I being from Virginia had an understanding of Southern customs and Negro capabilities."[6] Marshall promoted the mediocre Almond, encumbered with racist sentiment, above his level of competency, and it proved to be disastrous. Jim Crow had flown across the desert and landed in Arizona.

The choice of Fort Huachuca to garrison the two black infantry divisions was due to its isolation. The historic ghost town of Tombstone is 26 miles away. The small towns of Bisbee and Naco are 42 miles away and the Mexican town of Nogales 68 miles away. The community of Fry, where civilian construction workers lived, stood just outside the main entrance to the fort. Here, prostitutes and their consumers gathered in unsanitary fleapits. This section, called the "Hook," operated with over a hundred prostitutes and hundreds of reinforcements on paydays. "At Fort Huachuca I couldn't do anything. We were over 100 miles from Tucson and we were approximately 60 miles from Nogales, Mexico. That was the only place where a soldier normally could go," said Corporal Thomas J. Mann.[7] Sergeant Willie Topps remembers, "We were just outside of Tombstone, Arizona. They had a unit of black WAACs there. They ran the Post Exchange. They had black nurses who ran the hospital under Lieutenant Colonel Nichols and Major Giles, both out of Chicago."[8]

To remedy the situation of limited recreation and to improve morale, a comprehensive program sprang up to meet the off-duty needs of the enlisted men. The program included physical training, boxing, drill competitions, entertainment, and spiritual development. The post field house became the center of activities until baseball diamonds and other outdoor facilities became available. Fort Huachuca had two service clubs where officers could enjoy their off-duty time. The white officers attended Lakeside and the black officers attended Mountain View. The black enlisted men patronized the post field house, which they called the Savoy Ballroom after the famous Harlem nightclub. There was no need for separate enlisted men's clubs because the white soldiers on base were all officers.

The Lakeside officers club had western-style murals that depicted Indian warrior Geronimo and the local area. These murals gave no indication that Buffalo Soldiers were stationed there when Geronimo and his men roamed the nearby mountains. For the mural unveiling ceremony, the famous singing cowboy and movie star Gene Autry led the white officers in singing cowboy songs. Indian scouts performed dances for the officers. The Mountain View officers club stood on a hill overlooking a creek and a view of the surrounding mountains and contained paintings and other pieces of art by black artists.

From 1892 until 1946 the original Buffalo Soldiers and most of their spiritual descendants served at Fort Huachuca. U.S. Army policy required black soldiers to serve in segregated units; thus all four of the congressionally mandated units for black soldiers, at some point, served at the desolate fort, starting with the 24th Infantry and followed by the 9th Cavalry, the 10th Cavalry, and the 25th Infantry regiments— the original Buffalo Soldiers. During World War II their spiritual descendants, the 92nd and 93rd Infantry divisions, trained there. For that reason, Fort Huachuca became known as the home of the Buffalo Soldiers. As the 92nd Infantry Division began preparation for overseas movement, the 758th Tank Battalion departed Fort Huachuca and returned to Camp Hood to begin final preparations for combat.

In 1946 Fort Huachuca, by that time nearly abandoned, became surplus and the state of Arizona briefly took it over. During the Korean War it was reactivated for training combat engineers. In 1954 a new era began: the Signal Corps found the area and climate ideal for testing communications equipment and in 1967 the fort became the headquarters of the Army Communications Command (USACC). Then in 1971 the post became the home of the Army Intelligence Center and School. Together they made Fort Huachuca a major military installation again.

7

Return to Camp Hood

The 758th Tank Battalion returned to Camp Hood on July 2, 1944. They arrived in time to have Second Lieutenant Jackie Robinson, from their sister battalion, transferred to them. The top brass at Camp Hood conspired with the 758th Tank Battalion's commander to court-martial Robinson. The alleged offense took place on July 6 when Robinson sat next to a friend's wife in the middle of the bus, a fair-skinned Negress who was obviously mistaken for a white woman. This outraged the civilian bus driver, who stopped the bus and ordered Robinson to move. Robinson, himself outraged that a civilian would order a commissioned officer, refused. Corporal Thomas J. Mann comments:

> What happened when they sent us to Camp Hood, Texas, we had more problems. That's where Jackie Robinson, they tried to court-martial him and Colonel Bates, the best colonel we had, told them he was not going to court-martial him. Then they transferred him from the 761st to the 758th, where we had a *half-prejudiced* colonel named Steele. Colonel Steele tried to court-martial him. Jackie beat the case and later he was discharged for convenience of the government.... From here I was transferred out. I went to a glider battalion. I was sitting there and a colonel came in and saw us there, just two blacks there. Then he said, "Where did these two black niggers come from? We have no niggers in this outfit." Then I was transferred to the 761st Tank Battalion. And my time with the 758th was over.[1]

Second-Lieutenant Harry Duplessis, C/758th Tank Battalion, speaks of Lieutenant Colonel Steele, who was half prejudiced and ambitious:

> Our commanding officer, Lieutenant Colonel Steele, was over age and under grade. It seems that he had been in a brawl in the Philippines and lost seventy slots toward promotion. The men called him "the bull." I understand that upon his arrival at Hood he called the men together and told them, "It's tradition at West Point that black soldiers can't handle mechanical equipment and can't soldier. I want you to make a goddamn lie out of that tradition and I am here to help you." There were mixed feeling about the colonel until his leadership began to pull the group together.[2]

Lieutenant Colonel Steele, despite no firsthand knowledge of Jackie Robinson, consented to the court-martial. Commanding officers are required to provide character testimony regarding their subordinates, but in this case Steele provided none. Then, after years of being passed over for promotion, he became a full colonel. His men had no clue of his involvement in the Jackie Robinson court-martial. According to Second Lieutenant Harry Duplessis, "When promoted to colonel [Steele] was transferred, and the men really hated to see him go. I must say the officer replacing 'the bull' was a sad specimen, also out of Louisiana. Our officer complement was five white officers and thirty-three blacks, five of whom were black captains, and they actually ran the unit. We were considered most unusual because of the number of black officers in our group."[3] The men of the 758th Tank Battalion were deliberately kept in the dark about the witch hunt against a man they considered a role model and who later became an American icon. They should have been given the chance to testify. Second-Lieutenant Duplessis didn't know what the "bull" had to do for his pipe-dream promotion.

The court-martial commenced on August 2, 1944. "I spent quite a bit of time there," said Jackie Robinson's former commanding officer—the one who actually commanded him—Lieutenant Colonel Paul Bates, 761st Tank Battalion, "and it was the first time in my life I was ever called prejudiced. After my testimony, the prosecuting attorney recommended that all of my testimony should be thrown out because I was too prejudiced in favor of the defendant. Isn't that a beautiful way to use that word?"[4] The court-martial lasted seventeen days and Bates had this to say about it:

> At the beginning of the trial there were many, many witnesses who were on the bus who made many derogatory statements about him, about the bad language he used.... It did look pretty bad until this very smart lawyer asked this enlisted man who claimed that Jackie Robinson had threatened him. He asked if he had ever called Jackie Robinson a nigger. He said, "Under no circumstances." "Did you ever use the word?" "No, I never used it." "Did any of you ever use that word?" He said, "No, I never used it." "I want you to tell me and this is very, very important so that we can punish this man properly. I want you to tell me the exact words he used when he threatened you." "If you ever call me a nigger again, I'll break you in two." At that the president of the court stood up and the others did and they had the charges and specification read. And to every one of them they said: "Not guilty, not guilty." We lost Jackie then. I didn't expect to stay in the Army and if they were going to throw me out that would be as good a cause as any. Well, we left here with a bitter taste in our mouths. Yes, he got off but it never should have happened![5]

After the acquittal, and with Robinson's unit on its way to Europe, Jackie ended up with the tank destroyers. Then due to a prior football injury his new commanding officer sent him for a physical and the army changed his status from temporary limited service to permanent limited service. In October 1944 he received a 30-day leave and was placed on inactive duty. From home he awaited his honorable discharge.

Training continued at Camp Hood for the 758th Tank Battalion. The grueling routine at the camp included close-order drill, tactical hikes (mounted and dismounted), training with artillery, setting up communications, performing reconnaissance, and digging hull defilades for their tanks. This kept the men in combat condition. "You know black soldiers were on the shorts in everything and in every way. In the blistering heat of a Texas summer the 'patty boys' had ice for their water, drinks, everything; we didn't have any. It was these little, petty things that really burned you and made you know just what a vicious, scheming character 'patty' has" (Sergeant Horace Evans, B/761st Tank Battalion).[6]

HEADQUARTERS XXIII CORPS

GENERAL COURT-MARTIAL)

ORDERS NUMBER   130)

APO 103
Brownwood, Texas
23 August 1944

Before a general court-martial which convened at Camp Hood, Texas, pursuant to paragraph 6, Special Orders Number 120, this headquarters, 10 June 1944, as amended by paragraph 1, Special Order Number 123, this headquarters, 14 June 1944, and paragraph 8, Special Order Number 164, this headquarters, 29 July 1944, was arraigned and tried:

Second Lieutenant Jack R. Robinson, O-1031586, Cavalry, Company "C", 758th Tank Battalion.

CHARGE I: Violation of the 63rd Article of War.

Specification: In that Second Lieutenant Jack R. Robinson, Cavalry, Company "C", 758th Tank Battalion, did, at Camp Hood, Texas, on or about 6 July 1944, behave himself with disrespect toward Captain Gerald M. Bear, Corps Military Police, 1848th Unit, Eighth Service Command, Army Service Forces, his superior officer, by contemptuously bowing to him and giving him several sloppy salutes, repeating several times "OK Sir", "OK Sir" or words to that effect, and by acting in an insolent, impertinent and rude manner toward the said Captain Gerald M. Bear.

CHARGE II: Violation of the 64th Article of War.

Specification: In that Second Lieutenant Jack R. Robinson, Cavalry, Company "C", 758th Tank Battalion, having received a lawful command from Captain Gerald M. Bear, Corps Military Police, 1848th Unit, Eighth Service Command, Army Service Forces, his superior officer to remain in a receiving room and be seated on a chair on the far side of the receiving room, did, at Camp Hood, Texas, on or about 6 July 1944, wilfully disobey the same.

PLEAS

To the Specification of Charge I: Not Guilty
To Charge I: Not Guilty

To the Specification of Charge II: Not Guilty
To Charge II: Not Guilty

MILITARY JUSTICE DIVISION, JAGO. FINDINGS

TO THE ADJUTANT GENERAL:
          Of all Specifications and Charges: Not Guilty

The record of trial in this case has been examined in this office. and found legally sufficient to support the sentence.

262476

For The Judge Advocate General: - 1 -

L. A. WHITENER
Major, J.A.G.D.
Chief Examiner.

Copy for A.G.   SEP 4 19

CCMO #130, XXIII Corps, 23 Aug 44 (Contd)

The court thereupon acquitted the accused on 2 August 1944,

By command of Major General WOGAN:

WALTER D. BUIE,
Colonel, G.S.C.
Chief of Staff.

OFFICIAL:

L. K. OLSON
1st Lt. AGD
Asst AG

DISTRIBUTION
"I"

In August 1944, during extreme temperatures, the 758th Tank Battalion took their final tank cannon qualification course with individual marksmanship training. This refresher training consisted of all battalion crew and individual weapons and lasted approximately three weeks. Each battalion member shot at single and pop-up targets from several firing positions. In extreme heat and with no ice water they had to pass with a minimum score in order to qualify for overseas movement. Platoon Sergeant John Weston explains further:

> I will name every part of a light tank that you want named, every bit of it. An M-5 Stuart light tank has three .30-caliber machine guns and one 37-millimeter gun. It is powered by two (twin) Cadillac automatic drive engines. Behind the driver you have a Delco Remy generator. When you go into battle you always turn it on because your equipment will drain the 12-volt battery. The 37-millimeter gun had a gyrostabilizer. That's the unit. If you remember as a kid you would see these gyros that you would wind up and spin like a top, and any which way you touched it, it always came back to its original position. That's what the gyrostabilizer is. I don't know the revolutions it spins at, but once you got into battle and take your 37-millimeter gun out of its traveling harness, this gyrostabilizer takes over. So it doesn't care what the tank does, this gyrostabilizer keeps your gun on target at all times. The Cadillac engines had carburetors on them with open valves that are oil sealed. So any dirt that comes in off the road will go into the

oil and then into the carburetor so it kept your engine clean. I'm not sure of the amount of gas it took but you could only travel 3 miles to a gallon. In our arsenal, to the rear of the driver and assistant driver, we carried 12 rounds of AP—that's armored piercing—and 12 rounds of HE shells—that's high explosive. But I took the armored piercing out because we were not going to fight anything like big tanks. But what I carried mostly—canister shells. Canister shells were like shotgun shells. I carried them because when you are firing against troops, the shell explodes and spreads like when you are firing at birds with a shotgun. It does more damage.[7]

Through the first phase they refreshed their knowledge on how to disassemble, clean, and reassemble their weapons. They practiced loading and unloading their weapons with safely foremost in mind. They followed with identification of parts, function checks, ammunition types and care, correcting malfunctions, sight adjustments, and so on. During the next phase they revisited correct handling of weapons. They practiced body positioning to support their weapons to where they felt the natural point of aim. Then they studied aiming fundamentals, correct sight alignment, and eye focus. Then came breathing control, as breathing will make the weapon slightly move and result in a missed target. And finally they had to learn trigger squeeze, as the trigger is not pulled but gently squeezed. They spent hours practicing how to group their shots and setting their sites. Range instructors provided feedback and advice on how to improve. During the final phase the troops fired their weapons as crews and individuals. The crews received qualifications on the 37-millimeter tank weapon and the .30-caliber machine gun, such as expert gunner, first class gunner, and second class gunner. As individuals they received qualifications on the M-3 submachine gun (.45 caliber) and the M1 carbine as experts, sharpshooters, and marksmen. The M-3 submachine gun was an American classic commonly referred to as the "grease gun" for its visual similarity to the mechanic's tool of that name.

During the final preparations for combat, lessons of teamwork, discipline, and attention to detail were redrilled and pounded home: "We had our final combat training up at North Camp Hood near Gatesville. We went under fire. They fired over our heads as we crawled under barbed wire down through gullies and up the other side. We did that for a week—every day we had to get combat acclimated" (Sergeant Willie Topps).[8]

The sprawling camp, with strictly enforced segregation, offered limited recreation for the men. After years of rigorous training and isolation they felt restless. The 758th Tank Battalion used its own trucks to take their soldiers into accepting towns for recreation:

Most of us took a truck and we went to Waco. That's where we had all of our refreshments and whatever we wanted. We were going there when some fellas robbed the PX. The Texas Rangers came there and took over everything. And they figured it was black soldiers. They called in two of us. I was a staff sergeant. And they mentioned the little town I was talking about and asked if we could check and see if we could get any information on who robbed that place. So we went into town and we had a good time there. We were not interested in who robbed that place—because they treated us so bad down there! Then we came back and said there were no reports to be made, but then I made out a report and filled out a form. And then it was time for us to leave, to go to Camp Patrick Henry, Virginia [Platoon Sergeant John Weston, A/758th Tank Battalion].[9]

On September 30, 1944, the over-trained and underutilized 758th Tank Battalion departed Camp Hood for Camp Patrick Henry, Virginia, their port of embarkation. Second Lieutenant Harry Duplessis recalls that time:

Our shipping orders were an open secret, so many men wanted passes to see their wives and sweethearts before shipping out. The white major was sure that these soldiers would not return in time to make the train. The black captains assured him the men would come back and he reluctantly granted passes. The following morning twenty-two men missed roll call. Just as I was about to turn in the roster a sergeant ran up and said, "They are coming sir!" Twenty-one of the missing men were running across the field. Due to the rule that whites were allowed to board the bus first these men had been unable to get seats even though they explained their predicament. Having no other choice and determined not to fail their black captains they had jogged and walked all the way back. The only guy who hadn't appeared was the "lover" of the battalion. Everybody knew where he was and nobody worried. He made the train with a flying leap just as it was getting started.[10]

8

Camp Patrick Henry

September 30, 1944: The 758th Tank Battalion departed Camp Hood, Texas, and arrived on October 3 at their port of embarkation (POE), Camp Patrick Henry, Virginia. "One of the most amusing things I ever witnessed was an American Indian who had been assigned to our outfit. Now Indians usually serve with white units; in wartime they are equal, but this fellow was quite dark. He went haywire on the train, in-route to our POE, and was running up and down the aisle shouting, 'Me no nigger, me Indian!' They got him off of that train like lightning. The men did not find it funny and his problem would have been solved tragically if he hadn't been removed fast," said First Lieutenant Harry Duplessis, C/758th Tank Battalion.[1] The 92nd Infantry Division passed through Camp Patrick Henry prior to the 758th and sailed to the Mediterranean Theater of Operations (MTO) with their three regiments in close connection: the 370th on July 15, the 371st on September 22, and the 365th on October 2.

Camp Patrick Henry served as a staging area for the Hampton Roads Port of Embarkation. At its max, it processed 35,000 troops at one time, generally replacement troops. Over a million men and women passed through here during World War II. In their spare time the men found their way around camp within walking distance. Sudden eruptions of brawls, especially between tankers and paratroopers, were common. Mistaking the double buckle combat boots of the tankers for the prestigious airborne jump-boots, and envious of their sole right to wear them, the airborne soldiers often assaulted the tankers, who fought back vigorously.

In addition to the boot crisis, this army camp had an extensive history of racial unrest. Four months prior to the 758th Tank Battalion's arrival, U.S. Army paratroopers had displayed their ignorance. Obviously all paratroopers are not ignorant, thus some took an open-minded approach. One example of this follows:

> While at Patrick Henry I observed my first real display of bad feelings between the blacks and the whites. I knew there had always been a problem between the two races, but I had been spared any actual wild demonstrations of the hatred or whatever existed. I knew there were no blacks in the paratroopers, but I never wondered why. Apparently, they weren't asked to join. Very likely, this had little or nothing to do with the fact that a small war stated right there between the blacks and the whites. I was in the middle of it for a while with bottles, rocks, and a few other things flying through the air. I soon realized just how stupid this was and got the

heck out of there fast. Some were not so lucky and landed in the hospital. I wonder if they took the blacks to the same hospital.... [T]hey bled the same color of blood, I noticed [Private First Class Eugene Brissey, 517th Parachute Infantry Regiment, 13th Airborne Division].[2]

Not every paratrooper viewed it as PFC Brissey did and took the conformist approach:

We were there for a few days, and we continued to train there in the athletic way, in other words running and doing all the physical stuff. We had terrible fights with other outfits there that were shipped out. They would all make fun of us as we'd run down the road, you know, pretty proud, and they'd holler at us. They would be over there resting, smoking their cigarettes; and the only thing was that didn't happen but once before our company commander would stop us right there in the road, and march us over to that group, and make us mingle in among all of them. And then when the guys were still sitting down including their company commanders and their officers and our company commander would look at their company commander and say: "You want to tell any of your men to get up, or do you want to leave them where they are?" And, as I recall, the order was never given for them to get up. Every once in a while an individual would get up and go back down. We had no toleration at all for any of that. We were good. I can't tell you, it's kind of hard to believe when you talk to a guy like me, just a guy, you can be good at what you're doing and better than most guys think they are. And better than those guys sitting on the ground think they are. If they just knew it they could probably get up and do what you could do. But they didn't know it. We knew it. We had a lot of that problem. We had problems at night as we were going to sleep with guys coming in there trying to get us in our bunks with baseball bats. I mean big time. We had some trouble with one particular unit, I won't mention that because of this [oral history], but they came in, four guys came in and started beating on our guys with baseball bats while they were asleep. And we had a real thing with them. I mean you could go to jail for what was happening there. So we had a bad time there for the few days we were at the Port of Embarkation [Sergeant Randolph Coleman, F/517th Parachute Infantry Regiment, 13th Airborne Division].[3]

Camp Patrick Henry's leadership paid scant heed to these warnings. No good-faith effort at training or discipline took place. This lack of moral direction fostered continued ignorance and allowed this repulsive pattern to metastasize. Thus, considering the deadly consequences of America's covert race war, black soldiers customarily squirreled away ammunition in clandestine ammo dumps for self-protection. This pattern continued as the 92nd Infantry Division arrived at Camp Patrick Henry:

They had a system in the theater where the white women ticket-takers made you put your money on the counter, and they would rake it in. They didn't want you to touch them by putting the money in their hands. One of them made a mistake with the change, and of course, an argument ensued. So somebody called the MPs, and they flooded the place. There was a black captain there trying to settle the thing, but that wasn't working. So the MPs announced: "We're closing this PX down now," and somebody in the rear said: "Well, then close the Mother-Fucker!" All of a sudden it looked like on cue, everybody just left there. It looked like somebody had just vacuumed everybody out of the PX. Everybody left there, and they went across the street. And when the MPs came out, there were BARs and machine guns and people laying up on the road with rifles and everything. The MPs called the regimental commander, and he came down there and got the issue quieted down. I tell you, the MPs never came back in our area again [Sergeant Bill Perry, 370th Infantry Regiment, 92nd Infantry Division].[4]

Finally, on October 6, 1944, the 758th Tank Battalion fought their final battle on the home front, with none other than the United States Army "*Fallschirmjägers.*" In official records the 758th's "Listing of Events" for the month of October, dated November

30, 1944, stated the following: "6 October 1944: There was a riot between Enlisted Men of this Battalion and a group of paratroopers. One Air Corps Enlisted Man was killed (name unknown).—signed: Major Lawrence F. Becnel, Executive Officer, 758th Tank Battalion."[5]

What follows is eyewitness testimony from participants and bystanders. Their detailed recollection shows what happened from their points of view. Memory recall is indeed a credible source, but sometimes memories and individual perceptions can be unreliable. At any rate, it is a fact that the deadly riot took place according to the 758th Tank Battalion's "Listing of Events." Now it is up to you to match the eyewitness accounts to the incomplete U.S. Army documents available at the National Archives and Records Administration (NARA). It is interesting to note that, during a review of Camp Patrick Henry's medical files, Box 168 was found to contain files up through 1943 and referred the researcher to Box 136 for 1944 activity. Box 136 contained no documents for October 1944 but referred me back to Box 168 for October 1944 holdings, thus establishing an error loop. The following eyewitness testimonies come from four diverse points of view: a platoon leader, a platoon sergeant, a supply sergeant, and a tank commander. You, the reader, are invited to draw your own conclusions.

Start of Eyewitness Testimonies

A Platoon Leader's Perspective

We finally arrived at Newport News, Virginia, a staging area. The camp, Patrick Henry, was divided into eight sections; area eight, the bottom of the barrel, was for us. Fifty-odd AWOLs from the 92nd Division, which had departed a month before, were attached to us for transit overseas. Now infantrymen and tankers don't get along too well; frankly they fight at the drop of a hat, officers included, meaning me too, but we were stuck with these guys.

We had reached our destination about 5:00 p.m., and settled down. Around 8:00 p.m. we heard a bunch of guys singing as they went by and we noted they were paratroopers from Fort Benning. Late that evening we heard a lot of commotion, swearing, and an occasional use of the word "Geronimo." Knowing that was a paratrooper expression we split for the enlisted men's quarters. Upon our arrival the CO of the paratroopers was gathering up his men and ordering them back to their own area. They left with the parting remark, "Niggers, we'll be back." One of our sergeants was sporting a hickey the size of an egg on the side of his head. Instead of being furious and full of invectives he kind of smiled as the crackers left.

The following morning a battalion of Puerto Rican engineers arrived to occupy area seven. Throughout the day I had noticed that our tankers were mighty tight with the attached infantrymen. I chalked it up to good sportsmanship or something since they, the infantry guys, were outnumbered. That night the men were given permission to go to the show. A few stayed behind but it appeared that the majority had gone off for some entertainment. We officers were in our quarters yakking, playing cards, relaxing, the usual routine, when at 8:30 a call came from our commanding officer, who had gone off to visit friends in the white area. The exec ordered all of the officers up to the enlisted men's area on the double; we took off!

The General Store, Camp Patrick Henry, Virginia, circa 1943 (U.S. Army Signal Corps).

We covered that block in record time. To our surprise it was apparent few if any of our tankers had gone to the show. Our guys were standing at our area entrance watching the paratroopers giving the Puerto Ricans a fit. They had run the poor guys out of their barracks and were beating them with all kinds of clubs or substitutes; it was like a witch hunt. The tankers' attitude was it was their fight, let them fight it.

It finally occurred to those poor devils that the only place they could escape to was our area eight. They cut for our section. The tankers let them through but when the paratroopers tried to follow it was a brand new ball game. You could actually feel the earth tremble when our black tankers and those white paratroopers collided. Just as this very real no-holds-or-weapons-barred encounter swung into action the lights went out. I mean all over camp. They stayed out for approximately three hours and during that time I fought harder than I did the whole time I was in Italy.

The Puerto Ricans did not fight. They had run into our barracks and that's where they stayed. I can understand this. They had just come into the camp and the attack upon them was sudden, with no warning; they were just plain bewildered.

We had a very dark officer who was a giant of a man. There was a tree behind the arms room and that guy took a running leap, grabbed a tree limb and plunged through a window into the building. The door was opened and we proceeded to arm ourselves with Thompsons, rifles, and side arms. Theoretically we didn't have any ammunition, but like magic our men furnished us with all the ammo we needed. It seems that those infantry guys knew where the bullets were buried, so to speak, and that was why the sudden friendship had blossomed between them and our men. Together they had carried out a combined operation of preparing for war. Not for one moment had the men doubted that those "crackers" would return and they meant to be prepared for all eventualities.

As the battle progressed several of the officers got their heads together and discussed a strategy. It was agreed that the enemy would undoubtedly attempt to infiltrate our lines. Where? The logical place would be the drainage ditch that ran alongside the barracks. One of our recon scouts, 6' 4" and an ex-football star, got a trench tool and stood right at the corner above the ditch. The first white face that came up got his features flattened like a pancake. With his screams of pain those behind scurried out of there like rats only to be greeted by men who had been sent to cover their retreat. The lights came on as suddenly as they went off and the battle ended. The tally was three dead paratroopers and one black tanker shot in the foot while loading his weapon. He was furious because he could not go overseas because of his wound.

The next day when I was receiving several stitches in the back of my head I was happy to note that the paratroopers being stitched and bandaged outnumbered us considerably. One thing certain, they didn't say anything about returning for a rematch, nor was the word "nigger" being bandied about [First-Lieutenant Harry Duplessis, C/758th Tank Battalion].[6]

A PLATOON SERGEANT'S PERSPECTIVE

When we got to Newport News, Virginia, we had the same practice again—that's when they raided us. Oh, yeah! One night we were at camp getting ready to go overseas. We packed our stuff and inspected our weapons that we left in the orderly room. And that time I went over to the telephone exchange to call home to let them know that I was leaving the country. And while I was having this telephone call, that's when the outfit—I won't name them because I wanted to make sure—well, it was actually replacements for the 101st Paratroopers. They raided our camp and soldiers were scattered every which way. A lot of guys got hurt just running. We were across from the drill field so those guys knew right away what was happening, seeing the paratroopers waving those knives. A couple of our men went into the orderly room and got a couple of Thompson submachine guns and fired across the drill field.

I could tell by the weapon they carried—you know, the paratroopers carried a knife that they used to cut the shroud once they landed. That is what they waved at us. Most of the outfits, when you go into camps like this and bivouac down, they have a place where you

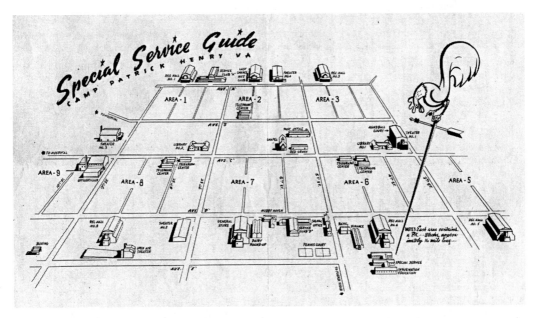

Special Service Guide Map of Camp Patrick Henry, Virginia (U.S. Army Service Forces, NARA).

put down all your weapons, usually the orderly room. And that is what we would usually do. We had no weapons. But over there where they were they turned in their weapons and they kept their knives. So we heard them across the field hollering "Geronimo!"

The paratroopers complained about our boots. That was the only way we could wear our pants was down in our boots. Now they had different type of boots. But what they really didn't like about us was that the PX and telephone exchange was on our side. So when they passed across the drill field to their side of the camp, they passed the PX. The PX had all white help and girls behind the counter. And what we were supposed to do, if you bought something, you picked out what you wanted and put the money down on the counter and step back. Then the girl picked up the money and you got your article. And we didn't think anything of those kinds of laws and regulations because we were fixing to leave the country. And so a couple of the fellows got familiar with the girls, they were laughing and the girls didn't mind—you know, laughing and talking. And when the paratroopers passed by they would see us and they said this was familiarization. So that's why they attacked us.

Platoon Sergeant John Weston (courtesy John Weston).

They kept us there an extra week and brought down the FBI and everybody else to find out who fired those shots. They finally found the guns that fired at them because the guns were thrown under the barracks. Our barracks at that time were built up on stilts. So they took all the guns and checked them ballistically and they found out that one of the guns was my gun. And so they called us all in to press charges, but they forgot one thing. I was staff sergeant and commander of the first platoon and it was my job to check each weapon every morning, and my fingerprints would be on every gun there. And then they found they couldn't get me on that. But what really saved me was a captain, a white captain, he was from Chicago too. We were looking out this big bay window together when all hell broke loose. So they had to let us go after they kept us there for one week. They were crying for troops overseas so they had to let us go.

To sum this up, my platoon was right across from the parade grounds, and the attack came right through there. I was across the street to call home, our last chance to call home. They came across the drill field right after chow time in the evening. According to my memory we were between the telephone exchange and the PX. And all the other places I don't know because we came in at night. They came across waving those big knives. A couple of the fellows went into the orderly room where we kept our guns and grabbed a couple machine guns and sprayed the field. The paratroopers ran back to their outfit and the next thing we knew a whole company of MPs and everything else appeared. The shooting came from our area. We just came back from chow and some of the guys were lying on their bunks when the yell rang out—the one the paratroopers use: "GERONIMO!" And our guys jumped up from their bunks and grabbed anything they could. But my platoon was near the first orderly room where all the weapons were kept. So some guys got machine guns and sprayed the field. That's all they could do. And then they took the guns and threw them under the barracks. And then everyone got quiet [Platoon Sergeant John Weston, A/758th Tank Battalion].[7]

A Supply Sergeant's Perspective

From Camp Hood we took the train to Camp Patrick Henry in Virginia. We had a confrontation there, a little problem at the post exchange. They had this policy that if you purchased things, the clerks wouldn't take the money from your hand if you were black. You had to put it on the counter. I've always been a person of—what I would say—stronger will. And I wouldn't put my money on the counter. I handed her my ten-dollar bill and she said, "Put it on the counter!" So I didn't put in on the counter and this guy from the 101 Screaming Eagles hauled off and hit me. Then Boyd from Chicago, when I got hit Boyd hit him. And that set off a riot.

The following morning the provost came to our outfit. I was not in our orderly room but this is what the clerk told me. He said he relieved Lieutenant Colonel Steele of command. Then he took our officer of the day with him, Captain Morgan. He started out of the orderly room with Captain Morgan. Our officer of the guard had alerted the battalion and our entire outfit had gathered around the steps. So we asked the provost where was he going. He told us that Captain Morgan was under arrest for failure to follow military procedures. So we politely told him, "Colonel, your best bet is to take your little cowboys and go back to your post!" So that is where it all began, although the night before we had a confrontation with the paratroopers. They entered our battalion area and they ran into quite a bit of problems. They thought we were a quartermaster or an engineer outfit. They didn't know that we were highly armed. We let them know that we were not to be run over [Sergeant Willie Topps, Service/758th Tank Battalion].[8]

A Tank Commander's Perspective

When we got to Camp Patrick Henry it was brewing. I could smell trouble, and I could see it too. When we went in for our indoctrination, the paratroopers on that base were antagonistic. They would gesture. They had shroud knives, the kind you use to cut your shroud when you drop in a parachute. They patted them, and they made gestures with those knives. We were told when we got there we could go anyplace on the post, because we are in the United States Army and all that. It was the post commander talking. "You are not confined to any area. You can go anywhere you want to." Well, that wasn't the case.

Some of our men had gone to the PX and were escorted out or run away from the area. The PX in our area was mixed, white and black soldiers. But the problem began because some white girls were overly friendly with the black solders, and the white paratroopers didn't like it. I was in the PX that night with a couple of sergeants, and I said, "Let's get out of here, I see some problems." So we got out.

The next night I was in charge of quarters, and, oh, about fifty of those paratroopers came down the road in front of our barracks. They were making a lot of racket. I said, "What do you fellas want?" "Well, your boys have their pants stuck down in their combat boots like us, and we feel that you are trying to emulate paratroopers." I said, "Well, these men are authorized for combat boots; And I told them to get back to their unit because they had no business over here. They left but the next night about two hundred of them came back. That night they said, "We're gonna kill some niggers tonight." Well some shooting started. I don't know what side started it. But I do know that my company commander was supposed to have been knocked down, and the key to the armory was taken. And guns were taken out. And we had a small gunfight. It lasted about a hot minute. Because when the shots rang out and people fell, those guys cleared out in about two seconds. One of my men in the company got shot in the foot. One of theirs got killed. So they more or less quarantined the company, and there was a large investigation. They took us in one by one and questioned us. They didn't have any evidence.... They couldn't figure out how my gun had been fired, and I said, "I don't know either."

We heard that paratrooper units had jumped on every black unit that had come through. They found some excuse to jump on the black units, and they had never been stopped. One officer said, "Your outfit was the first to stop them." Yeah, my bunch of boys in the 758th Tank Battalion were crazy, I tell you. We had fellas from Chicago, New York, Detroit, Cleveland, Philadelphia, all, mostly, city boys, big city boys [Sergeant Allen Thompson, A/758th Tank Battalion].[9]

This is one of the sadistic amusements white soldiers ran on their black comrades-in-arms. But in this tremendously rare case, it backfired in their faces: "You don't bring a knife to a gun fight." The white soldiers did not squirrel away ammunition like their opposite numbers. They did not share the same fears and had no reason to risk a court-martial. They enjoyed the full force and protection of the law in a social system that protected them. This begs the question of why the army's leadership would allow and, more than likely, encourage this? This may never be answered, but at any rate at least one poor mother never knew how her brave but manipulated son perished. Clearly, some individuals in the U.S. Army or NARA, or both, felt these documents were too sensitive for public consumption and removed them.

9

Destination Mediterranean Theater of Operations (MTO)

On October 21, 1944, the 758th Tank Battalion embarked from their port of embarkation at Newport News, Virginia—Destination: Mediterranean Theater of Operations (MTO), Leghorn, Italy. Able, Headquarters, and Service companies, along with elements of the Medical Detachment, boarded the SS *John W. Brown*. Baker and Charlie companies, along with the rest of the Medical Detachment, boarded the SS *Joseph Warren*. "We thought we would go across on the *Queen Mary* but we got the Liberty Ship *John W. Brown* and another ship," Sergeant Willie Topps (Service/758th) recounted with a chuckle.[1]

As the ships pulled away from the rickety wooden piers, salty air breezed as waves slammed directly into them. Within 30 minutes Newport News had snuffed out under the horizon. The two ships joined a convoy for the transatlantic passage. The rough Atlantic, which could turn intestines inside-out, lay ahead. Platoon Sergeant John Weston later recalled the voyage:

> We were on the water for about 29 days. The Liberty Ship *John Brown* was tough going over. We were in the Bermuda Triangle and the ship's steering rudder jammed and we went in a big circle for a day and a half before they fixed that thing. And then we started overseas and I got seasick. I recall Lieutenant Colonel Steele. I don't know if he was relieved of duty after the riot at Camp Patrick Henry, but he went overseas with us on the same ship. He got so seasick that they put him in the infirmary. He was a big fellow and must have lost 50 pounds going over-seas. I think a Major Becnel took over the battalion. He came from the 4th Armored Division.[2]

Adding to this misery the threat of German U-boats emerged. They sank many American ships off the U.S. coast. In their pursuit of these targets they brushed up against American shores so close that the submariners could smell the pollution from factory smokestacks, watch automobiles travel the roads, and tune in to American radio stations playing the jazz and swing music many of them enjoyed. They inflicted such lethal pain that body parts, oil, and wreckage washed up along America's eastern seaboard. To combat this threat, the U.S. Navy employed convoys, a maritime strategy where armed escorts protected groups of vessels sailing together. As convoy escorts increased, sinking by U-boats dropped to nearly zero. On November 8, 1944, while their younger sister battalion, the 761st, underwent its baptism by fire in France, the convoy completed the Atlantic crossing. They approached Europe below Portugal and Spain directly above Morocco, North Africa. From there they entered the Strait of Gibraltar, where the convoy began to split up.

The SS *John W. Brown* anchored at Augusta, Sicily, on November 14. Then on the 17th she steamed through the Strait of Messina, the narrow passageway between the eastern tip of Sicily and the southwestern tip of Italy. At its narrowest point, this strait measures less than two miles in width. From there the troops sailed up the western coast of Italy and anchored briefly at Naples. The men viewed Mount Vesuvius from the gulf of Naples six miles to the east. This legendary volcano known for its eruption in the year 79 AD led to the burying and destruction of the Roman cities of Pompeii and Herculaneum. An estimated 16,000 people perished and are preserved in stone. From this historic sight, the vessel steamed away and docked at Piombrina before arriving at the port of Leghorn on November 25 "We bivouacked until our tanks and the rest of the battalion caught up with us. Then we went to Pisa," said Platoon Sergeant John Weston.[3]

Aerial photograph of the SS *John W. Brown* (National Archives and Records Administration).

Meanwhile, the SS *Joseph Warren* took a different route and on November 9 the sea-battered ship laid anchor in Oran, North Africa. The troops disembarked and embarked on the French ship *Governor General Lepinx* and steamed on. They sailed without Private Junior L. White, of Charlie Company, who they sent from the ship's infirmary to a general hospital for follow-up for an emergency appendicitis surgery aboard. On November 14 the *Lepinx* anchored in Naples, Italy. The troops disembarked and set up bivouac in nearby Bagnoli and performed guard duty for the port staging area. On November 26 the troops embarked on a U.S. Navy Landing Craft Infantry (LCI) called *Elsie Items*, a seagoing amphibious assault ship. They sailed on the USS LCI 525 at a clip of 15 knots per hour and anchored at Leghorn, Italy, on November 28. "It was Thanksgiving Day when we dropped anchor but we were not allowed to go ashore; our Thanksgiving dinners were sent out to us. When we finally got ashore we were put in some woods near Pisa," recalled First Lieutenant Harry Duplessis, C/758th.[4] Baker and Charlie companies, along with elements of the Medical Detachment, made an amphibious landing from the LCI and joined the rest of the battalion at the staging area.

The Liberty Ship *John W. Brown* is one of two operational and one of three preserved as museum ships. She was named after the Canadian-born American labor union leader John W. Brown (1867–1941). As a Liberty ship, she operated as a merchant ship of the United States Merchant Marines during World War II and later as a static vocational high school training ship in New York City. Now preserved, she is a museum ship and cruise ship berthed at Clinton Street Pier One in Baltimore Harbor, Maryland. The Liberty Ship SS *Joseph Warren* survived World War II, was sold to private industry in 1947, and was scrapped in 1969. The surviving operational Liberty ship besides the *John W. Brown* in Baltimore, Maryland, is the SS *Jeremiah O'Brien* in San Francisco, California. A third Liberty ship, the *Hellas Victory* (ex–SS *Arthur M. Huddell*) is preserved as a static museum ship in Piraeus, Greece.

USS LCI-525 was decommissioned and transferred to the Soviet Union at Cold Bay, Alaska, in July 1945. She participated in the Soviet invasion of Japan in the Kuril Islands in August and September 1945. Returned to the U.S. Navy in 1955, she received two battle stars for World War II service and was struck from the naval register. Her days of service ended and her whereabouts are unknown.

The surviving USS LCI-713 is located in Portland, Oregon, near the I-5 bridge over the Columbia River and is currently being restored. Another survivor is the USS LCI-1091, which is moored in Eureka, California, and is owned and operated by the Humboldt Bay Air and Sea Museum.

Many former LCI amphibious assault ships were modified for use as sightseeing boats after World War II for the New York City Circle Line. Other LCI vessels have been located around the world. The Argentine navy had at least three in service as of 1998. Another one was used in Alaska as a fishing boat. Three are rotting in the Witte Marine Salvage Yard in Staten Island, New York. Unfortunately, the situation of LCI-525 is unknown.

At any rate, the 758th Tank Battalion reunited after their sea-sickening voyage, mindful that their fathers and grandfathers sailed this route to fight World War I only two and a half decades earlier and that this was the same ocean voyage endured by their ancestors as African slaves when an estimated 25 percent did not survive the journey. On the slave passages the sick were thrown overboard so as to not infect others. Now these brave warriors who had proved their mettle on the home front landed in Italy prepared to fight for democracy. Their M-5 Stuart light tanks would roll over some of the same ground as the great North African warrior Hannibal, in the spirit of armored warfare, had traversed on elephants centuries earlier.

10

Battle Indoctrination
at the Gothic Line

In December 1944 the 758th Tank Battalion, in the vicinity of the ancient town of Pisa near the Arno River, prepared for combat operations in support of the 92nd Infantry Division. Between December 1 and December 23 the battalion received classroom and field training while their tanks, equipment, and supplies arrived. First Lieutenant Harry Duplessis, C/758th, takes up the story:

> The great day came when we were to go down to tank ordnance and pick up our tanks. We had checked out on every tank in the army so we were ready. As we walked along we could see row upon row of brand new tanks and could hardly restrain ourselves in getting through the proper procedure and secure the tanks assigned to us. Our joy quickly turned to disappointment with the realization that the army transported its separate and unequal campaign ideas wherever it went. The equipment given us had been used in the African campaign. The tanks were covered with layers of dust, full of sand, and corroded in every possible crevice. Our mechanics worked night and day, draining and cleaning gas tanks, removing sand from every conceivable and inconceivable place, to mention a few of the problems confronting them, in order to get these beat-up hulks into a usable condition. We watched white units come in and leave with brand-new equipment of all kinds. When we inquired about the new tanks just standing there and were told they were not available for us. It was heartbreaking to see our guys working like dogs without let-up and those brand new beauties just sitting there.[1]

On December 10 and December 11 the 92nd Infantry Division's inspector general (IG) inspected the battalion. By December 17 the battalion had corrected all deficiencies. On December 23 it completed final preparations and began decomposing and attaching as smaller units to elements of the 92nd Infantry Division.

The 92nd Infantry Division, which had arrived prior to the 758th Tank Battalion, had its units thinly deployed along a twenty-mile front. "The troubles that would dog the division, surfaced immediately: Almond's staff sent one of the lead infantry regiments to the front without Ammunition! The mix up arose from Almond's policy of not allowing black troops to have live ammunition unless absolutely necessary—he simply didn't trust them," said Second Lieutenant Joseph Hairston, C/599th Field Artillery Battalion.[2] The men of the 92nd believed that the measure of success for their commanding officer, Major General Edward "Jim Crow" Almond, would be a body count—not dead enemy soldiers but their own. According to Hairston, Almond

74

announced to them, "You people constitute ten percent of the population of this country, and I'm going to see to it that you suffer ten percent of the casualties."

The 92nd Infantry Division operated with three organic infantry regiments, the 365th, 370th, and 371st, with a complement of supporting units. Each regiment had three battalions. Each battalion contained a headquarters company and four letter companies. The 1st Battalion had letter companies: A (Able), B (Baker), C, (Charlie), and D (Dog); the 2nd Battalion had E (Easy), F (Fox), G (George), and H (How); and the 3rd Battalion had I (Item), K (King), L (Love), and M (Mike). There is no J (Jig) Company. The 92nd Infantry Division also had the separate 366th Infantry Regiment attached. Captain Hondon Hargrove, 597th Artillery Battalion, had this to say:

> Now the 366th got into the act when the 92nd command desperate for black replacements, suddenly remembered the 366th, which had been on airfield guard duty for almost a year. It had once been an infantry unit. That unit thrown on the front line with no preparation had been hit hard so my friend was a replacement for them. In less than twenty-four hours from the time they swooped him up in Rome he was on the front line trying to learn how to use the M1 and not shoot himself or one of the men around him. I assure you his opinion of the army is unprintable.[3]

758th Tank Battalion being indoctrinated and trained in a movie theater, Leghorne, Italy, December 1945 (courtesy Willie Topps).

The 92nd operated with four organic artillery units: the 597th, 598th, 599th, and 600th Field Artillery battalions. They also had other artillery units attached to reinforce their fire missions. The organic units form the permanent structure of the 92nd. The attached units are temporarily fastened and referred to as "bastard battalions." The 92nd also had the 760th Tank Battalion (Medium) attached. Now the 758th Tank Battalion (Light) would become its latest attached unit. Able and Charlie companies (758th) attached to the 760th Tank Battalion, a medium-tank battalion that operated mainly with Sherman tanks and provided the main armored support to the 92nd Infantry Division. They attached in the vicinity of the seaside town of Forte Dei Marmi. This posed the question of how the light tanks would assist the medium tanks. Platoon Sergeant John Weston comments:

> They always wanted a light tank outfit, especially in Italy because when you went through one of those towns you noticed the roads were narrow. When a medium tank went through a town it could not traverse its gun. So we would go through in front and in back to protect the medium tanks. We always stayed in the towns because our 37 millimeters could not do much against tanks anyway. So we maneuvered mostly against pillboxes, machine-gun emplacements, and troops. We always wanted to have something between us and our enemy. Our light tanks could protect us against anything under a 40-millimeter gun. Anything above that, we were dead meat.[4]

The 758th in Leghorne, Italy (U.S. Army Signal Corps).

Baker Company (758th) attached to the 92nd Reconnaissance Troop, a company-sized unit that operated with armored scout cars, jeeps, and motorcycles, with the mission of reconnaissance, surveillance, and target acquisition. They attached in the vicinity of the medieval Tuscan town of Camaiore. The light tanks assisted the reconnaissance and cavalry units by providing swift-moving armored support. Together they swept wide, taking side roads to clear the flanks of Highway 1.

The Assault Gun Platoon (758th) and the Mortar Platoon (758th) reported to the 371st Infantry Regiment in the vicinity of Pietrasanta, a coastal town in the foothills of the Apuan Alps, about 20 miles north of Pisa. The assault guns fired harassing shots at general enemy positions while the mortars fired on predetermined enemy targets.

The 758th command post moved to forward position in the vicinity of

Lt. John R. Fox (courtesy Arlene Fox).

the sandy beaches at Lido Di Camaiore. At this point the 758th Tank Battalion received a request to employ light tanks as stationary pill boxes. The battalion commander, Major Lawrence Becnel, responded:

> It is questionable whether or not tanks are satisfactory as stationary outpost or armored pill boxes because of their high silhouette and the difficulty in out-posting them with Infantry. Most counter attacks are made at night when tanks are particularly blind. It does not seem practical to jeopardize such valuable equipment by subjecting it to night raids, when the same mission can be performed equally as well by Ground Mounts which can be dug in. Whenever tanks are used for outpost at night an adequate amount of Infantry should be used or provided for their protection. When used in this role, the tanks should form a support for the Infantry outposts. In every case the Tank-Infantry team work must be emphasized.[5]

On December 23, the winter's first major snowfall blanketed the area where the 92nd Infantry Division stood with orders to hold at all costs. Major General Almond would not see that his "boys" were spread too thin and reserves positioned too far behind to be deployed in a timely manner. In the predawn hours of December 26, following several probing thrusts along the Gothic Line, the enemy attacked in force, striking the U.S. Fifth Army's left flank in the 92nd Infantry Division's zone of operations. They assaulted astride the Serchio River through Sommocolonia on the east and through Molzanna on the west and swept southward.

Operation Winter Storm, nicknamed the Christmas Offensive, battered the 92nd Infantry Division with heavy mortar and artillery barrages. Immediately following this barrage, German infantry and elite white-clad Mountain units, along with Fascist Italian Alpine and Marine units totaling over 9,000 men with 100 light artillery pieces and no tanks, attacked through the rugged mountains and down the riverbanks. During this attack, enemy long-range artillery barrages landed, including on the coastal sector where the 758th Tank Battalion's command post (CP) stood. The CP displaced immediately.

From approximately one mile north of Sommocolonia, a battalion of the German 286th Infantry Regiment overran the windswept mountain village held by only two platoons of Easy Company and forward observers of Cannon Company, 366th Infantry Regiment. Frantic hand-to-hand fighting in the streets ensued. First Lieutenant John Fox, the Cannon Company forward observer, reasoned that the only way to stop the enemy was to call artillery fire on his own position. First he called for a smoke screen to cover the escape of the overwhelmed troops in the area. He remained behind and adjusted Cannon Company's short barreled 105-millimeter howitzers and the 598th Field Artillery Battalion's 105-millimeters howitzers to "walk" high explosive shells to his observation post. "Fire it! There are more of them than there are of us. Give them hell!" Fox commanded.[6] No further communications came from him. The survivors of the two Easy Company platoons fought their way through the rapidly closing escape route. Only 17 of approximately 60 men escaped. The others were killed or wounded.

The loss of this position forced other elements of the 366th Infantry Regiment to relinquish ground to avoid being outflanked. This put the command post of the 370th Infantry Regiment and the advance command post of the 92nd Infantry Division in danger of being captured. They displaced to the rear as the 598th Field Artillery Battalion fired on the advancing enemy columns. Despite this the enemy outflanked the 370th Infantry Regiment and overran their positions on a six-mile front on both sides of the river as the 366th and 370th Infantry regiments fell back to a new line established by the 366th Infantry Regiment.

With the Battle of the Bulge underway in France, Belgium, and Luxembourg anxiety grew among Allied commanders in Italy. Anticipating an enemy offensive, the U.S. Fifth Army moved the South African 6th Armored Division into the area and placed other units on alert. Additionally they ordered the Indian 8th Infantry Division to reinforce the 92nd Infantry Division: "On December 22nd a dramatic call came. Once again the High Command had anticipated trouble,—this time on the Fifth Army front, where the American 92nd Division held a sector fifteen miles in front of Lucca, a provincial town which covered the main American supply base at Leghorn. 19th and 21st Brigades suddenly found themselves in Lorries, skidding their way down the slippery Apennine switchbacks, on a ride one hundred miles to the west" (War Department, Government of India).[7] By the time the 8th Indian Division arrived, the Germans had already broken through and routed the Americans.

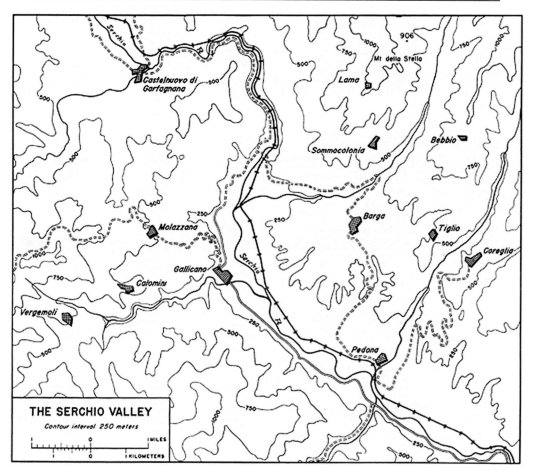

92nd Infantry Division battle map (National Archives and Records Administration, courtesy Davide Del Giudice).

Bewildered by this breakthrough, Lieutenant General Truscott, who had taken over command of the U.S. Fifth Army from Lieutenant General Clark on December 16, immediately ordered additional troops to the vicinity, the 1st Armored Division along with regimental combat teams from the 34th and 85th Infantry divisions. Truscott reinforced them with additional artillery, which caused a severe dislocation of the entire U.S. Fifth Army front.

Prior to Operation Winter Storm, German intelligence, well aware of the racist leadership of the 92nd Infantry Division, learned the circumstances of the thinly spread 366th and 370th Infantry Regiments in the Serchio sector. They took full advantage of the situation. In a postwar interview, Lieutenant Colonel Thomas Arnold, the 92nd Infantry Division's G-3 (Plans and Operations Officer), obtained a German officer's statement: "The weakness of your deployment in the Serchio Valley in December 1944 were that your troops were deployed on a front which was too long for the number of troops available, and your reserves were too far in the rear area which prevented their being deployed immediately" (Lieutenant General Otto Fretter-Pico, Commanding Officer, 148th German Infantry Division).[8] The enemy diverted Allied troops from their central front to their western flank as they had set out to do. From there they broke off the attack and withdrew and formed a new line of resistance about one mile south of their original line. They returned with stockpiles of captured weapons, food, and equipment along with 250 Allied prisoners.

By January 1 the enemy threat to the U.S. Fifth Army supply line no longer existed. The Indians, in direct contact with the enemy, regained most of the terrain east of the river including Sommocolonia. In the rubble they found the shattered bodies of First Lieutenant Fox and his men along with over 100 enemy troops. Meanwhile, the 370th Infantry Regiment regained most of the terrain west of the river.

During this period negative reports reinforcing the army's prejudices poured into the War Department. This alarmed the civilian advisor on Negro Affairs, Truman K. Gibson, Jr. He asked Major Oscar Magee, of the War Department's Intelligence Division, who was on his way to report back to Italy, to investigate. The investigation turned up the phrase "melts away." Magee's report quoted: "Too frequently the infantry 'melts away' under fire and an abnormal number of men hide in cellars until they are routed out by their officers."[9] The civilian advisor's reaction follows:

> For four hours I interrogated Magee and turned up the ugly stench of bigotry emanating from commanders in Italy. White officers detailed to black units felt they were doing penance. The ranking officers in the division had no faith in the black GIs they commanded. "I don't trust Negroes," Major Theodore Arnold was quoted as saying. "There have been many examples of individual heroism on the part of Negro officers and soldiers," said Colonel William J. McCaffrey, the chief of staff of the 92nd. "However, I believe that the Negro generally cannot overcome or escape his background [of] no property ownership, irresponsibility and subservience. The Negro is panicky and his environment hasn't conditioned him to accept responsibilities." What would be the effect on fighting morale of officers who dislike their assignments and don't believe in the troops they commanded?[10]

Major Magee returned again with more conflicting evidence such that a person with a bias could prove or disprove anything he desired. He also brought back an invitation form Lieutenant General Mark Clark, then commander of the Fifth Army, for Gibson to come to Italy to see the deeds of the 92nd Infantry Division in person. Gibson told Assistant Secretary of War John McCloy that they should consider his accepting the invitation.

In the meantime, Clark filed a disturbing report on the first elements of the 92nd to engage the enemy. Clark stated that most of the junior officers failed to show the "leadership, initiative, responsibility and aggressiveness" needed for "offensive combat against determined opposition." The enlisted men "exhibited more nervousness and less aggressive will to fight in the face of danger than do white soldiers.... Experience so far has shown that unless the men are under the immediate control and guidance of effective leaders they are apt to shrink from danger and to fall away from their units as they close with the enemy. The most flagrant cases are malingerers who, in several instances, have been found to have hidden rather than go forward." In the interim, fifty soldiers had been court-martialed for "misbehavior before the enemy."[11]

It was not difficult to envision that preconceived prejudices against black soldiers were being expressed and reinforced.

As December 1944 ended, the 758th Tank Battalion completed its battle indoctrination. Completely attached to the 92nd Infantry Division, they had engaged the enemy together. Mindful of their training period together at Fort Huachuca, they witnessed the infantrymen's degradation by their racist commanders. Despite this, the tankers concentrated on Tank-Infantry teamwork.

11

Probing the Gothic Line

For nine months Field Marshall Kesselring directed the construction of the Gothic Line fortifications in the rugged mountains of the Apennines. They were built by the slave labor of approximately 15,000 Italians forced to dig or blast antitank ditches, gun emplacements, machine-gun nests, rifle pits, and trenches. The entrenched positions, drilled out of solid rock and reinforced with concrete, ran from the coastal area to the mountains and beyond. These fortress-like positions could produce interlocking fields of fire and their observation posts commanded views from which practically anything that moved could be spotted.

In January 1945 the main line of resistance stabilized along the Gothic Line as the 92nd Infantry Division held their positions, intensified patrolling, and improved their defenses. Heavy snowfall and arctic temperatures impeded movement. The two opposing forces thinly spread both laterally and in depth, sat across from each other and deployed patrols to probe for intelligence, take prisoners, and inflict lethal pain. The 758th Tank Battalion operated in a complex environment. Platoon Sergeant John Weston explains: "I was with Company A, 758th Light Tank Battalion, platoon sergeant for the first platoon. We had five tanks and a medic jeep. But our platoon was never with the company after we left Pietra Santa. From there the outfit split up and different platoons went in different directions. We went up into the mountains to support the infantry and I don't know what happened to the rest of the outfit. We didn't come together again until we came to Genoa."[1]

The breadth of the Gothic Line and its temperament of terrain in the 92nd Infantry Division's zone compelled two separate fronts, i.e., the rugged mountains east of the Serchio River and the seaside west of the river. The steep mountains were generally impassable except by mule and troops on foot. "We went up into the mountains" said platoon Sergeant Weston. "That was quite a trip because we had to take those tanks up into the mountains along those narrow roads. We stayed up there for about a month. We fired our guns—we only had 37-millimeter guns and the enemy had big artillery guns. We could fire across the valley and places like that but not any distance firing. The mountain roads were just wide enough for our light tanks to get through safely and you had to hug the mountain side of the road because on the other side you don't have a railing. You are looking straight down into a valley."[2]

East of the Serchio River in the rugged terrain a ten-man patrol from Easy Company, 371st Infantry Regiment, patrolled east of Mount Strettoia seeking an enemy observation post. They found nothing in the hilltop hamlet. Then three scouts from the patrol climbed farther to investigate and found a cluster of five bunkers. The first four contained nothing. As the scouts approached the fifth, an enemy soldier rose and fired his burp gun wildly. Before the patrol could take cover the German begged to surrender. The patrol held its fire, and then suddenly two more Germans appeared and opened fire. In the ensuing firefight, the patrol killed all three of the enemy and then pulled back in time to avoid German mortar fire that came crashing down.

Love Company, 371st Infantry Regiment, patrolled from Mount Strettoia to Seravezza being supported by B/758th

Gothic Line historical marker at the mouth of the Cinquale Canal, where the February 1945 battle took place. Mount Folgorito is in the background (courtesy Davide Del Giudice).

light tanks. They fired on enemy positions north of Barga, the picturesque medieval walled fortress town with clay-tiled roofs. Three enemy deserters of Polish decent capitulated and divulged that an Allied fire mission shot out their observation post. As they were speaking, a huge explosion from behind enemy lines shook the entire area, followed by plumes of billowing smoke. Meanwhile, a patrol from Item Company, 371st Infantry Regiment, on their way to search buildings in Pian di Lago got pinned down by plunging enemy machine-gun fire. They called and directed mortar fire on the enemy positions, which allowed their escape with only one casualty. On the other side of the mountain a patrol from Easy Company shot two enemy soldiers standing guard outside a house on the western slope of the mountain. The enemy fired back with well-aimed small arms that overwhelmed the patrol and forced a withdrawal.

West of the Serchio River along Highway 1, elements of the 366th Infantry Regiment reconnoitered the village of Strettoia and the surrounding hills. They were

John Weston brandishing his Model 1911 Colt pistol as his tank driver looks on (courtesy John Weston).

supported by elements of the 758th Tank Battalion including the Assault Gun and Mortar platoons, who fired harassing salvos on enemy positions. The streets in Strettoia were too narrow for a light tank and the off-road mountainous terrain too steep and jagged, so they stayed behind. The Mortar Platoon lobbed high explosives over the hills and made direct hits on enemy positions but left trails in the sky from their rockets. The enemy quickly spotted them and returned fire, destroying the ammunition stockpile and damaging a half-track. The advance came to a halt in the Strettoia hills due to accurate enemy artillery and machine-gun fire.

Along the sea, tanks from the 758th and 760th Tank battalions surveyed the Cinquale Canal for fords that would support an armored crossing. Item Company, 366th In-

Sergeant William H. Smith (courtesy William H. Smith).

fantry Regiment probed, across. "Arriving at the company area I found everybody loading up with hand grenades and extra rounds of ammo, and stripping down to just the necessary equipment for a raid. I reported to Captain Overall, who told me I was leading the company across the Cinquale Canal.... When I was given the order to pull out, I started saying my prayers, knowing I am the first to cross into enemy territory and being exposed, searching for good cover and a place to cross the canal. Thinking of my family back home, where I wished I was right then. Well, I swallowed a couple of times and started across the canal," said Sergeant Harold Russell, Jr., Item Company, 366th Infantry Regiment.[3] Spot-on mortar and machine-gun fire prevented their advance on three attempts. Machine-gun fire hit Sergeant Russell in the hip and he was evacuated to an aid station: "About this time some of the wounded patrol starting coming in. I learned Captain Overall didn't make it, nor did Sergeant Mahaley. The 2nd Platoon I was told got captured. Other names were being called off, were either missing, wounded, or dead. I was getting sleepy and must have dozed off. I don't remember the trip to Pisa General Hospital."[4]

Able Company, 758th Tank Battalion, sent their Second Platoon to support elements of the 894th Tank Destroyer Battalion along the coast between seaside resort towns. Enemy artillery spotted their forward movement and stopped their advance. Private Willie L. Cox was wounded and three deuce-and-a-half trucks were damaged.

January 1945 came to an end with continued heavy snow and freezing temperatures. The big picture remained unchanged as patrols and sporadic artillery fire continued. Enemy espionage increased and resulted in too-accurate artillery fire upon the 758th Tank Battalion and units they supported. Extreme caution was taken to insure loyalty of civilians in 758th areas of operations and all were prohibited from the command post area. Sergeant William Smith, A/758th, saw firsthand the damage that could be done:

> After we came back from fighting we would take the tanks and clean them out and then we could go to town. And that was in Italy. We went to town and we had a good time. We met people and learned the language. I learned the dirty part of the language. We had a good time over there but of course you had to watch out because the Germans would slip one in on you to get information or they would kill one of the fellas. I remember when we were in Italy and we were getting ready to go into another place to fight. The lieutenant went through the tents and found one of the guys dead, stabbed. And none of us knew anything about it, that's how they slipped in and slipped out of the camp.[5]

The battalion reported four men in January 1945, wounded in action and hospitalized: Technician Fourth Grade Clarence Lee, Private Willie Gorham, Private Emory Cox, Jr., and Private Albert Martin. Eight vehicles were lost. Two trucks and two half-tracks were lost to enemy actions. Two tanks, one truck, and one jeep suffered mechanical failure, all of which were repaired and put back into service.

12

February Offensive

Up to February 1945 offensive actions by the 92nd Infantry Division took place in a piecemeal fashion. Major General Almond remained anxious to launch a combined attack and pierce the Gothic Line. The plan called for two phases in a three-pronged assault preceded by a diversionary attack in the Serchio Valley. The diversion took place three days prior to the principal attack and consisted of the 365th Infantry Regiment with elements of the 366th Infantry Regiment.

Their plan was to engage, absorb, and draw enemy reserves into the Serchio while the three-pronged attack proceeded. The first phase of the two-phased attack was to capture Montignoso and Mount Folgorito; the second was the capture of Massa and the Frigido River line. The three prongs were as follows: (1) on the west flank, a tank-infantry task force named Task Force 1 built around the 3rd Battalion of the 366th Infantry Regiment and commanded by Lieutenant Colonel Edward Rowney, the commanding officer of the 317th Engineer (Combat) Battalion, and facing the Cinquale Canal (the 760th Tank Battalion and Able Company, 758th Tank Battalion, prepared to spearhead Task Force One); (2) in the center, the 370th Infantry Regiment faced the Strettoia hills; and (3) on the east flank, the 371st Infantry Regiment faced the rugged terrain on Folgorito Ridge.

Prior to the diversionary attack, Baker and Charlie companies, 758th Tank Battalion, sent unit commanders to reconnoiter routes of approach to support the 366th Infantry Regiment west of the Serchio River and the 365th Infantry Regiment east of that river. The light tanks moved into position under the cover of darkness and the following morning elements of the 366th Infantry Regiment attacked toward Gallicano while the 365th Infantry Regiment attacked towards Barga, Sommocolonia, and Bebbio. They set out to retake some of the land lost to the enemy's offensive—Operation Winter Storm.

The diversionary attack began on February 5. Elements of the 366th Infantry Regiment west of the Serchio River advanced half a mile over mine fields and scattered resistance to capture the village of Calomini. Baker Company's 1st Platoon had three light tanks destroyed by mines:

Seven February 1945, my platoon—1st Platoon, Company B—being attached to the 1st Battalion, 366th Infantry Regiment, was given a mission to patrol the road running from Gallicano to

Broglia. On the return trip to Gallicano the second tank in column hit a mine, which blew the right suspension system off, continuing on my mission the fifth tank in column hit a mine. This road had been reported to me as being cleared of mines. The tanks were ordered over this road by the battalion commanding officer, which my unit was attached. The mine platoon was to have cleared the mines. A day or so later the mine platoon was sent out to clear mines on the Gallicano—Molazzana road, due to the weather the platoon progress was slow. The platoon leader reported that he would not have the mines cleared because they were buried deeply. I was ordered through the battalion commanding officer, 366th Infantry to go ahead with my mission whether the mines were cleared or not. Another vehicle struck a mine and was disabled. This terrain is no place for tanks, the reason being that I have no freedom of maneuver and the vehicular guns cannot elevate enough to cover the crest, and cannot depress enough to bear fire on the draw which the enemy occupies. Vehicles at this point are perfect targets for all flat trajectory weapons which are reported in the vicinity. The vehicle disabled by mine is a total loss because of the impossibility of the recovery vehicle to get there [First Lieutenant William Hannah, B/758th].[1]

East of the Serchio River, elements of the 365th and 366th Infantry regiments jumped off approximately five miles east of Gallicano with the objective of capturing the Lama di Sotto ridge. The assault surprised the enemy and the ridge fell quickly. However, the ridge afforded excellent observation toward German strong points that the enemy could ill-afford to relinquish. Fierce counterattacks ensued and control of the ridge changed hands several times. When the smoke cleared on February 11 the Lama di Sotto ridge belonged to the enemy. The 365th Infantry Regiment set up forward outposts, with a net gain of three-quarters of a mile.

During the night of February 7 the attacking elements of the 92nd Infantry Division moved into assembly areas. At 0600 hours the following day they jumped off. Major General Almond had with him the U.S. Fifth Army commander, Lieutenant General Truscott, and the IV Corps commander, Major General Crittenberger, along with staff members. They assembled at an observation post to watch the attack after a concentrated artillery and mortar barrage. To conceal the forward movements of the tanks, large plumes of smoke were intermingled with the high explosives. The division's three-pronged attack focused on breaching the remaining Gothic Line positions that fiercely guarded the La Spezia naval base and the road to Parma, Reggio, and Modena.

In Prong 1, on the 92nd Infantry Division's west flank, Task Force 1 traversed a mine field before reaching the Cinquale Canal. "The mine field was extensive and thick, with one layer just below the surface and a second layer about three feet below the surface with a baseball-type stick on top of it. Anti-personnel mines were also scattered through the antitank mine field," said Lieutenant Colonel Edward Rowney, the Task Force 1 commander.[2]

Task Force 1 jumped off ahead of schedule, traversing a large marsh area to the mouth of the canal. The plan of attack called for engineers and infantry to ride on the tanks of the 760th Tank Battalion across the shallow waters of the Ligurian Sea at the mouth of the canal. Since the beaches were heavily mined, the first tanks carried combat engineers who dismounted and cleared the way for the other tanks. The infantry dismounted to protect the combat engineers while they removed mines.

They had a platoon of light tanks and a platoon of tank destroyers attached who deployed to the flanks to meet enemy crossings and counter attacks. Lieutenant Colonel Rowney recalled the event later:

> By 0430 I was at the starting point for the attack. I made a last minute check on all arrangements and gave the artillery the go ahead signal to begin their preparatory fire. Covered by the noise of the artillery barrage the tanks began to turn over their motors. A few minutes before the lead tank was to move out the smoke generators began to belch their heavy white clouds and smoke hugged the ground as though painted into the landscape. Promptly at 0500 the first wave shoved off. My command group, totaling ten persons including myself, was to follow this first wave. The remaining two companies were to follow me. In about ten minutes the first company had cleared past me. The job of clearing mines in the gap to the sea had been done well and as far as I could see, no trouble had been encountered almost up to the mouth of the canal.[3]

Elements of the 758th Tank Battalion supported Task Force 1. First Lieutenant Harry Duplessis, A/758th, continues the narrative:

> While the mechanics were still trying to get our tanks into shape, an order came through for us to move them out, on the double, up to the Cinquale Canal sector. Infantrymen of the 366th and 370th were to make an assault across the canal. We could only put five tanks on the road because of the terrible condition of our assigned equipment. We arrived at the canal and had to walk out into it to see about the footing; it was in February. Tanks will sink without a solid base. We asked for a load of gravel or anything to assure our being able to make it to the other side. We had found places, especially on the other bank that once wet could cause sliding, thus holding up those behind and causing them to drown out. We were told, "To get those damned tanks across the canal."[4]

Able Company 758th Tank Battalion, ordered their 1st Platoon over the canal first. The platoon sergeant's light tank went first and tipped over. The noise of artillery fire was deafening as geysers erupted from explosions that sent columns of seawater splashing over the tanks. The front end of the second tank dipped and disappeared into the canal as seawater rose over its running boards and spilled inside and sloshed around. As water began seeping into the engine crankcase, reality suddenly overtook the tankers. They felt their hearts pounding and cold sweat beading on their foreheads. Then the second tank tipped over. "One of the mortars hit underneath the bridge and that's what capsized my tank. We left the tank sitting there and they zeroed in on it and knocked it out. I waved the other tanks to go around me. We had jumped into the water and it was pretty deep there. We had to go back to shore. The Cinquale Canal was about as wide as a football field. It was along the Mediterranean seaside. Men from the 760th Tank Battalion picked us up and took us back to our staging area," explained Platoon Sergeant John Weston (A/758th).[5]

The commander of the third tank, Sergeant Jefferson Hightower, A/758th recalled the following:

> In my memory it was February 12, 1945, and the Germans were retreating to the north and the 92nd Infantry Division wasn't able to break through. There was a canal that went down to the Mediterranean Sea. 758th, A Company, 1st Platoon, which I was a part of, was given the job of crossing that canal and picking up the infantry and making an advance up the coast. I was in tank number three—Lieutenant McClain was in tank number one. When he hit that canal he turned over and all of them jumped out into the cold water and made it back to the beach. Tank

number two tried to pass him and they turned over too. I'm in tank number three and I'm sure he is going to tell me to turn around and go back. He is lying there in the sand on the beach cursing and waving me to go across. My driver, who was very good, went around those two tanks and kept his foot on the gas long enough to keep water from sucking up into the engine and we made it across. Tank number four turned over and tank number five, commanded by Sergeant Seymour Miller of New York, make it across. As soon as we made it across some officer from the 92nd told us to go back. "We can't go any farther right now and all you guys do is draw fire." He was right, we were drawing fire. We drew fire from those big naval 12- and 14-inch guns. And then the officer insisted that we go back because he had infantry out there and he didn't want their positions given away. We made it back across the canal by taking the same route. I will never forget that, because the shells were coming so close to us that I could see fire coming out of the tail ends. They came right at us and we had to maneuver through them. If they caught you—you were gone![6]

Able Company's commanding officer was wounded in the canal:

Captain Morgan got out of his tank and walked so the tanks could follow his for a sound bottom. Just as he reached the other side he stepped on a mine and got a back full of fragments. There was a group of medium tanks, white, behind us and every one of us that managed to get across slipped and slid around that opposite bank and got the hell shot out of us, rendering our tanks absolutely useless. The others, backed up in the canal, just as we had predicted, drowned out. You had some pretty angry tankers, black and white; the utter waste because of rank stupidity. We lost one officer, who covered his men so they could escape. The infantrymen we were supposed to cover had waded on across, when I say waded I mean waist-high on the average man; they got the hell shot out of them once they moved up from the north bank of the canal [First-Lieutenant Harry Duplessis, A/758th].[7]

The infantry crossed the canal. However, once they were across the tide came in fast. There were only a few places the tanks and vehicles could cross. It appeared that every time a tank reached those fording places the German artillery on top of the mountains zeroed in. Most of the tanks were either hit or drowned out. "As far as I could tell, there had not been a single casualty up to this point. While comforting myself with this thought, the first of several long-range shells from the Punta Bianca naval guns near La Spezia began to land right in the mouth of the canal. The first one hit squarely in the middle of my little command group and when I looked around there were only two others who had not been hit. The shell had killed seven. The entire mouth of the canal appeared to turn red with blood," said Lieutenant Colonel Rowney.[8]

The foot soldiers who made it across the canal stayed for three days with practically no tank support, being methodically cut to pieces by enemy artillery. "Let me explain something, from an artillery man's viewpoint, above the Cinquale Canal," said Captain Hondon Hargrove (C Battery, 597th Artillery Field Battalion). "Our guns faced the mountain ranged called Cauala. Now we were up in the mountains but we were looking up at the Germans ... and he was always looking down at us. Cauala was a series of razor back mountains that got higher the further north you went.... Directly left and in front of us was La Speza, an Italian naval base. Naval guns there were still operating and they could bring fire to bear on the Cinquale but we damned sure couldn't reach them with our field pieces. There was other German artillery throughout these mountains; the Germans could bring tremendous fire power to bear upon that little canal."[9]

A German coastal defense battery in the same specifications as the one at Punta Bianca (Bundesarchiv Bild 146–1986–104-10A).

From another vantage point, First Lieutenant Joseph Hairston, Charlie Battery, 599th Field Artillery Battalion, observed:

> If you can imagine an ocean on the west, flat lands, and then a mountain going up, then a canal running from the base of the mountain to the sea on the coast and then swamp land on both sides of the canal. Now if you commit tanks, you can't commit tanks in a mountain. Tanks operate on flat or nearly flat terrain. Our Division Commander ordered a tank attack along the flat lands. Now we had to cross the Cinquale Canal. The Germans had mined both sides of the canal so the General sent in the engineers to clear the mines. The engineers cleared a space about wide enough for a tank to go through on both sides of the canal, under fire but they cleared the mines and the tanks were committed. So the Germans were sitting up on the hill, well enforced, watching all this action throwing a round over every now and then. But no serious opposition, the tanks started going through. When about six or eight tanks had gone through, the Germans knocked out the first tank then they knocked out the back tank. And mines are on both sides. We lost more tanks in that engagement I am told than in any other single engagement of the whole war. But the stupidity of engaging tanks in single file through a mined area, it makes no sense. Even a non-military person could see that you don't want your tanks lined up like ducks, you want your tanks spread out because of the rotating tank turrets could cover a lot of ground, but if you line them up, and like the Germans did, knock out the first one and the others are sitting ducks. We witnessed that as I was actually supplying artillery support for that attack which failed miserably.[10]

The infantry kept digging into the flat, soggy terrain as the praying and moaning became audible. The engineers cleared the dead and wounded from the lane. They removed ten dead soldiers, to a clump of trees and out of sight, and then transported twenty wounded agonized men to the basement of a bombed-out house. By noon the first wave had cleared the beach and moved forward. "While this was going on," said Lieutenant Colonel Rowney, "Major Willis D. Polk, the battalion commander, came toward me. I noticed that he had been shot in the shoulder. He told me that he wanted to reassure me that he was up forward doing everything that he could to get the men into position and that he would have to be hit harder than he was to make him stop. There was no bravado in his voice—it was filled with sincerity. Later that afternoon, I found him lying in the vicinity of the lead tank with a bullet hole between his eyes."[11]

The 3rd Battalion, 366th Infantry Regiment, the unit that Task Force 1 developed around, sustained heavy casualties among the rank and file and had its top leadership wiped out. Their commanding officer, executive officer, and operations officer were all killed in action. Troops were scattered about and completely disorganized. It became apparent that further attempts to advance would be futile and Task Force 1 was called off and withdrew back across the canal.

Lieutenant Colonel Thomas Arnold, the 92nd Infantry Division's plans and operations officer, conducted a postwar interview with the German commanding general responsible for this area, Lieutenant General Otto Fretter-Pico, 148th Genadier Infantry Division. Fretter-Pico said, "My initial reaction to the attack of the 92nd Division on 8 to 11 February 1945 was that of not too much concern as I knew that

Punta Bianca ruins as seen from the Ligurian Sea today (courtesy Davide Del Giudice).

the 92nd Division had not received front line replacements for this attack. I did not consider this action as a major offense, but only as an attack to relieve the fight at the main front. I was right in that the attack was halted and no other attacks followed immediately."[12]

Prong 2 was the 92nd Infantry Division center, and the 3rd Battalion of the 370th Infantry Regiment jumped off near Querceta at 0600 hours on February 8 following an artillery barrage by the 598th Field Artillery Battalion. The foot soldiers moved in two columns along ridges through the Strettoia Hills towards Canal Montignoso. The other battalions followed this narrow path through the Strettoia Hills, designated Hills X, Y, and Z. They crossed Hill X first, followed by Hill Y to the north until it intersected with the east-west Montignoso draw. Hill Z, called the Ice Cream Cone, stood east of Hill Y. Their heights ranged from approximately 450 to 600 feet.

Ruins of a Punta Bianca small arms pill-box destroyed by air raids (courtesy Davide Del Giudice).

To divert the enemy's attention from the advance in the Strettoia Hills, a tank force pushed up Highway 1 spearheaded by a company of medium tanks from the 760th Tank Battalion and the 2nd and 3rd platoons from Able Company, 758th Tank Battalion—light tanks. They transported elements of the 317th Engineer (Combat) Battalion and the 370th Antitank Mine Platoon on their backs. The lead tank hit a mine and the advance came to a halt. Accurate enemy machine-gun fire prevented the combat engineers from clearing the mines and the tanks became sitting ducks for antitank fire.

Back in the Strettoia Hills, antipersonnel mines and wire entanglements slowed the advance on Hill Y, the second hill. The 3rd Battalion's Love Company on the left and King Company on its right encountered heavy automatic weapons fire that brought the advance to a halt. King Company, to the rear, dug in and called for artillery support while Item Company advanced on Hill Y. The 2nd Battalion moved up behind the 3rd Battalion and ascended Hill X, with orders to dig in and prepare to attack Hill Y in the morning. The Germans observed this troop positioning from Hill Z, the

Observation bunker at Punta Bianca today (courtesy Davide Del Giudice).

tallest peak in the area. They waited until reinforcement arrived, a complete Grenadier-Infantry Regiment, and before dark they unleashed hell. They launched an inferno-like mortar barrage of incendiary rounds (white phosphorus) that stuck and burned fiercely as it ignited clothes and ammunition. The enemy followed with accurate machine-gun fire that inflicted heavy casualties, including killing a company commander and wounding two other officers. Confusion and panic followed in the evacuation of Hill Y as some withdrew to Hill X and others scattered about. The 2nd Battalion, on Hill X, came under the same mortar barrage and machine-gun fire. With Hill Y completely evacuated, what remained of the 3rd Battalion, 370th Infantry Regiment—approximately 80 men—consolidated their positions with the 2nd Battalion, 370th Infantry Regiment, on Hill X. Most of the officers took part in rounding up their men scattered by this inferno-like rout.

The following day's activities consisted of rounding up scattered troops, reorganizing formations, and consolidating positions on Hill X. When the IV Corps commander, Major General Crittenberger, got word of the rout he insisted that the attack be scrubbed. The 92nd Infantry Division's commander, Major General Edward Almond, arrogantly rejected his superior officer's instruction. "The Division will resume the attack tomorrow unless there is a new division commander here before that time," Major General Almond said.[13]

What remained of the 3rd Battalion, 370th Infantry Regiment, moved back to Hill X during the night and at dawn attacked the still-smoldering Hill Y. The attack began at 0630 hours on 10 February. The 3rd Battalion, a skeleton crew of eighty men led by two officers, ran directly into another mortar inferno. This disrupted their

Ruins of the tunnel under Battery Punta Bianca that housed a large artillery piece on railway tracks. It would come out under cover of darkness or smoke to fire and then immediately retreat back inside (courtesy Davide Del Giudice).

formation to the extent that scattered soldiers had to be organized into lines set up in the rear. With this setback, Major General Almond finally called in reserves. He ordered the 371st Infantry Regiment Reserve (3rd Battalion) to assist the 2nd and 3rd battalions of the 370th Infantry Regiment. The 3rd Battalion, 371st Infantry, established a foothold on Hill Y by mid-morning. The troops held their ground in a vicious firefight. Around noon, the commanding officer of the 3rd Battalion, 371st Infantry Regiment, Lieutenant Colonel Arthur Walker, was killed in action.

At 0730 hours on February 11 the enemy launched a counterattack in force and the Americans evacuated Hill Y in disarray. A determined enemy, supported by effective machine-gun, mortar, and artillery fire, extracted a heavy toll on the infantrymen and wiped out their leadership. This severely demoralized and disorganized the 370th Infantry Regiment and the reserve battalion from the 371st Infantry Regiment. At the end of the four-day operation, the survivors of the regiment found themselves back at the original jump-off point.

Prong 3, on the 92nd Infantry Division's east flank, the 371st Infantry Regiment, faced the rugged terrain of Folgorito Ridge. There the enemy had a system of interlocking fortifications with machine guns, mortars, and artillery emplacements chiseled into the rock. Deep ravines cut through peaks and shrubs dotted the landscape. Here the 1st and 2nd battalions attacked the Gothic Line through barbed wire and mine fields while their 3rd Battalion remained in reserve.

The jagged ridge of Mount Folgorito runs north from Vallecchia to Genoa and overlooks the Ligurian coastal area. Its peaks rise to over 4,500 feet and while it was in enemy hands the route to Massa and Genoa remained closed. The uneven rises leading up to Folgorito peak had been given code names: Rocky-Ridge, Maine, Florida, Georgia, and Ohio.

The 1st Battalion attacked the emplacements on Maine, where the approaches were almost straight up. They quickly gained a foothold until a small but determined enemy force drove them out. The 2nd Battalion attacked Rocky-Ridge and quickly gained a foothold until George Company got strafed by friendly fire from American fighter bombers. This resulted in a number of casualties, including the company commander. Fox Company came up to sustain the attack and cover the reorganization. There they inflicted casualties on the enemy and took twenty-five prisoners. Shortly thereafter enemy resistance increased and halted the American advance. When the enemy counterattacked in force, they was disrupted by accurate artillery fire assisted by the 758th Tank Battalion's Assault Gun Platoon. Progress on both sides came to a standstill.

The Allies needed maneuvering room to take advantage of their superior resources and materiel but the mountainous terrain of the Gothic Line would not allow it. It was becoming trench warfare similar to that of World War I. The Germans established machine-gun and mortar positions in rock formations at one end of an opening, and when the advancing infantry began to make progress against them they fell back to similar well-prepared positions before counterattacking. Despite their lack of sufficient airpower, the Germans gave ground sparingly. The highly experienced German troops knew the complexities of the battlefield.

Inside the bunker at Punta Bianca today (courtesy Davide Del Giudice).

Throughout the four-day operations, the troops fought skillfully and the scattering of troops was negligible. Despite not reaching all objectives, they advanced 800 yards and held their positions against determined resistance. The 371st Infantry Regiment suffered approximately 129 casualties: eight officers and 121 men killed, wounded, or missing, of which four officers and seventeen men were killed in action.

In summary, the four-day, three-pronged divisional attack that began with a diversion ended in a stalemate in the mountains and on the coast. The 92nd Infantry Division sustained casualties of forty-seven officers and 659 men killed, wounded, or missing in action. The division achieved a slight improvement in its positions, but the main contribution came from pinning down enemy forces and perplexing them as to future Allied intentions. Additionally, a considerable amount of information on enemy strength and disposition was revealed. This proved to be valuable for the upcoming spring offensive.

As the negative reports flooded in to Washington from Italy, it was time for the civilian aide to the secretary of war, Truman Gibson, Jr., to take Lieutenant General Mark Clark up on his invitation. "That opportunity came in early February 1945, when the Ninety-second hurled into the Gothic Line. Alas, the attack failed after several days and the word reaching us in Washington was that the black soldiers had 'melted away' under fire from the Germans. It was time for me to take Clark up on his invitation. [Assistant Secretary of War] McCloy wrote him that I would be visiting

The roof of the bunker at Punta Bianca today (courtesy Davide Del Giudice).

The Cinquale Canal today (courtesy Davide Del Giudice).

Europe 'to observe the performance of Negro troops, their attitudes, and the attitudes of their officers towards them,'" said Gibson.[14]

Gibson boarded a U.S. Army Air Forces DC-3 and took off over the Atlantic Ocean. He was strapped into an aluminum bucket seat and bounced around in transit. They stopped in the Canary Islands for refueling and then took off for Casablanca, where Gibson got acquainted with ancient-era personal hygiene. The toilet consisted of a mere hole in the floor. At any rate, he got a few hours of sleep in a bed before taking off on the final leg of the journey. They landed in Caserta, Italy, on February 26, 1945.

Gibson's old friend from the War Department, Major General Otto Nelson, now deputy commander of the Mediterranean Theater of Operations, greeted him upon landing. Together they climbed into an army sedan and sped off to the Royal Palace of Caserta, the king of Naples' winter palace, then being used as the headquarters for the MTO. There Gibson met with the theater commander, Lieutenant General Joseph McNarney.

McNarney handed Gibson a report from Lieutenant General Clark. The report stated that the division had been capably commanded by Almond and praised the regimental and battalion commanders, i.e.: the white officers. Everything else was disparaging. It expounded that the 92nd was subpar to the seven other U.S. divisions in northern Italy. They failed to stand firm under counterattack. The troops were disinclined to close for hand-to-hand combat and entire units had disintegrated under artillery fire. The noncommissioned officers and the junior commissioned officers, i.e., the black leaders, had failed. Clearly the 92nd was being characterized as a failed division.

Gibson immediately objected to praising only white officers and completely laying the failure on the black junior officers and men. McNarney denied the objections and informed Gibson his officers had recommended that the division be pulled out of the line and the order was awaiting his signature. Gibson implored him to wait and took off to see Lieutenant General Clark, who also refused to rescind the order to take the 92nd out of the line. Clark believed that the failure of the 92nd had stalled the entire Allied effort to breach the Gothic Line. Clark had recently been promoted to commander of the Fifteenth Army Group, and Gibson then went to see Lieutenant General Lucian Truscott, Jr., who was Clark's successor as Fifth Army commander. Truscott wrote his own devastating report about the 92nd. Again Gibson's plea was rejected.

For Gibson's final attempt, Major General Otto Nelson took him to the battlefield commander, Major General Willis Crittenberger, IV Corps. Gibson's friendship with Nelson made these impromptu meetings possible and Gibson later recalled the event:

> Then came one of those peculiar episodes that make the recounting of history so enjoyable. Crittenberger said he would help me out if I could give him a hand with a problem he had with Major General Joao Baptista Mascarenhas de Marais of the Brazilian Expeditionary Force. Those troops had been "bloodied," and afterward their general would not visit them. "What can I do?" I asked. Crittenberger produced two bottles of cognac and said, "Let's go see him." So off we went to the Brazilian command. Otto and I were introduced to Mascarenhas, and Crittenberger pulled out the bottles, opened them, and poured a glass for everyone. Then commenced one toast after another. We toasted President Roosevelt, the president of Brazil, Secretary of War Stimson, the Brazilian minister of war, General Crittenberger, Otto, and finally I was treated to a toast. The bait had been taken. Then Crittenberger dropped this one: "Truman, would you like to review the Brazilian troops?" The trap

General of the Army George C. Marshall visits the U.S. Army's senior leadership in Italy at the 92nd Infantry Division's headquarters on February 14, 1945. Standing, left to right: Major Gen. Alfred M. Gruenther, chief of staff, 15th Army Group; Lt. Gen. Mark W. Clark, CG of 15th Army Group; General of the Army George C. Marshall; Lt. Gen. Lucian K. Truscott, CG of Fifth Army after Dec 1944; Major Gen. Edward M. Almond, CG of 92nd Division; Lt. Gen. Joseph McNarney, U.S. Army Mediterranean Theater of Operations; and Major Gen. Willis D. Crittenberger, CG of IV Corps (courtesy George C. Marshall Foundation, Virginia Military Institute).

was sprung. I said yes, working up all the enthusiasm I could. How could Mascarenhas refuse! We piled into a jeep, and off we went. Unknown to us, the Germans were watching through high-powered binoculars. The wind blew Mascarenhas's parka back, exposing the gold on his cap. The Germans saw they had a high value target, and one of their eight-eight guns belched out a shell. It exploded close to us, fortunately not harming anyone but leaving us all with a good scare.

Well, I had done my part, and Crittenberger delivered on his end, dispatching a recommendation that McNarney hold off on signing that order until I had conducted my investigation. McNarney gave me two weeks to supply him with any pertinent information that might change his view, including the influence of racial attitudes on the performance of the enlisted men and officers of the Ninety-second in combat.[15]

From the first to the eighth of March, Gibson spent his waking hours with the 92nd traveling from Leghorn to Viareggio. He interviewed over a thousand soldiers, both officers and enlisted men. The company officers informed him that there was

John Weston's platoon members: Sergeant Seymour Miller (second from the left) and three unidentified others.

little or no pattern in the tendency of "melting away." At times an entire platoon or company would fold but the entire unit would not break. Additionally, the twenty-six hundred recent replacements in the 92nd came from service organizations and had no infantry training: "No other single observation was repeated [by company officers] in more instances than this one," Gibson told Nelson. "No white soldier had ever been sent into combat without undergoing the infantry basic training course. Of course, Almond denied that untrained troops had been sent into battle. Furthermore, 89 percent of the replacement troops fell in the two bottom categories of the Army General Classification Test. The Ninety-second was manned by many troops who had the bare minimum of schooling and who were illiterate."[16]

Gibson pointed out that the racial arrogance of segregated America had a profound effect. The discriminatory promotion policies convinced the black GIs that the high command had no confidence in black officers, thus undermining the black leadership and with it the division's fighting spirit. Being that no white officer could serve under a black officer, inexperienced white officers were catapulted into command positions. White officers scapegoated their black troops with all the prejudices of men who resented their duty—being stuck in the 92nd. Promotions for black soldiers were not made on the basis of merit but went to subservient Negroes who lived up to stereotypes, i.e., the white officers were advised to have a "mean coon" to keep your "niggers" in line.

The affliction of Fort Huachuca resurfaced in Italy through segregated officers' clubs. One white captain who invited two black officers into his club was officially reprimanded for having "an improper social attitude,"[17] and the two African Americans were ejected. The white club boasted having dances with local women, while women were not permitted in the black club. "After outlining those findings," recounted Gibson, "I suggested a number of recommendations. At the top of the list was the vital need for a fair promotion policy that elevated officers on the sole basis of ability. Separate officers' clubs had to be abandoned. The army should stimulate race pride in black troops. Training courses for replacement troops should be strengthened to account for black troops coming from service units. Finally, the Ninety-second Division should be reorganized so that it could stay on the front line."[18]

For the entire month of February, the 758th Tank Battalion supported the 92nd Infantry Division and witnessed unimaginable carnage as the division lost sixty-two officers and 1,191 enlisted men killed, wounded, or missing in action. The 758th Tank Battalion lost eight tanks—five to mines and three to self-destruction to avoid capture. The battalion sustained four battle casualties, wounded in action: Captain Henry Morgan, Sergeant Harold Luckie, Private Emory Cox, Jr., and Private William Bunch.

13

Reorganization of the 92nd Infantry Division

Following the 92nd Infantry Division's failure to capture Massa in early February, Major General Almond had what he needed to finally convince his close friend and fellow Virginia Military Institute alumnus General (of the Armies) George C. Marshall to allow him to cannibalize what was left of his undesired division. The common belief at that time was that Almond's division was the worst division in Europe and hung the blame on its black soldiers while Almond and his staff escaped accountability. This was coupled with Lieutenant General Clark's sentiment that the division was "less favorable than any of the white divisions."[1] Taken together, the sentiment was that although it was vital to launch an offensive up the Italian west coast the black soldiers were inherently inferior and thus incapable of this task. This led to a series of discussions among Generals Marshall, Clark, Truscott, Crittenberger, and Almond. Finally General Marshall found common ground with the recommendations of Truman Gibson, Jr., and endorsed that the most reliable elements of the three regiments of the 92nd Infantry Division were to be combined into one regiment and that the 473rd (white) and the 442nd (Japanese-American) regiments attach to the 92nd Infantry Division to complete the required three regiments. On General Marshall's return trip to the United States from the Yalta Conference with Roosevelt, Churchill, and Stalin he took time to visit the 92nd Infantry Division and gave his final approval for its reorganization.

From late February to mid-March, seventy officers and 1,359 enlisted men with infantry training qualifications or holding decorations for valor, or both, transferred into the 370th Infantry from the 365th and 371st Infantry regiments. Subsequently, fifty-two officers and 1,264 enlisted men transferred out. "Only the 370th, with its casualties replaced from her sister regiments took part in the spring offensive. What was left of the 371st and the 365th carried supplies, stretchers, and so forth, for white outfits," pointed out Staff Sergeant David Cason, Jr., 365th Infantry Regiment.[2]

The 473rd Infantry Regiment, which was activated on January 14, 1945, at Montecatini, Italy, attached to the 92nd Infantry Division on February 24. The soldiers came from the 434th, 435th, 532nd, and 900th Antiaircraft Artillery Automatic (AAA)

Weapons battalions. With the far-reaching decline in Luftwaffe targets, AAA soldiers converted to other specialties to bring under-strength units up to full strength. The 434th and 435th had already undergone their baptism by fire as infantry for several months when they fought along the Arno River and up to Strettoia.

The 473rd Infantry Regiment moved into the Serchio Valley and gradually relieved the 365th and 366th Infantry Regiments. The 473rd wanted no association with the stigma of the 92nd Infantry Division and did not wear the buffalo unit insignia. In its place they wore the U.S. Fifth Army insignia. Following its relief, the 366th Infantry Regiment moved to an area south of Viareggio and turned in their infantry equipment. According to Sergeant Harold Russell, Jr., I/366th Infantry Regiment, "At the staging area the 366th Infantry Regiment was deactivated, and became the 224 and 226 Combat Engineers. I was assigned to the 224th Engineers."[3]

At that time the U.S. Fifth Army had a critical need for engineers. In addition to employing Italian civilians (Partisans), it converted several antiaircraft units to engineers. The Partisan movement in Italy began as an impulse reaction to Fascist and German dominance. It drew its strength from ex-Italian military personnel and the underground organizations of various liberal and progressive parties, augmented by young men determined to evade forced labor into Germany. The movement expanded to about 60,000 patriots who risked their lives to free Italy from the Fascist grip.

Ruins of the German observation post on Mount Folgorito (courtesy Davide Del Giudice).

Top: View of Mount Folgorito from the Cinquale Canal today(courtesy Davide Del Giudice). *Bottom:* Truman K. Gibson, Jr., government photo ID, property of U.S. government (courtesy Truman K. Gibson, Jr.)

When the Allies realized the great advantage of nurturing the Partisan movement, they supplied them with food, weapons, and clothing. The results were instrumental in accomplishing the overall missions, especially when the Partisans routed the German soldiers before the Allies even got there.

The famed 442nd Regimental Combat Team (Nisei) arrived in Leghorn after an exhausting sea journey from France in open landing crafts. As a Regimental Combat Team they carried their own artillery, the 522nd Artillery Battalion (105-millimeter). They moved in secrecy to a training area north of the walled city of Lucca and attached to the 92nd Infantry Division on March 25. They accepted the infantry equipment that the 366th Infantry Regiment had turned in. Intensive training followed as Major General Almond conducted command and training inspections. The 442nd did not want be associated with the stigma of the 92nd Infantry Division either. They wore their own regimental insignia, the liberty hand holding a torch in the national colors of red, white, and blue.

Tank manned by black trainees. Back left to right: PFC Dewey McClain, Jacksonville, Florida; Pvt. Hulet MacHenry, Salina, Kansas; and PFC Lester Baker, Alexandria, Louisiana, Armored School Detachment, Replacement and Training Command, Naples, Italy March 1, 1945 (National Archives and Records Administration).

During the winter stalemate both sides prepared for the spring offensive. The light ground combat action left units with adequate personnel, equipment, and well-stocked forward ammunition dumps. The major difference came in constant air bombardment on German positions. This constant pounding destroyed enemy positions and impeded their logistics. It weakened transportation systems to the point that resupply became infrequent and inadequate. To make matters worse for the Nazis, the Partisans increased sabotage and guerrilla activity.

During the reorganization the 758th Tank Battalion sent Able and Baker companies to the 473rd Infantry Regiment as Charlie Company reported to 92nd Infantry Division headquarters. The Mortar Platoon took up position with the 92nd Reconnaissance Troop while the Assault Gun Platoon attached to the 371st Infantry Regiment and took part in patrolling and shooting harassing fire at the enemy. Sergeant Willie Topps later remembered once such event: "From the canal we climbed the Apennines Mountains and dropped down into the Po Valley. We left there and went briefly to Florence. We ran into the Senegalese troops just outside of Florence. They had just killed a farmer's cow and they were having a bar-b-q out in the open right up under a hill. We told them that there are Germans up there. They said, 'Yeah! We know. We ran them up there.' And they continued to roast that cow."[4]

The month of March displayed a noticeable slow-down of enemy activity in all sectors where the 758th Tank Battalion stood. However, enemy artillery still landed with deadly effect. Many casualties inexplicable in nature manifested during and after combat. Platoon Sergeant John Weston recounted one such situation:

> In my tank there was myself and a fellow named Meyers. At first I had Clarence Lee—he was originally my tank driver. Then I had Jones, my new driver. My assistant driver was Wright and he also operated the radio. In the turret I had Meyers. He operated the 37-millimeter gun. He was on the left and the tank commander is always on the right. Clarence Lee, when we got overseas he drank a lot. He got wild one time and didn't want to go on duty so he turned his machine gun on me. So I had to get rid of him and send him back to headquarters. I got a new driver by the name of Jones. He became a real good driver and he remained for the duration of the war. I can't think of his first name because we called everyone by their last names. But I do remember Clarence Lee because when in the states he was my favorite driver. I guess when he got into battle that stuff got a hold of his mind and he went off the deep end.[5]

The 758th ended the month with the loss of one tank destroyed by enemy artillery and two men wounded in action and hospitalized: Private Murriel Robinson and Chief Warrant Officer Samuel Byrd.

14

Spring Offensive

Favorable weather finally arrived April 5, 1945. This allowed the Allied 15th Army Group to launch its long-awaited offensive, the final offensive to evict the German forces from Italy. Meanwhile, the Third Reich continued deteriorating. Soviet and American forces, along with other Allied units, closed in on Berlin. The Americans halted at the River Elbe as the Soviets stood poised to storm Berlin. Hitler sent frantic telegrams to his supreme commander of armed forces, Field Marshal Keitel, demanding that Berlin be relieved by nonexistent forces. For the final drive back in Italy, the Allies positioned the 92nd Infantry Division on the west, the British Eighth Army on the east, and the U.S. Fifth Army in the center. Intermittently from April 5–14, following the heaviest air bombardment in the Mediterranean Theater of Operations, the final offensive to extricate Italy from the Nazi grasp jumped off.

The reorganized and reinforced 92nd Infantry Division stood south of Massa with its 370th, 442nd, and 473rd regiments poised to lead the assault. Operation Second Wind jumped off at 0500 hours on April 5 behind an intense air bombardment on the enemy's big guns at Punta Bianca. This well-entrenched position, known as the Green Line, anchored the Gothic Line to the Ligurian Sea. The enemy enjoyed excellent fields of fire with maximum observation. Their artillery and mortars dueled with American artillery, pounding the hillsides. However, the only way to take out these positions was for the infantry to root out each observation post, battery, and bunker. Platoon Sergeant John Weston describes the action from his point of view:

> Up in Italy you have a lot of mountain areas, in one position the enemy is in front of you, and in another position he is behind you because of how the terrain is situated. That's where the light tank had an advantage over the medium tank because of the narrow roads. The leader of the platoon was in the lead tank and his assistant was in the third tank. So we would get together and go up and see who would need support and which way we would have to go, forward or retreating. When we first went up into the mountains to this outfit, when we walked in there it looked like he had a slur on his face. He said, "Where is your commanding officer?" And I said, "Well, I am the commanding officer." I was a staff sergeant. And I said, "I'll tell you what we need. Can you string us a phone?" You see, every outfit had to have a phone so you would know who you were supporting and so on. He said, "We don't have a phone like that." That just turned me off, so we left as I saluted and told him where we would be if he needed any help. So that night, Jerry, as they called the Germans, rained down on the area all night, so the next morning

they were stringing us a phone line. That was the only opposition we had at that particular time. When in combat you don't have too much of that because you are only thinking of yourself and your outfit, and all we had to do was try to get home. That was the main thing. You see, you are young, you got these guns and everything to do, and you are in another country, and you are the law there—when you go to them other countries, you are the law. That was better than my country, where I was not the law. I was running from the law.[1]

The 370th Infantry Regiment and the 442nd Regimental Combat Team moved out abreast on April 5 at 0500 hours. The 370th advanced single file through the lower hills towards Massa, avoiding the Cinquale Canal. On their right flank, the 442nd traversed the jagged ridges over and around Mounts Altissimo and Brugianna. Meanwhile, the 473rd Infantry Regiment conducted aggressive patrols and remained in strategic reserve ready to exploit any opening created by the 370th and 442nd. Preparations had been made with stealth during the moonless night. Air attacks on enemy positions around Massa and on the guns at Punta Bianca preceded the attack. The recovering enemy offered weak resistance at first but grew stronger as the attack progressed. Then intense counter battery fire, including the guns of Punta Bianca, opened up and forced the attacking forces deeper into the mountains and away from the coast.

Castle Aghinolfi today (courtesy Davide Del Giudice).

So as not to repeat the previous disasters in the coastal area, the 92nd Infantry Division safeguarded their attacking elements from the heavy caliber guns at Punta Bianca. The major thrust spearheaded by the 370th, 442nd and 473rd regiments pushed through the rugged peaks. They advanced along the sharp ridgelines and shale-covered trails of the northern Apennine Mountains. Several men were injured and one mule fell to its death as they cleared the treacherous ridges where tanks could not tread. However, the light tanks of the 758th traversed the narrow mountainside roads.

With olive trees green again, the back roads were soft and muddy from the spring rain. The light tanks bogged down constantly between hamlets and isolated houses scattered throughout the area.

Remains of a German bunker directly below Castle Aghinolfi (courtesy Davide Del Giudice).

Fortunately, their training at Camp Claiborne made the 758th experts in extricating tanks from this natural muddle. German soldiers could be seen moving around their concrete bunkers directly behind tiny hamlets where women could be seen performing their farm chores. Rounds were fired at the bunkers to the rear of the hamlets, sending the Germans into their bunkers and the women into their cellars. With dark and seemingly moonless nights, the tanks advanced by day and bivouacked by night: "When we went into battle, me in the first tank, I moved to the third position and each tank moved up. The second tank becomes the first tank and so on. When we were bivouacked I always had my tank to go on guard duty first. I didn't want the men to think we were playing favorites. Then the other tanks will fall in behind. The two hours on and four hours off rule, with the entire platoon you would only have to go on watch one time per night," recalled Platoon Sergeant John Weston.[2]

In order to neutralize the accurate enemy artillery, their observation posts had to be destroyed. On the high grounds east of Highway 1 stood Castle Aghinolfi, which overlooked the coastal area. Barbed wire, minefields, and dugouts housing machine-gun and sniper positions surrounded it. This position enjoyed a commanding view of the Gothic Line, and the 12th-century castle boasted robust walls, tunnels, and towering bastions. The uppermost area consisted of a parade ground surrounded by extensive walkways supported by numerous arches. The Germans modified this castle into a mountain bunker complex and key observation post that directed accurate artillery fire on the 92nd Infantry Division.

On the cold, dreary morning of April 5 near Viareggio, Second Lieutenant Vernon Baker, Charlie Company, 370th Infantry Regiment, led his 25-man platoon up the mountainside leading to the intimidating Castle Aghinolfi. Baker's platoon negotiated their way through the obstacles, low-crawling for hours. Baker was mindful of the life-threatening wounds he had received when the 92nd Infantry Division was nearly decimated attempting frontal assaults on the Gothic Line. Now his platoon climbed up the mountain to within yards of the castle, where he noticed binoculars sticking out of a slit in the rock. In coordination with artillery exploding in the distance, Baker stuck his rifle into the porthole and fired off his entire clip, killing the two occupants. Moving on, he stumbled upon a camouflaged machine-gun nest, where he killed the occupants as they ate breakfast.

From there Baker returned to his platoon and positioned them for an assault and then sprinted back to the rear to receive orders from the company commander, Captain John Runyon. Runyon gave orders to advance on the castle when out of nowhere a German potato-masher grenade clanked off Runyon's helmet. The grenade failed to explode and Baker shot and killed the fleeing German soldier. Baker left the shaken Runyon and returned to his platoon for the assault.

Ruins of a well-fortified machine-gun emplacement above Aurelia Road at Porta ridge (courtesy Davide Del Giudice).

On the return trip Baker went down into a draw, where he blasted open a concealed entrance to another bunker and shot one German soldier who emerged after the explosion, then he tossed another grenade into the bunker and killed two more Germans. This alerted the enemy to the presence of Baker's platoon and they opened up with machine-gun and mortar fire. With nowhere safe to go, outflanked on both sides, and with Castle Aghinolfi looming ominously in front, Baker rushed his platoon into the olive groves at the base of the castle for cover. Then all hell broke loose. Machine guns, snipers, and mortars plunged fire on his platoon, killing or wounding two-thirds of them. Cut off from their lines and being picked off from every direction, Baker refused to go down without a struggle.

He radioed for artillery support and pointed out the coordinates of the enemy positions. The fire direction center denied his request because they deemed it impossible that Baker's platoon had reached Castle Aghinolfi. Baker went to the rear and asked his white company commander to order artillery support. Instead of radioing for artillery support Runyon ordered a withdrawal. Baker argued to no avail. He then volunteered to cover the withdrawal of walking wounded carrying the seriously wounded. Baker, supported by covering fire from what remained of his platoon, low-crawled to within range of two camouflaged machine-gun positions previously bypassed during the assault. Two well-thrown grenades silenced them.

Runyon told Baker that he would go back and return with reinforcements. When Runyon arrived at the command post, he reported Baker's platoon had been annihilated. Left for dead and low on ammunition, Baker withdrew his men, stood in view of the enemy, frantically shrieked, and fired. The enemy then concentrated their fire on him as Baker's platoon escaped. Baker was hit during this diversion. When he and his platoon finally reached safety, the commanders volunteered Baker to lead a follow-up assault. Despite having two bullet wounds, he complied. He escorted a full-strength battalion of the all-white 473rd Infantry Regiment in a night attack through the enemy obstacles right up to Castle Aghinolfi.

Baker never set eyes on the cowardly Runyon again. As was to be expected, the overtly racist leadership of the 92nd Infantry Division awarded Runyon the Distinguished Service Cross (DSC) and nominated him for the Medal of Honor. In order to justify Runyon's Medal of Honor recommendation, Baker also received a DSC recommendation. Clearly racism prevailed in the 92nd Infantry Division. The "leadership" of Major General Almond demoralized the entire 92nd Infantry Division. "A competent leader can get efficient service from poor troops; while, on the contrary, an incapable leader can demoralize the best of troops" (General John J. "Black Jack" Pershing).[3]

On April 7, the 2nd Battalion of the 473rd Infantry Regiment passed through the 370th Infantry Regiment's position and took over the assault against the Strettoia hill mass and Castle Aghinolfi. Artillery and mortar pounded the hill mass and the enemy replied in kind. The 473rd sent their companies Easy, Fox and George to climb the steep terraced hillside. They moved without difficulty for about a hundred yards before all hell broke loose. From an innocent looking vineyard a blast of machine-gun fire erupted and swept from flank to flank. Seconds later from a higher hill another machine gun erupted and swept as if demonstrating a page in the manual depicting traversing and searching fire on exposed troops. Seconds later a barrage of enemy artillery landed.

The infantry battalion commander, Lieutenant Colonel Hampton Lisle, remained with his forward troops in the heavy fighting. He gave orders, advice, and encouragement and directed accurate artillery fire. While performing his duties he was killed by enemy mortar fire. The infantrymen of his command felt a heavy loss but reorganized quickly as the castle and the surrounding hills fell silent. When they reached the castle they found it deserted. "When we were with the 473rd Infantry Regiment up in the mountains, they gave us a couple of corpses to bring back. We returned to the rear headed to grave registration. We were going down the road, strictly a hair-pinned curve. One of the supposedly dead men raised up: "Will one of you give me a cigarette?" WHEW!!! The wheels of our weapons carrier sharply turned. It turned into the mountain. Had he turned the other way, we would have plunged over 500 feet down the mountainside and we all would have been killed!" (Sergeant Willie Topps, Service/758th Tank Battalion).[4]

At this point elements of the 370th and 473rd Infantry regiments moved their attacking troops on tanks from the 760th and 758th Tank battalions up Highway 1. The 849th Tank Destroyer Battalion transported reserve elements. However, the big guns at Punta Bianca stopped them in their tracks. During this phase and from another direction the 442nd Regimental Combat Team, on the same mission to neutralize the accuracy of the enemy's artillery, attacked. They directed their assault toward the observation posts along the high grounds of Mount Belvedere. Elements of the regiment attacked to the north behind a tremendous demonstration of artillery. The 599th and 329th Field Artillery battalions, the Regimental Cannon Company, Company B of the 84th Chemical Battalion (4.2 mortar), and the Assault Gun Platoon of the 758th Tank Battalion had all let fly a ten-minute concentration on the enemy positions. "The 92nd Infantry Division had an attached artillery unit, with the big 155-millimeter guns and we had to support them. There was this Lieutenant Colonel Ray. You see on the big 155-millimeter guns, they had to be dug in. So we had to go ahead of them and protect them until they could dig in these guns. That's the way we went up the coast" (Platoon-Sergeant John Weston).[5] Steady artillery barrages, air attacks, and infantry pressure forced the enemy to reluctantly withdraw from the coastal sector as they desperately clung to key observation posts.

On April 10, the 442nd Regimental Combat Team crossed the Frigido River in a three-pronged attack. The 1st Battalion (the famed 100th Battalion), took Ancona and continued over difficult terrain to occupy the mountain hamlet of Colonnata, three miles east of Carrara. The 2nd Battalion captured Mount Brugiana overlooking the city of Carrara. The 3rd Battalion moved through the foothills above the coastal plain and then down into Carrara and found the city controlled by the Partisans. Other elements of the 442nd blocked off the road leading to Massa from the east.

"We went up into the mountains to support the Nisei regiment. That was quite a trip because we had to take those tanks up into the mountains along those narrow

Aghinolfi hill today. The old customs authority building of the Medici Dynasty along the ancient Aurelia Road, today known as Highway 1 (courtesy Davide Del Giudice).

roads. We fired our guns, we only had 37-millimeter guns and the enemy had big artillery guns. We could fire across the valley and places like that but not any distance firing. The mountain roads were just wide enough for our light tanks to get through safely and you had to hug the mountain side of the road because on the other side you don't have a railing. You are looking straight down into a valley," said Platoon

Sergeant John Weston.[6] First Lieutenant Harry Duplessis also spoke of the situation: "In April we were attached to the 442nd Nisei. Our biggest problem with the little Japanese-Americans was keeping up with them; they moved like greased lighting. Instead of following the paths, which tanks have to do, they went up and across those mountains like crazy. We worked out a system. As they took out across the mountains we'd wind our way along until we received a signal from them. Then we would lay down a barrage as a diversionary. Jerry would be concerned about us and the Nisei would move in swiftly from the rear and mop up. I do mean mop, they turned those Germans every way but loose."[7]

In the coastal sector, the enemy covered their withdrawal with accurate artillery fire, particularly from the big guns at Punta Bianca. Both Massa and Carrara came under heavy fire along with the avenues of approach.

In an effort to speed the advance, Major General Almond narrowed the zone of the 473rd Infantry Regiment by assigning the flat land between the coast and Highway 1 to a tank/infantry task force. Highway 1, the principal north-south road, connected Rome to the principal cities along the coast. This task force came under the command of Major Claire Curtis (760th Medium Tank Battalion). It consisted of elements of the 760th Tank Battalion; elements of the 758th Tank Battalion; A/894th Tank

Hills X, Y, and Z in 1945 (U.S. Army Signal Corps, courtesy Davide Del Giudice).

Hills X, Y, and Z today (courtesy Davide Del Giudice).

Destroyer Battalion; E/370th Infantry Regiment; A/317th Engineer Battalion; and the antitank company of the 473rd Infantry Regiment. Task Force Curtis fired upon Mount Strettoia and the Porta ridge and dodged counter battery fire from enemy self-propelled guns as they cleared the coastal sector west of Massa. The following is according to Platoon Sergeant John Weston:

> We supported the medium tank battalion—Sherman tanks. When we went into a town, you had to have light tanks in front. You know, in Italy the roads were narrow and the houses were right on the street. A medium tank in the town could not traverse its 75-millimeter gun. So our job was to go into each town with our tanks in the front and the back of the medium tanks. The medium tanks and anything larger were all for open field. They could bombard a town but they would not go into a town unescorted because they would get trapped. You see, our tanks were small. We could go into these towns and lay down fire. We had .30-caliber machine guns and the 37-millimeter gun on our tanks.[8]

Additionally, four task forces consisting of medium and light tanks along with tank destroyers were established. The 758th Tank Battalion and the 894th Tank Destroyer Battalion augmented Task Forces Bradshaw, Crowder, Turner, and Barr, with the objective of advancing up Highway 1 in support of the infantry. That morning Task Force Bradshaw, commanded by First Lieutenant Roland Crouse, with a tank-bulldozer advanced up Highway 1. A *Panzerfaust* (bazooka) knocked it out and blocked the advance. A tank recovery vehicle attempted to retrieve the tank bulldozer and hit a mine. Then one B/758th tank struck a mine and another took a *Panzerfaust* hit. The platoon leader, First Lieutenant Hannah, was given the mission of leading the rest of his light tanks in continuing the attack. Hannah had penetrated hostile lines when his light tank took *Panzerfaust* fire that knocked it over and set it ablaze in a ditch. Tech-5 Samuel Berry perished in the burning tank and the other two crew members, PFC Olin Cubit and PFC Buford Tyler, had serious wounds. Hannah and his surviving men quickly dismounted and sought cover. Hannah assessed the state of affairs and prepared to evacuate his men. He observed three German soldiers nearby as he returned to the burning tank, in which ammunition was now exploding. He helped the two wounded men, who could not walk, to a safer location. When he returned to the task force for assistance he was fired upon. While returning the fire he was killed in action. Hannah was posthumously awarded the Silver Star, dated August 23, 1945.

After this setback, Task Force Bradshaw withdrew back across the Cinquale Canal. The following day this task force continued up Highway 1 until heavy artillery from Punta Bianca forced it off the highway. The Task Force moved across Highway 1 and ran into a minefield approximately 2,500 yards west of Montignoso. Three tank destroyers hit mines and became immobilized by blown tracks. B/758th continued supporting the Infantry and lost two light tanks, one to *Panzerfaust* fire and one to enemy mines. PFC William Miles was killed in this action when artillery and mortar fire hit these immobilized vehicles and destroyed them completely as their crews scrambled to safety. The task force stopped dead in its tracks.

On April 8, Task Force Crowder, commanded by Captain Herman Crowder, Jr., moved up Highway 1, was also forced towards Montignoso, and proceeded toward the coast just north of the dreaded Cinquale Canal. The task force crossed the canal and advanced to the Mogliano Canal, crossed it and pulled up 300 yards south of the Frigido River. Intense enemy artillery fire forced them to withdraw just north of the Mogliano Canal. Task Force Turner, commanded by Second-Lieutenant Pickney Upchurch, moved up Highway 1 on April 8 with the objective of breaking into Massa. The tanks reached Turino but withdrew in the face of heavy enemy fire.

In the meantime, Task Force Barr, under command of First Lieutenant Charles Barr, moved up Highway 1 to the Montignoso Road about 600 yards from the coast. They turned north and negotiated the connecting roads between the coast and Highway 1 up to a position south of the Mogliano Canal. The Partisans and doughboys augmented the engineers in repairing road demolitions, and Task Force Barr worked across the canal and consolidated positions with the other task forces south of the Frigido River.

Tanks from the 760th and 758th Tank battalions spearheaded elements of the 473rd Infantry Regiment to the outskirts of Massa on April 10. There they fired in support of the infantry who had crossed the Frigido River in front of Massa. Machine-gun nests and sniper positions stopped the infantry's advance until the tanks provided suppressing fire that allowed them to continue. When they reached the center of the city they found the Partisans had mopped up and were in control.

Platoon Sergeant John Weston in turret (courtesy John Weston).

Moving on from the marble city of Massa, on April 13 combat engineers cleared the mines between Highway 1 and the coast. Conjointly the task forces moved out of the now cleared minefields up the highway. As the battle ensued, an enemy ammunition dump went up in a spectacular detonation. Platoon Sergeant Walter Jones (B/758th) was seriously wounded during the counterattack and later died of his wounds. The enemy resistance proved too stiff and the advance came to a halt. Artillery fire had to be called in to soften up the enemy's positions. The barrage neutralized numerous enemy machine-gun nests and strongholds.

Brigadier General William Colbern, the 92nd Infantry Division's artillery commander, engaged his 155-mm guns in a duel with enemy antiaircraft batteries protecting the coastal guns at Punta Bianca. In addition, almost daily attacks on Punta Bianca by American bombers added to the overwhelming bombardment. However, this bombardment did not hinder the operations of the Punta Bianca guns.

Punta Bianca is a peninsula between the mainland and La Spezia. Enemy naval guns there neutralized the 92nd Infantry Division. Besides harassing and interdicting the emplaced and advancing troops, the guns covered the enemy's withdrawal. Organized into batteries and protected by antiaircraft artillery, tanks, and self-propelled guns, the big guns were emplaced in concrete casements and could fire to the southern

Two knocked-out 758th light tanks near a blown bridge over Canal Magro on the Aurelia highway between Montignoso and Massa. Notice Castle Aghinolfi in the background (April 10, 1945) (National Archives and Records Administration, 196th Signal Photo Company).

As elements of the 442nd Regimental Combat Team (Nisei) advance up Mount Belvedere, the assault gun platoon of the 758th Tank Battalion fires in support with self-propelled 75-millimeter howitzers from the village of Seravezza. They are firing on Fascist Alpine Italian troops around Mount Altissimo, April 8, 1945 (National Archives and Records Administration, 196th Signal Photo Company).

limits of the 92nd Infantry Division area. Until the fall of Massa, 92nd artillery did not have sufficient range to reach them, and air missions were met by German 88-mm FLAK guns.

On April 14 leading elements of the 92nd Infantry Division advanced sufficiently to permit smaller and more accurate artillery pieces to come into range. Enter the 679th Tank Destroyer Battalion (Cld.) with towed 76-mm antitank guns. They placed all 36 of their guns into action against the coastal guns of Punta Bianca. First they knocked out the enemy's smoke generator used to screen their position. Then they aimed at the bunker ports. The heavy steel doors that quickly opened and closed to permit the guns to fire became targets. Each time an enemy gun fired, it received a barrage of 76-mm high-velocity rounds. When the forward observer saw gun smoke, they called for fire that struck the ports within 45 seconds before they could close. Enemy self-propelled guns attempted to duel with the 679th tank destroyers and got knocked out. Then 92nd Infantry Division artillery brought an eight-inch howitzer to assist. This duel went on until April 19, when all of the guns at Punta Bianca finally fell silent.

Elements of the 370th Infantry Regiment pursuing the retreating Germans through the Po Valley, April 11, 1945 (National Archives and Records Administration).

On April 21 the 1st (100th) and 2nd battalions of the 442nd Regimental Combat Team attacked along Golle Musatello Ridge, which was heavily defended by elements of the enemy's crack 361st Panzer Grenadier Regiment. Second Lieutenant Daniel Inouye led his platoon in a flanking attack on the ridge near San Terenzo. Inouye's platoon got caught in the cross-fire of three MG-42 machine guns that systematically cut them to pieces. Inouye emerged from his low-crawl position to sight cover for his men when a bullet passed through his abdomen just inches from his spine. Ignoring his wound, Inouye proceeded to destroy the first machine-gun nest with hand grenades and his Thompson submachine gun. When informed of the severity of his wound he refused treatment and rallied his men for an attack on the second machine-gun position. He destroyed it in the same fashion and then collapsed due to blood loss. Then his platoon distracted the third machine gunner as Inouye, who had regained consciousness, crawled to within ten yards of the final machine-gun nest. He raised himself up and cocked his arm to throw his last grenade and took a bullet in his right elbow, leaving his primed grenade clenched in his fist. Inouye's horrified platoon moved to his aid, but he told them to keep back out of fear that his severed fist would involuntarily relax and drop the grenade. While the German inside the bunker reloaded his rifle, Inouye pried the live grenade from his useless right hand and transferred it to his left. As the enemy soldier aimed his rifle at him, Inouye tossed the grenade into the bunker and killed the German soldier. Then he continued forward, silencing the last German resistance with a one-handed burst from his Thompson. He took a bullet to the leg and tumbled to the bottom of the ridge. He came to and saw his worried platoon hovering over him. Before being evacuated he ordered his platoon back to their positions, saying, "Nobody called off the war!"

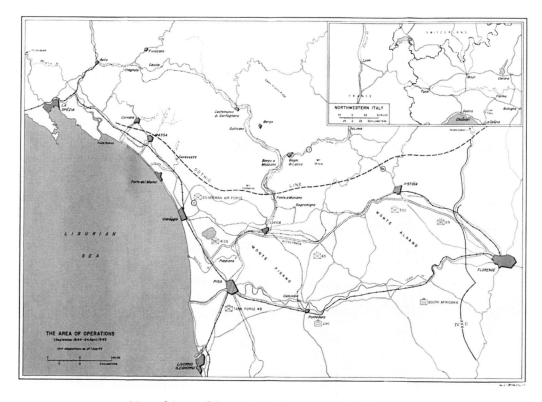

Map of Area of Operations, Sept. 1944–April 1945.

Inouye made it to a field hospital, where the remainder of his mutilated right arm was amputated. "The doctors looked at me," he said later with a chuckle, "[and] they're mumbling among themselves. Two minutes later a chaplain comes up—opening words: 'God loves you.' I said: 'I know that. I love Him too. But I'm not ready to meet Him yet!'"[9]

This action cleared the way and the dash was on with the end in sight. Task Force Curtis, spearheaded by tanks of the 758th Tank Battalion, crossed the Margra River and moved up Highway 1 until it ran into a delaying force. The Germans fought for a few hours and then withdrew to Aulla on the evening of April 23. Resistance gave way and when the task force entered towns and cities the Partisans had already defeated the Germans there. By the time La Spezia and Aulla fell, the enemy was too badly disorganized to launch an offensive. They continued to withdraw, leaving behind small delaying forces and large quantities of materiel.

The spring offensive that jumped off on April 5 ended on May 2. The 758th Tank Battalion assisted the 92nd Infantry Division's advance of nearly 100 miles and opened the major seaports of La Spezia and Genoa. Jointly they captured an estimated 22,000 enemy troops and significant amounts of materiel and inflicted hundreds of casualties on enemy troops.

On April 27, as Allied forces closed in on Milan, Italian dictator Benito Mussolini fell into the hands of Partisans as he fled with a German antiaircraft battalion. He and his cohorts were executed the next day and their bodies taken to Milan and hung up for viewing. Then on April 30, the day Hitler committed suicide, Mussolini's minister of defense, Rodolfo Graziani, surrendered all remaining Fascist Italian forces in Italy. On the same day, German SS General Karl Wolff signed the surrender document on behalf of General von Vietinghoff. The instrument of surrender stipulated a cease-fire and surrender of all forces under the German command effective at 1400 hours, May 2, 1945. After bickering between Wolff and Albert Kesselring in the early hours of May 2, nearly 1,000,000 men in Italy and Austria surrendered unconditionally to General Harold Alexander of Britain. The war was finally over in Italy and the beginning of the end of the Third Reich. Days later, on May 7, the Nazi high command signed the unconditional surrender documents in Rheims, France, and announced it the next day. World War II officially ended in Europe on May 8, 1945 (VE Day).

On April 29, the 758th Tank Battalion secured and occupied the town of Voltri and remained there until hostilities ceased in Italy. The battalion came together for the first time since being committed to combat operations. During the month of April they had lost nine light tanks, five to mines and three to *Panzerfaust* fire, along with one to mechanical failure. They also lost a jeep, a half-track, and two trucks to enemy action. Baker Company, 758th Tank Battalion, suffered four soldiers killed as a result of enemy action. Three soldiers were killed in action: First Lieutenant William Hannah on April 7; Tech-5 Samuel Berry on April 7; and PFC William Miles on April 9. In addition, Staff Sergeant Walter Jones died of his wounds on April 15.

15

Back to the Home Front

Throughout the month of May the 758th Tank Battalion remained attached to the 92nd Infantry Division with the mission of maintaining order in the Ligurian area by clearing enemy forces from its zone, collecting prisoners, and administering to displaced persons. The 758th occupied the Italian towns of Voltri, Pegli, and Albisola, where they guarded critical points, bridges, and ammunition dumps. They performed maintenance on vehicles and equipment and participated in organized athletics and sightseeing. Each battalion-size unit within the 92nd Infantry Division was subjected to command inspections by Major General Almond and his staff. Nightly retreat parades were held at the Piazza della Vittoria in Genoa along with decoration cere-monies and memorial services. Platoon Sergeant John Weston comments:

> The war was about over when we hit Genoa. We didn't stay there long, maybe a few hours and then we went down to a town called Voltri. That's where the war ended for us. We didn't know what was going to happen to us. Next thing we knew they told us to clean up the tanks and line them all up and we took them to a big staging area and turned in the tanks. Then they gave us orders. Those that had enough points went one way and those that didn't went another way. Then we went to a little town where they made small ships. I had a platoon of men, and they sent us up to the 92nd Engineers where they were building a bridge across the Po Valley River where it emptied into the Mediterranean seaside. They were building one of the longest Bailey bridges using German equipment. They took our tank drivers to grade the ground. I had the day detail. My group had to drive piles and all of the construction it took for a Bailey bridge. I had the day set. Then we had an evening set and a midnight set. I stayed there for about three months. We were just out of a city called Pavia, a nice little town. They treated us royally. Since I had the day shift I would go there after chow time. We could always get a ride anywhere because they always had trucks going somewhere. I had a lot of Italian friends. When we first went into the town of Voltri, they never met us before. That was the funny part of it. We were at this big hangar where they built fishing boats and they would stand outside and peep in there because I guess the white soldiers told them we had tails. Then they found that everything is good. Most of the young people catered to us. The old people stayed away for some time. And the kids, they all flocked around us. We had a pretty nice time there.[1]

The 758th Tank Battalion had little trouble within its area. The leaders of the five Partisan brigades that had operated in the 92nd Infantry Division's sector were debriefed by Major General Almond. Of those five brigades, three were Communist, one was Christian Democrat, and one was composed of escaped felons. The 92nd and the Partisans cooperated well in turning over authority to the Allied Military

Top: Mother's Day 1945, from left to right, front row, in uniform: Major Roy Chatham, Adjutant; Captain Hall, company commander; Captain Williams, deputy commander; Major Wright, battalion commander; Jack Parren, Service Company Commander. Others are unidentified (courtesy Willie Topps). *Bottom:* Notice the children peeping from underneath the parade stand, Mother's Day 1945 (courtesy Willie Topps).

Top: "Captain Morgan [A/758th] leading pass and review in Volterra, Italy, on Mother's Day, 1945. The others are fellow 'dog faces' (like myself)," said Willie Topps (courtesy Willie Topps). *Bottom:* Captain Morgan [A/758th] leading the review (courtesy Willie Topps).

Government. "I came in contact with several individuals who were the Partisans," said Sergeant Willie Topps:

> They wore red armbands to indicate that they were against Mussolini. I was able to meet an old Partisan—we called him Pisano. He followed the outfit all the way to the Po Valley. I went fishing with him one day and he caught a big deep-sea fish. And when they brought it up out of the water, it burst wide open. He said that happens all the time. He made me a friendship ring out of nuts and bolts. I still have it.
>
> From the canal we climbed the Apennines Mountains and dropped down into the Po Valley. We left there and went briefly to Florence. Then we went all the way up north to Venice. We stayed there and a lot of us went on leave. I went on a three day pass to Switzerland. I went to Geneva, Montreux, and Interlochen. I visited the ice cave. Then we convoyed back down to Pisa. And from Pisa the outfit went to France to be broken up and dispersed. I didn't go. I came home because I had enough points.[2]

On June 6, 1945, the 92nd Infantry Division conducted an impressive ceremony in the Piazza della Vittoria in Genoa, the birthplace of Christopher Columbus. They restored the urn containing the mortal remains of what was believed to be the explorer. During the war, the urn containing these ashes and accompanying official documents had been removed and hidden in the mountains. Columbus (1451–1506), later disgraced but best remembered for his 1492 voyage, died in Spain and his remains were sent back to Hispaniola. From there things get murky. Two cities, Seville, Spain, and Santo Domingo, Dominican Republic, claim that they have his remains.

A/ 758th marching by (courtesy Willie Topps).

Top: M5 tank, Volterra, Italy, Mother's Day, 1945 (courtesy Willie Topps). *Bottom:* A/758th marching away (courtesy Willie Topps).

Top: Officers of the 758th Tank Battalion at war's end. From left: Becnel, Allen, Singley, Bennett, Chatham, Bobo, Klein, McFall, Cline, and Leigh (courtesy Willie Topps). *Bottom:* At the shipyard in Volterra, Italy, just before turning in their tanks and the men being split up and sent to other units (courtesy John Weston).

Tanks are lined up and ready to be turned in at Volterra, Italy (courtesy John Weston).

The triumphal arch at the Piazza della Vittoria stands as a World War I memorial that commemorates the 680,000 Italians killed in that war and also the workers who died constructing the arch. Built in the 1930s, it symbolizes classic Italian Fascist imagery that includes a depiction of Mussolini. It has two side doors leading to a crypt. Down in the sanctuary are statues and sculptures representing Italian victories, Saint George, and the Genoa coat of arms. An altar of red marble is located center stage with a bronze crucifix hanging above it. The exterior monument rests on four cornerstone pillars with eight ornate supporting pillars decorated with sculptures. Two large columns located inside the arch are dedicated to peace and the family. Off from there is a terraced walkway displaying three anchors on the first, followed by three tiers depicting Caravelle di Colombo: the *Nina*, the *Pinta*, and the *Santa Maria* caravel ships.

Sergeant Willie Topps (far right) with the U.S. Army Air Forces before it became the U.S. Air Force taking time out for posterity with two friends at a Japanese photo studio, 1947 (courtesy Willie Topps).

Sergeant Willie Topps (left) at happy hour in Japan at an integrated noncommissioned officers (NCO) club 1947/48 (courtesy Willie Topps).

All elements of the division stood in formation in the plaza as a horse-drawn caisson, draped with the flag of the City of Genoa and bearing the urn, came through the Arco della Vittoria (Victory Arch) accompanied by the honor guard of the 370th Infantry Regiment. The division band played a slow solemn march and the field artillery fired an eleven-gun salute. Major General Almond laid a wreath and made remarks in tribute to the memory of Columbus. John Weston later recalled, "We brought Columbus' ashes back. They had put them somewhere in a vault because they didn't want the Germans to get them. We had a big review and we were given a citation."[3]

Remnants of the 758th Tank Battalion remained attached to the 92nd Infantry Division in Italy until September 22, 1945, when it was deactivated. The battalion never came home as a combined unit. Personnel transferred to other units and rotated stateside. "So coming home we had to pass over a bridge and had to go slow. And going slow I have never forgotten that as far as you can see, these crosses, white crosses in both directions. And I thought about, thank God for those men ... [tearing up] their sacrifice ... made it possible for me to be coming home," said Platoon Sergeant Weston.[4] William H. Smith, A/758th, had this to say:

> After the war I came back to Detroit and got on with the DSR and I ran a streetcar and a bus. I left Detroit and went to California, where I did odd jobs. Then I went back and forth to Pitts-

burgh for a while. I worked for a couple of years with the Vern Stern Band. When I left the band, I went on back to Detroit and worked in an auto factory. I hated the way those guys in the band acted. A lot of times, in the white man's face they were grinning, but if you say something they wanted to cuss you out. So I said the hell with this mess. So I got out of there and was glad when it was over. I wouldn't back down from them. If they wanted to fight Bill Smith, Bill Smith was ready for them. As you see, they couldn't run over me. During that time I was headstrong and I would fight at the drop of a hat and they didn't want that. But a whole lot of fellas that I knew never tried to get along. They wanted to be bullies. But outside of that I got along OK. But like I said, back then I would fight at the drop of a hat, but no more. When I started getting older my Dad kept telling me, "Billy, you are getting too old for that—you are going to run up on some youngster who's going to whip the hell out of you if you don't quit." I quit before then. After California, I lived in North Carolina for the later years of my life [43 years]. I've since moved to Georgia. And that's the end of my story.[5]

Mr. Smith's story didn't end there. In 2016 he became a centenarian. "Being 100 years old feels good, like being 70," he said. "I still feel young. A lot of them who came along with me aren't here anymore. And a lot of folks that I met along the way are gone. I am glad and thankful to have lived this long. Although some people say I am evil as hell, I hope they don't expect me to take everything they put on me. I tell them to

From left: Willie Topps, his daughter Juanita Hayes, and John Weston at the 761st Tank Battalion Monument dedication, Fort Hood, Texas. November 10, 2005 (courtesy Ivan Harrison Jr.).

Willie Topps holding the 761st banner. "For many years, each Memorial Day, veterans would march to remember fallen comrades. This march took place at Oak Woods Cemetery, on 67th & Stony Island, in Chicago, Illinois. I don't remember the particular year," recalls Juanita Topps Hayes (courtesy Willie Topps).

stop it and if they don't listen to me I tell them, "Hell! Stop it!" And mean it. And they would say, "Oh." I try to be nice. I will give a person anything I have that they want."[6]

Not much has changed on the home front but the war opened a new window of opportunity in the struggle for equality. A number of civil rights leaders had been trained in the military where they acquired a renewed sense of pride and leadership with organizational experience. John Weston returned to Chicago:

> For a while I didn't do too much of anything. I ran out of my leave money and one Christmas I stopped by the post office to work the holidays and they kept me. I had the round-table team, one of the hardest teams they had. Then we automated the post office around 1973–74 and they sent us down to Oklahoma for training on computers to automate the post office. That's where the ZMT—Zip-code Mail Translator—was organized. When we came back to Chicago we organized with eight people on a console that fed letters into a machine that was continuously moving. It dropped them in bins on the other side by particular zip code. While working at the post office I went back to school and I didn't have time for too much of anything else. I had a television shop and I repaired televisions up until the time I retired in 1977. By then they became so cheap you could almost buy a new one instead of repairing it. I went to Midway Television and later American Television schools. I dropped out because I got bigheaded and thought I could repair anything. I got to be pretty good. When I went to the school for the post office, they taught me electronics. If you could tell me what it did, I could fix it.
>
> Most of the civil rights organizations, I belonged to them but I didn't go out to march. I had a family and I was working and repairing televisions. I didn't have much time to do too much of anything else. I lost my wife in 1997 and didn't do too much of anything after that. After I got together with the 761st Association we went around to high schools and told students of the things we did in the service and why they should go to school because you may never realize what you will need later in life. I told them that I hated geometry but when I got overseas, geometry was a great help. When you are firing at something you have to know the distance, what they are traveling at, and stuff like that.[7]

William H. Smith celebrating his 100th birthday with his daughter Delores Williams, May 22, 2016 (courtesy William H. Smith).

"Tee Jay would spend time at the close of the war in Nice, France, which served as a post of respite for U.S. Soldiers…. He loved this country and his fond recollections prompted [his daughter Kim] to take him back in 2002 where they found the hotel he was stationed at. During his later years, this period of service would be a defining chapter of his life," said Kimberly Mann (courtesy Thomas J. Mann).

T.J. Mann returned home and resumed his job as a lifeguard for the Chicago Park District. A few years later he became a police officer for the park district and then in 1953 joined the Chicago City Police Department and served until his retirement in 1981. He was an active member of the Mr. & Mrs. Club of Chicago, comprising police officers and their wives. As a member of the Chicago chapter of the 761st Tank Battalion and Allied Veterans Association, Tee Jay met regularly with chapter members in the basement of Mr. Willie Topps' Southside residence. Their unofficial headquarters displayed memorabilia depicting their history. They began with about thirty members and in 2006 seven remained, of which only four could attend the meetings: Mr. Willie Topps, Mr. T.J. Mann, Mr. John Weston, and Mr. Johnny Holmes. Through the decades they conducted chapter business, made preparations for their national conventions, and introspectively discussed their experiences echoing humor and heroism. Over Memorial Day weekends they would lay a wreath at the Oak Woods Cemetery in memory of their fallen comrades. "Father Time and Mother Nature are beating the living hell out of us," said Willie Topps, who in 2016 became the lone survivor of the Chicago chapter. These men had somewhat comparable experiences in that they returned to their hometowns, in this case Chicago. Willie Topps recounts his situation:

I returned in December 1945 back to Newport News, Virginia. I came home! I had married my wife in 1943 in Chicago. The best job you could get back then was $3.50 a week, and you bought those jobs. I didn't stay home long because there were no jobs so I went back into the military, the air force this time for a tour of duty in Japan. I was base supply sergeant at Japan Air Materiel Area (JAMA) located northwest of Tokyo. I went to Iwo Jima after the hurricane hit and there was nothing left except the generators. Then I came home for good. For 18 years I worked two jobs, one as a die setter and one as a pipe fitter. And when Tootsie-Roll came here from back East, I was hired by them as a pipe fitter. And I retired from Tootsie-Roll.

I have a 35-millimeter camera that I took from a German colonel and I never used it. It is in a drawer in my room. But one of these days I will take it to a place to learn how to use it and see if it will still work. I was cadre with the 761st and so I joined them in their reunions. I've been going practically every year. But I think 2008 may be my last. We are having it here in Chicago near O'Hare Field. My wife and daughters go with me; they support me as I support them.

I donated to civil rights causes but I didn't march because I was too quick tempered. I couldn't stand it when Reverend Martin Luther King—over here in Chicago on Western and 71st Street—they threw a brick and hit the Reverend King. I couldn't take that standing up. I never bothered anyone and I always tried to treat everyone like I wanted to be treated. But it didn't take too much to set me off. I raised a family. They are all doing well. We have four children. I think I have about seventeen grandchildren and eleven great-grandchildren. I see most of them every week. They come here, they sit here in the house, and we'll have dinner sometimes. They play records, watch television, and they sit and talk to my wife and I. On the 10th day of August 2008, we will be married 65 years. And we are doing as well as can be expected for our age. So, Mr. Wilson, our race of people has been mistreated all down through the years and it is not getting any better. I just hope Obama makes it. I believe he will make a good president. McCain was tutored by Goldwater and came up in Arizona. And they never had any love for us.[8]

16

Whatever Happened to the 761st Tank Battalion?

In October 1944, after two years of intense armored training, the 761st Tank Battalion landed in France. The tankers received a welcome from the Third Army commander, Lieutenant General George Patton, Jr., who had earlier observed the 761st conducting training maneuvers. "Men, he told them, "you're the first Negro tankers to ever fight in the American Army. I would never have asked for you if you weren't good. I have nothing but the best in my Army. I don't care what color you are as long as you go up there and kill those Kraut sons of bitches. Everyone has their eyes on you and is expecting great things from you. Most of all, your race is looking forward to you. Don't let them down and damn you! Don't let me down!"[1]

On November 8, 1944, the 761st Tank Battalion became the first African American armored unit to enter combat as they supported the 26th Infantry Division in the Alsace-Lorraine region of France. During the attack, Staff Sergeant Ruben Rivers, in Able Company's lead tank, encountered a roadblock that held up the advance. With utter disregard for his personal safety, he courageously climbed out of his tank under direct enemy fire, attached a cable to the roadblock, and removed it. His prompt action prevented a serious delay in the offensive and was instrumental in the success of the attack.

On November 9, Charlie Company ran into an antitank ditch at Morville-les-Vic. The crack German 11th Panzer Division began to knock out tanks one by one down the line. The tankers dismounted with their M-3 submachine guns ("grease guns") and crawled through the freezing, muddy waters of the ditch under pelting rain and snow while hot shell fragments fell all around them. When German artillery zeroed in on the ditch, the tankers' situation appeared hopeless.

First Sergeant Samuel Turley dismounted his burning tank and organized a dismounted combat team. When the team found itself pinned down Turley entered a burning tank and retrieved the large .30-caliber machine gun. He ordered his men to retreat as he climbed from the ditch and provided covering fire. He stood straight up with the machine gun, an ammo belt around his neck, and fired. His accurate fire caused the German gunners to pull back. He remained standing and covering for his men until German machine-gun bullets ripped through his body. Turley crumpled to the ground. The next day he was found sitting straight up with the large machine gun on his lap and his finger still gripping the trigger. An eyewitness from the 26th Infantry Division, PFC Bill Houle, I/104th Infantry Regiment, recalls this battle:

> The battle of Morville-les-Vic, to get right down to the brass tacks here. We spent the night before in the woods on a sloping hill and dug in for the night. In the morning we went across a wide flat area almost like a marsh. We went across on a wooden footbridge that the engineers built. Then we came to a hill and we had a very difficult time capturing that hill. We lost a lot of guys. I believe about eight in my company were killed. I remember John La Forte from Sacramento, California. The platoon sergeant yelled, "That's La Forte! He's dead!" And sure enough, it was La Forte and he was dead or dying. I wasn't sure when I got there so I rolled him over and tried to do what I could, but it was useless—he had blood coming out of his ears. That was from a shell blast, and I could see where the shell blasted in front of him. Colonel Dwight D. Collie was severely wounded—he was about 100 feet from me. He was a national guard colonel from Massachusetts. He was yelling at us to get moving up the hill. And the next thing I know, someone yells, "Your colonel got it!" He was severely wounded but he survived and was sent back to the states. And I'll be darned, before the war was over he was back over here with us. Anyway, we finally took that hill. We started out with 200 men and after we took the hill, we had 30 to 40 left.
>
> November 1944, that was the big drive, our first major battle. We took a hill and lost a lot of the guys doing it and when we came down the reverse slope, to the right the Germans were waiting and they opened up. And of all things, I hear these motors running. The black tank battalion was coming up behind us over the crest of the hill and they went after the Germans. There is one thing I will say about the black tankers, they can pull a trigger faster than anyone in this world. And they hit! They laid a barrage on those Germans and they saved us. Here we are, at the bottom of the hill, the tankers are coming down the hill towards the town of Morville-les-Vic. I'll always remember the town. There we were lying on the ground and they are shooting right over our heads while we snuggled as close to the ground as we could. That lasted for a while. Then one of our tanks got hit. I don't know how many of the tanks got hit. In this case, an 88 armor-piecing round went into the front. I couldn't see it go into the front, but I saw it come out the back. When the Germans withdrew and retreated out of that area, several tanks were hit—bad. Our first sergeant yelled at us, "Help those soldiers get out of those tanks!" We rushed over and helped them out of the tanks and did whatever we could, which wasn't a lot. Another soldier and I, we took a black tanker whose leg was cut open from his knee to his hip. We got him out of the tank and put him on a stretcher. All tanks had stretchers attached to the back. He wasn't bleeding very much because his wound was seared. We carried him to the first-aid station that seemed like a mile. It was probably only a half a mile. We couldn't carry him nonstop, we had to stop and take a rest a couple of times. We took him into that tent and laid him on the ground and the medics went right to work on him. I saw an empty chair and I was so pooped I sat down. Then a medic said to me, "What's wrong with your foot?" I looked at my right foot and the shoelaces were torn and the top of the boot was torn open. My foot was bleeding slightly. He took my boot off and said, "You have trench foot! You have a wound but you have trench foot too." He took the other boot off and I had trench foot there too. Then I stayed in the hospital for three or four days and then back to the front lines. We fought together with the 761st daily until around December third when we headed to the Bulge, and the 761st went up to the Bulge too but they were attached to a different unit. That's about all I can tell you at this moment.[2]

On November 10 Sergeant Warren G.H. Crecy fought through enemy positions to aid his men until his tank was destroyed. He immediately took command of another

First Sergeant Samuel Turley (courtesy Thomas J. Mann).

vehicle, armed with only a .30-caliber machine gun, and liquidated the enemy position that had destroyed his tank. Still under heavy fire, he helped eliminate the enemy forward observers who were directing the artillery fire that pinned down the American infantry. The next day, Crecy's tank became bogged down in the mud. He dismounted and fearlessly faced antitank, artillery, and machine-gun fire as he extricated his tank.

While freeing his tank, he saw that the accompanying infantry were pinned down as the enemy began a counterattack. Crecy climbed up on the rear of his immobilized tank and held off the Germans with the tank's .50-caliber machine gun while the foot soldiers withdrew. Later that day, he again exposed himself to enemy fire as he wiped out several machine-gun nests and an antitank position with only his machine gun. The more fire he drew, the harder he fought. After the battle Crecy had to be pried away from his machine gun. The war correspondent attached to the 761st Tank Battalion, Trezzvant Anderson, illustrates:

> To look at Warren G.H. Crecy (the G.H. stands for Gamaliel Harding) you'd never think that here was a "killer," who had slain more of the enemy than any man in the 761st. He extracted a toll of lives from the enemy that would have formed the composition of 3 or 4 companies, with his machine guns alone. And yet, he is such a quiet, easy-going, meek-looking fellow, that you'd think that the fuzz which a youngster tries to cultivate for a mustache would never grow on his baby-skinned chin and that he'd never use a word stronger than "damn." But here was a youth who went so primitively savage on the battle field that his only thought was to "kill, kill, kill," and he poured his rain of death pellets into German bodies with so much reckless abandon and joy that he was the nemesis of all the foes of the 761st. And other men craved to ride with Crecy and share the reckless thrill of killing the hated enemy that had killed their comrades. And he is now living on borrowed time. By all human equations Warren G.H. Crecy should have been dead long ago, and should have had the Congressional Medal of Honor, at least![3]

Warren G.H. Crecy, age 17, graduate of Solomon M. Coles High School, Corpus Christi, Texas. At 150 lbs. he was a star football player. His coach said that pound for pound Crecy was the greatest player he ever coached. Crecy enlisted in the Army on December 12, 1942 at Fort Sam Houston, Texas (courtesy Mrs. Margaret Crecy).

The 761st Tank Battalion pushed on. It was rough going through the rain, mud, and cold, driving sleet, fighting an enemy who bitterly contested every inch of ground. The 761st spearheaded through more French towns, with Rivers leading the way for Able Company (A/761st). Ruben Rivers, a tank platoon sergeant, became adept at liquidating the enemy with the .50-caliber machine gun. The dashing young man from Oklahoma soon became a legend in the battalion. One lieutenant recalled telling Rivers, via radio, "Don't go into that town, Sergeant, it's too hot in there." Rivers respectfully replied, "I'm sorry, sir, I'm already through that town!"

761st Tank Battalion map, by William Kaiser, Jr. (National Archives and Records Administration).

On the way to Guebling, France, on November 16, 1944, Rivers' tank ran over a Teller antitank mine. The explosion blew off the right track, the volute springs, and the undercarriage, hurling the tank sideways. When the medical team arrived they found Rivers behind his tank holding one leg, which was ripped to the bone. There was a hole in his leg where part of his knee had been, and bone protruded through his trousers. The medics cleansed and dressed the wound and attempted to inject Rivers with morphine, but he refused. He wanted to remain alert. The medics informed Rivers' commanding officer, Captain David Williams II, that Rivers should be evacuated immediately. Rivers refused. Pulling himself to his feet, he pushed past the captain and took over a second tank. At that moment a hail of enemy fire came in. The captain gave orders to disperse and take cover.

A/761st was to cross a river into Guebling, after combat engineers constructed a Bailey bridge. The Germans tried desperately to stop the construction, but the 761st held them off. The bridge was completed on the afternoon of November 17. Rivers led the way across, and the 761st took up positions in and around Guebling. On the way into town, Rivers, despite his wounds, engaged two German tanks and disabled them both. Still in great pain, he took on two more tanks and forced them to withdraw. A/761st spent that evening under fire. Before dawn on November 18 the captain and

PFC Bill Houle taking time out for posterity, posing with his brother's .22 caliber rifle, Newbury, Massachusetts, spring 1944, right before going to the European Theater of Operations with the 26th "Yankee" Infantry Division (courtesy William W. Houle).

the medical team visited each tank. When they reached Rivers, it was obvious that he was in extreme pain. Rivers' leg was reexamined and found to be infected. The medical team said that if he was not evacuated immediately, the leg would have to be amputated. Rivers still insisted that he would not abandon his men. Throughout the day, both sides held and defended their positions.

At dawn on November 19, A/761st began an assault on the village of Bougaltroff. When they emerged from cover, the morning air outside Guebling lit up with tracers from enemy guns. Rivers spotted the source and directed a concentrated barrage on them. He continued to fire until several tracers were seen going into his turret. At a range of approximately 200 yards, the Germans threw an AP (armor piercing) round that hit the front of the tank. It penetrated and left ricocheting fragments confined inside its steel walls. "The first shot had blown Rivers' brains out against the back of the tank, and the second went into his head, emerging from the rear, and the intrepid leader, the fearless, daring fighter was no more," said Trezzvant Anderson.[4]

Artwork of Medal of Honor Recipient Ruben Rivers by military artist Jody Harmon (courtesy Jody Harmon, jodyharmon.com).

Ruben Rivers did not have to die on that cold, dreary November morning in France. Three days earlier, he had received what GIs called a "million-dollar wound." He could have been evacuated to the rear and gone home a war hero with his Silver Star and Purple Heart, knowing that he was admired and respected as an outstanding soldier and comrade. But he stayed—and he died.

The 761st Tank Battalion pushed on. From December 31, 1944, to February 2, 1945, the 761st took part in the Battle of the Bulge. In a major battle at Tillet, Belgium, the 761st operated for two continuous days against German panzer and infantry units. The operations of the 761st in the Bulge split the enemy lines at three points, the Houffalize-Bastogne road, the St. Vith-Bastogne highway, and the St. Vith-Trier road, preventing the resupply of German forces.

Later, as the armored spearhead for the 103rd Infantry Division, the 761st took part in assaults that resulted in the breech of the Siegfried Line. From March 20 to March 23, 1945, operating far in advance of friendly artillery and in the face of vicious German resistance, elements of the 761st attacked and destroyed many defensive positions along the Siegfried Line. The 761st captured seven German towns, more than 400 vehicles, 80 heavy weapons, 200 horses and thousands of small arms. During that three-day period the battalion inflicted more than 4,000 casualties on the German army. It was later determined that the 761st had fought against elements of 14 German divisions. On April 16, from Bayreuth, 40 miles from Leuchtenberg, elements of the 71st Infantry Division with supporting 761st tanks formed Task Force Weidenmark. Their objective was to extend the Third Army's Eastern front to Czechoslovakia.

Dateline, November 11, 2006, by PFC Vernon Schmidt, 90th Infantry Division:

> Sixty one years ago in a German village named Leuchtenberg, WWII was winding down at a fast pace. A nine year old Hitler Youth kid, named Bruno Ehlich, was an ammunition carrier on a German antitank gun positioned in the woods just outside this village. Their orders from the SS soldiers were to fire on any oncoming American tanks hoping to slow down their advance. An American Sherman tank rumbled up into view and Bruno's crew fired on this tank but caused no damage. Return fire from the tank wiped out the German crew, either killed or wounded. Bruno, wounded and scared, ran to the castle in this village only to find the SS troops gone, now leaving the defense of Leuchtenberg into the hands of these Hitler Youth. Bruno, running from the castle down to the village center, found himself staring up into the huge barrel of the 76 gun on the tank. A black tanker jumped to the ground grabbing Bruno by the neck and demanded to know the location of the German troops or where they were hiding. Bruno revealed a secret underground passage and shortly the village was in American hands and little nine year old Bruno found himself a prisoner of this black tanker. Bruno's story, *Born on the Wrong Side of the Fence*, written in 2004, had a chapter missing. Who was this black GI tanker? Was he still alive? Can I find him or his unit? Persistent searching by Vern Schmidt, a combat veteran of the 90th Infantry Division and a friend of Bruno, found Joe Wilson, Jr., author of a book, *The 761st "Black Panther" Tank Battalion in World War II*. Joe's father was in this unit and familiar with much of its history through France and Germany and Joe Wilson Jr. became very involved in trying to find the tanker who had grabbed Bruno on that April day back in 1945. Following several phone calls to Mr. Johnnie Stevens, Jr. of Carteret, N.J. and he being a former tanker from the 761st Tank Battalion, Mr. Stevens said, "I believe that probably was me." Now, after sixty-one years Bruno Ehlich, a retired Sergeant from the Royal Australian Air Force, sent Mr. Johnnie Stevens, Jr. a letter of congratulations and thanking him for liberating this little Austrian kid from Hitler's Nazi army. Poor health and continents apart will probably prevent these two gentlemen from meeting each other, but perhaps now Bruno can realize his long search is complete. Our congratulations to Mr. Johnnie Stevens, Jr. on receiving the coveted French National Legion of Honor award for his exemplary service in WWII to the French people. May God Bless Johnnie Stevens, Jr.[5]

Vernon Schmidt reported that he questioned whether 761st tankers came into Leuchtenburg on April 24, 1945—because that was in the 90th Infantry Division's sector and the 90th set up a divisional command post at 1600 hours in that little Bavarian town. Several 90th Infantry Division veterans told him that African American tankers were there. He has been recently told by a World War II veteran that the 71st Infantry Division was just west of Leuchtenberg that day, and he confirmed that the 761st was supporting them. Vernon's thinking is that a 761st tank may have gone down the road into the 90th area. As a side note, the tanker demanded information from Hitler Youth Bruno Ehlich about where the German soldiers were. Bruno showed them a hidden passage into the castle and when the tankers blew the lock off the door to this passageway all kinds of people came out, including a lady whose sons were on an antitank gun trying to stop the tank. She had a pistol in her hand and pointed it at the tank like she was going to take it prisoner. Vernon has been back to Leuchtenberg four times, staying in a guest house that was then owned by the same lady.

From here the 761st moved on to towards Austria, where the war ended for them. They were among the first American units to link up with Soviet forces. On May 5, 1945, the 761st reached Steyr, Austria, on the Enns River, where they met the Soviets.

Through six months of combat duty, without relief, the 761st Tank Battalion served as a separate battalion with the 26th, 71st, 79th, 87th, 95th and 103rd Infantry divisions and the 17th Airborne Division. Assigned at various times to the Third, Seventh, and Ninth armies, the 761st fought major engagements in six European countries and participated in four major Allied campaigns. During that time, the unit inflicted exorbitant casualties on the German army and captured, destroyed, or aided in the liberation of more than 30 towns, several concentration camps, four airfields, three ammunition supply dumps, 461 wheeled vehicles, 34 tanks, 113 large guns, and thousands of individual and crew-served weapons. This was accomplished despite extreme shortages of replacement personnel and equipment, with an overall casualty rate approaching 50 percent and the loss of 71 tanks.

On June 1, 1947, the 761st Tank Battalion, after conducting occupation duty, deactivated in Germany. On November 24, 1947, it reactivated at Fort Knox, Kentucky, as a segregated training battalion. Finally on March 15, 1955, the 761st deactivated.

In 1978, thirty-three years after the end of World War II, the 761st Tank Battalion received the Presidential Unit Citation. In 1997, fifty-three years after giving his life on the battlefield, Staff Sergeant Ruben Rivers was posthumously awarded the Medal of Honor. The motto of the 761st Tank Battalion has always been "Come Out Fighting." In World War II, that is exactly what they did.

17

Whatever Happened to the 784th Tank Battalion?

The 784th Tank Battalion, the last of the three "Negro" tank battalions to be activated, landed in France on Christmas Day 1944. A medium-tank battalion, they consisted of six companies, A (Able), B (Baker), C (Charlie), D (Dog), Headquarters and Service. Able, Baker, and Charlie operated with the Sherman medium tanks, Dog with the M-5 Stuart light tanks, and Headquarters with the 105-millimeter Assault Gun Platoon, the Reconnaissance Platoon, and the 81-millimeter Mortar Platoon. Service took charge of maintenance, transportation, administration, and other tasks.

On December 26, 1944, approaching Soissons, France, while en route to join the 104th Infantry Division, the battalion heard bomb blasts. As the explosions increased in intensity and rapidity, they discovered the source, a flaming ammunition train. An ammunition company officer requested and received their help in saving the remaining rail cars from detonation. Using tanks as recovery vehicles, the tankers worked all afternoon while the explosions continued. They saved 160 of the original 300 rail cars. After this diversion, the 784th Tank Battalion continued its road march and joined the 104th Infantry Division near Eschweiler, Germany, on December 31, 1944.

Along the Roer River in the Duren area the 784th supported the 104th as they held and defended their positions. The tankers fired along with division artillery. On February 3 they were released from the 104th and assigned to the 35th Infantry Division. While en route to their new assignment, elements of B/784th served as infantrymen. Staff Sergeant Franklin Garrido, B/784th Tank Battalion, continues the narrative:

One of the things that can happen and usually does happen to tankers when spearheading without stopping to lube the bogie wheels is that they burn out. That's what happened to me. We were spearheading, going as fast as we could without stopping when the bogie wheel, at least one, in my tank burned out. We pulled over to the side where an armored division was bivouacked. Two other tanks from the battalion also pulled over because they too had burned-out bogie wheels. I was the highest-ranking noncom there so I took charge. The first thing we did was to beg the armored division for a couple of cases of ten-in-one rations, which they gave us. The next thing we did was to get "Preacher," who was a member of another crew, to evacuate the civilians in a house so that we could use it as a command post. He was a preacher. He was always quoting the gospel. He is the one person who could really evict people from their houses. Within minutes he had them flying out the

Top: Merode Castle, 1945 (National Archives and Records Administration, courtesy Albert Trostorf). *Bottom:* 784th Tank Battalion command center in the basement of the Merode Castle, February 1945 (National Archives and Records Administration, courtesy Albert Trostorf).

door. While we were there waiting for Service Company to come up and put on our new bogie wheels an infantry lieutenant came up to ask if he could borrow one of our machine guns. I was a little bit leery because I might not get it back. I told him, "How about us taking it and going with you. I'll ask my gunner if he will go with you." That was okay with him just as long as he had the machine gun. They were notified that on a hill a few kilometers away was a German encampment. He was ordered to capture the hill. The lieutenant had a squad of infantrymen, which we called doughs, from doughboy. When we had to shoot at German infantrymen coming toward us, we referred to them as doughs. Any infantry, we called doughs.

We loaded up on a weapons carrier and drove to the base of the hill. We spread out and charged. I was in armor, the whole time being in tanks. I was not used to running against the enemy without any protection around me. I felt naked. We were ordered to fall and fire. We fired. I had my grease gun with me and fired along with the machine gunner I was commanding. I fed ammunition to the machine gunner. We did that about three times before reaching the top of the hill. There were two Germans there. One was intact and the other was wounded. He was laying on the ground moaning. The wounded man was shot by a dough. He just walked up to him and dropped his M-1 on his temple and let go. The other must have been drinking a lot of schnapps because he acted as if he was intoxicated. We left the dead on the top of the hill and took the other German prisoner. On the way back, one of the doughs took his canteen and smelled it and sure enough, he smelled alcohol.[1]

On February 8 the 784th Tank Battalion joined the 35th Infantry Division at Geilenkirchen, Germany. Together they prepared for a major offensive. On February 26, they assisted elements of the division in the capture of Hilfarth and Wassenberg. On February 28 Task Force Byrne, organized with the mission of liberating the town of Venlo, crossed the border into Holland. This task force consisted of the 320th Infantry Regiment, the 784th Tank Battalion less A/784th, the 654th Tank Destroyer Battalion, artillery support, plus attached engineer and medical units. Colonel Bernard Byrne, commanding officer of the 320th Infantry Regiment, commanded this task force. On March 1, the 784th Tank Battalion spearheaded down the road to Venlo, bypassing pockets of resistance except in towns and villages. The task force moved so swiftly that the enemy did not have time to destroy bridges. The coordinated assault of tanks and infantry surprised and quickly wiped out enemy positions. The task force entered Venlo on March 1.

The 134th and 137th Infantry regiments, along with A/784th, followed Task Force Byrne, mopping up bypassed enemy forces. The task force then set out in the direction of Straelen, Sevelen, and Rhineburg, Germany. The battalion had little trouble moving ahead except for scattered resistance and blown bridges. In Straelen a tank was knocked out by *Panzerfaust* fire. The burning tank was pushed aside and the task force continued.

The 8th Armored Division stabbed toward Rheinberg in the afternoon and received a jolt. Now it was the 35th Infantry Division and the 784th Tank Battalion's turn. A night attack was planned, a plan which only a veteran, experienced unit could fulfill. In a daring and shrewd move, elements of the 35th Infantry Division entered Rheinberg at 1930 hours followed by other elements of the division at 2012 hours. The 784th Tank Battalion preceded their entry with a dash through five miles of enemy territory to the Rhine River itself. After dismounting from trucks, the infantry followed and worked their way down the main street, advancing on both sides of the street flushing out dark cellars and buildings. There were firefights until 0600 hours the following day when the city was finally secure.

For the remainder of the day, the advance was checked outside of Rheinberg due to a blown bridge. Without tank support, the infantry couldn't move against the heavy enemy fire directed at them from across the flat expanses of terrain. The tanks couldn't cross a stream that flowed into the Rhine River until a bridge was built. The drive continued at 1800 hours as soon as the bridge was put in. Ossenberg was the next objective. This area was referred to as "88 Alley" because of the heavy presence of German 88-millimeter guns. The 35th Infantry Division's artillery pounded Ossenberg day and night so that it might be taken and the enemy's retreat across the river above the town halted.

Sevelen, Germany, March 4, 1945, Dog Company, 784th Tank Battalion, during a maintenance break (courtesy U.S. Army Military History Institute, Carlisle Barracks, Pennsylvania).

From another location, a force that consisted of D/784th light tanks, a company of medium tanks, the assault-gun platoon, and a company of infantry entered Sevelen around midnight on March 2. When they reached the center of town, the enemy blew the bridges behind the troops and launched a counterattack. The *Los Angeles Times* reported:

> With a bridge blown behind them, a Negro tank battalion task force staged a miniature "Bastogne" in Sevelen today, mauling Nazi parachute units in savage street fighting while cut off for 18 hours. The following day, March 3, reinforcements [C/784th] entered Sevelen and counterattacked. When the smoke cleared, 53 enemy soldiers lay dead, 27 surrendered, and a large supply of food and ammunition fell to the task force. The 784th Tank Battalion was fighting its first offensive beside the 35th Infantry Division. The battalion won a place in the hearts of the men of the battle hardened 35th Division, who fought from St. Lo to Venlo and beyond, by the battle it put up here and the spearhead fighting it did to get here [Wes Gallagher, Associated Press].[2]

On March 4, 1945, C/784th departed Sevelen to assist in the attack on Kamperbruch with elements of the 320th Infantry Regiment. They were stopped dead in

Sevelen, Germany, in 2015, the location where Dog Company, 784th Tank Battalion, took its maintenance break in 1945 (courtesy Uwe Sewing).

their tracks by a sustained fury of antitank fire and lost three tanks. Hatches opened and men accompanied by flames scampered out. Three tankers perished inside their blazing tanks: tank commander Sergeant James Laurie; tank driver Private Willmore Mack; and tank driver Private Raymond Womack. "When we got hit," said Technician Fifth-Grade James Hamilton, C/784th Tank Battalion, "me and Irby—the driver next to me—got out of there together. His right arm got split all the way up. The lieutenant said he never saw anyone who could run that fast. He said, 'They were shooting at you and they couldn't hit you.'"[3]

Early the next morning the remainder of C/784th once again attacked Kamperbruch, but this time the enemy had withdrawn. They pushed on and assaulted two small villages before stopping outside of Millingen. There they broke up into a two-pronged attack. One tank platoon went along the soggy road leading through evergreen woods. The lead tank got knocked out on the approach to this village by a concealed self-propelled antitank gun. Then they became sitting targets for automatic, small arms, and mortar fire. The tanks in the rear provided covering fire to effect the withdrawal.

The other C/784th tanks were not as fortunate. They went straight down the main road into Millingen. Then all hell—in the most vivid meaning of the term—broke loose! Concealed antitank guns and *Panzerfausts* appeared from out of nowhere. Muzzles flashed all around. The antitank rounds had tracers that could be seen streaking from the enemy, hitting the tanks, and the ineffective ones careening hundreds of feet into the sky. Then the thumping sound of the *Panzerfaust* roared and swished as its rocket-like projectile unsteadily streaked toward the tanks in perceived slow motion. The ones that hit the road threw up dirt and rocks along with searing shrapnel from their phosphorus warheads. The tanks directly hit by this deadly fire shuddered and stopped in the middle of the road before erupting into flames. Smoke hissed from the neatly pierced holes in the armor. The enemy antitank guns, in typical fashion, knocked out the lead tank to block the advance, then took out the rear tank to prevent the others from backing out. One by one they went after the other tanks, destroying four.

C/784th suffered the loss of four tanks. Tank gunner Corporal Wilson Griswell and platoon leader First Lieutenant Art Solow perished. Platoon leader Second Lieutenant Alex Carr, along with three other men, went missing in action. Platoon leader First Lieutenant David Crawford and others were medically evacuated. This left C/784th without officers in command. Fighting continued at a fierce and savage pace as this tank company regrouped and launched several assaults to liberate their trapped comrades:

> On the 5th, Captain Watkins of F Company was killed while his company was leading the advance with the colored tankers. The tank company commander had a leg blown off and a tank platoon leader was wounded. By yesterday afternoon one company of our tanks had lost all its officers except the maintenance platoon leader, whose duties were more or less somewhat to the rear of the front elements. The company lost eight tanks, five yesterday, three day before.... A great part of a platoon of Negro tankers were either killed or captured when they spearheaded into a town and were cut off. The bodies of some were found, badly beaten about the

face, and one shot through the forehead. One was recovered alive after other troops fought into the town. He was badly bruised from beating. He said the Nazis beat them after they were made prisoners. He was in too bad a condition to question further and was rushed on back to the hospital [Major Orval Faubus, HQ/320th Infantry Regiment].[4]

Corporal Claude Sharrieff-Frazier, B/784th Tank Battalion, recalled the following:

The difficult thing for me—it was around 1946—this brother came to my house. He told me about the battles over there and the losses. A statement he made, the 784th, especially C Company, was bottled up in a place outside a town in Germany. And in this battle he claimed that orders were misconstrued by the commanding officers and a lot of men got killed and captured. That is where Art Solow got killed and I believe that Whitbeck got killed there too. I was trying to put that together because I didn't remember Whitbeck being an active tank crewman. The point he made to me as that there was so much carnage in such a vicious battle that somehow or another, with officers being wounded and killed, Ora Burns took command of the company and he safely, either offensively or defensively, saved a lot of members of C Company. What I was told was that some of the men were treated very badly when captured. They were brutalized, so it is possible that some of them were killed as prisoners. This brother told me this and he is like a mystery to me. I am so sorry that I didn't keep in touch with him. He would break down when he was telling me this. He was crying when he said that if it wasn't for Ora Burns they would have been totally wiped out. He said there was a lot of screaming. Art Solow got messed up because they saw on his dog tag that he was Jewish. I recall Ora Burns was from the Midwest, either Kansas or Missouri. He was about medium height, close to 6 feet, dark-skinned, and very pleasant and an excellent noncommissioned officer. So it didn't surprise me to any great extent when this person told me how he handled himself in the heat of battle. But I was shocked to hear that they suffered such a tremendous loss. And when I look at the graves of the men, I see that most of them died between March the 1st and 5th when the battle was at its peak.[5]

The 784th Tank Battalion continued its push toward the Rhine River with the 35th Infantry Division. On March 26, A/784th, attached to the 134th Infantry Regiment, crossed the Rhine River to exploit the XVI Corps Rhine bridgehead. The remainder of the battalion crossed later. Resistance became less frequent as the enemy became disorganized and withdrew through the Ruhr towns. Then the Germans began surrendering by the hundreds. "We crossed the Rhine at night," said Staff Sergeant Garrido. "They were still bombing and machine gunning, sending artillery into the area. We crossed on a pontoon bridge. Being a Southern Californian, I'm not used to seeing wide, deep, swift rivers and it scared the heck out of me. At midnight with no lights I had to lead my tank across this deep, wide, fast-flowing river under fire. I was scared. I was a good swimmer and I kept telling my crew, if the tank goes down or if a shell hits one of the pontoons, just ride with the flow of the current. We made it across the bridge. It was scary."[6]

The 784th Tank Battalion continued the offensive, supporting the 35th Infantry Division. On April 10, B/784th and C/784th attached to the 17th Airborne Division for a brief period for an attack on Oberhausen and Mulheim. On April 13, they reattached to the 35th Infantry Division, where they patrolled the wooded area around Blatz on the west bank of the Elb River. There they mopped up pockets of resistance and took prisoners.

SS troops evacuating Jews and political prisoners from the east discovered American troops advancing in their direction. They herded their evacuees into a hangar on the edge of Gardelegen. They poured gasoline on the structure, set it afire, and waited outside with their machine guns at the ready. Caught between a blazing fire and machine-gun bullets, many of the prisoners burned alive as they pressed on the walls. The ones that made it out got cut down by a deadly blanket of machine-gun fire. Others died as they emerged from underneath the walls after desperately clawing and digging themselves free. According to one report, only 12 of the 1,100 prisoners survived.

As the war in Europe began grinding to a halt, elements of the 784th Tank Battalion became eyewitnesses to the holocaust, Staff Sergeant Garrido being one of them:

Corporal Claude A. Frazier (courtesy Claude Sharrieff-Frazier).

One of the last large cities that we captured was the medieval city of Hanover. We entered without firing a shot under a plethora of white sheets, pillowcases, towels, underwear, socks, anything white—signs of surrender. When we reached the edge of town we stopped, reloaded, and prepared to jump off at 0600 the next morning. At 0600 we were lined up for what we thought would be Berlin; it was only 100 kilometers away. We took off in a convoy, traveling along at a clip of about 35 miles per hour. The sun was out. It was a beautiful spring morning. The sky was clear, dew was on the ground, and I was lulled into daydreaming about Los Angeles and the California girls. And then I saw this large tall spiral of black greasy smoke ascending into the sky. When we rounded the curve, I saw this compound. There was a large hangar-like building surrounded by a wire fence. On the nearest corner there, what I thought was laundry, clothes hanging on the fence. As we got closer, I saw the clothes, to my horror, was human skeletons—alive! Human skeletons were clinging onto the fence begging us with their eyes to help them.

At that time the radio crackled and we heard an urgent message over the air telling the tanks not to run over the bodies. We hadn't reached the gate yet and the urgent-sounding voice said, "Slow down! Don't run over the bodies!" The convoy slowed down from 35 miles per hour to 5 miles per hour. And sure enough, as we came closer to the gates of the compound we had to thread our way through the bodies. When the barn-like structure was set on fire, it was where the inmates were kept. The doors were locked. As the inmates scrambled to escape the fire, they were machine-gunned. Some of them made it to the road, but they were machine-gunned and their bodies were strewn all over the place. We didn't stop. In fact, the same urgent voice, probably an officer said, "Don't stop! There are people in the rear echelon who can help these people. Your job is to continue to pursue the enemy. It was the SS that did this and we want to catch them. Don't stop!"

Years later I had a librarian at the Holocaust Museum in Los Angeles do some research for me. I told her that the only name I could remember about the area was Gardelegen. The concentration camp was on the outskirts of the town of Gardelegen, Germany. Gardelegen was not a concentration camp. It was a satellite camp where they farmed out forced laborers to the various war industry factories in the area. One of the factories was Wolfsburg. Wolfsburg was—and still is—the home of Volkswagen. After we threaded through the bodies, we continued pursuing the retreating Germans until we reached the Elb.

The Elb River was approximately 40 or 50 miles from Berlin. I told my crew to get ready for the big one, we are going in to Berlin. But unknown to us the "Big Three" had already made a decision that the Allies on the west side of the river would halt. That would give the Russians the honor of capturing Berlin, which was all right with us. My company, Company B, was held in reserve. Two companies of the 784th were at the Elb River when the Russians swept through Berlin. They swept through Berlin with a vengeance. Hitler committed suicide, and the war ended. The Soviet army met the American army at the Elb River. Company B was not there but two other companies were.[7]

On April 26 the battalion moved to Immensen, where it performed occupation and control over the surrounding communities. On May 26 it moved to Kelberg and the surrounding communities. With the loss of 140 men in battle, of which 24 were killed in action, the 784th Tank Battalion returned to the United States and was deactivated on April 26, 1946, at Camp Kilmer, New Jersey. Wes Gallagher, the AP correspondent, gave his opinion of the battalion:

> I had studied the brilliant history of the outfit, and among the ranks of its enlisted men, I had formed some of my most cherished friendships. But I had not seen the battalion under actual combat conditions, the skill and daring of the battalion's colored tank commanders. There were countless stories of how these Negro sergeants carried on alone in the heat of battle, even when their white commanding captains and lieutenants had been wounded or lost in action.... Along the lonely German fields and roads that beckoned to the Ruhr, I had a chance to test the truth or falsity of those stories, and I found that the glowing tales of heroism which had been attributed to these brown warriors were only a small part of a greater truth.[8]

In reference to the March 4, 1945, picture depicting Dog Company, 784th Tank Battalion, taking a maintenance break, notice the soldier walking out of the garage at the half-track. He is positioned between the tanker smoking a cigarette and the tall tanker. That is Sergeant Bill Hughes, the communications sergeant. He is wearing the typical winter gear of a tanker, one of his most cherished World War II possessions. He describes it in his final e-mail:

> ... those clothing were worn every day by me during the bitter winter of 1944, and also saw the horrors of war.
> There are a couple of blood spots the cleaners could not get rid of because I waited many years before having it cleaned as it was stored in a basement trunk. The blood had caked when I put it away. Since it was mine, I did not try to remove it because it reminded me of a very lucky day. Enemy snipers latched to high trees fired on our tank column in a wooded area. One bullet hit my tank turret and all I heard was a loud PING. I ducked and closed

the hatch. My arm felt numb and I thought I had hit my elbow on the tank in my haste to close the hatch. I did not think any more about it but I felt a warm sticky substance in my glove. It was my blood so I wondered where in the devil did it come from. I found a torn hole in my jacket and took it off. A bullet fell to the floor of the tank. Blood was coming from my arm where the bullet had grazed it. A little Sulphur and bandage took care of the bleeding. It was never reported as a combat wound. I don't know if I was the intended target or not. If so, I was lucky to have a bad shooting sniper pulling the trigger that day.[9]

18

Legacy

On June 14, 1946, the 758th Tank Battalion reactivated at Fort Knox, Kentucky, as part of the Armored Force School. The battalion trained recruits in basic armored-infantry tactics initially with M4A3-E8 ("Easy Eight") Sherman tanks. The "Easy Eight" weighed 37 tons and mounted a 76-millimeter main gun. Soon the newer and heavier M26 Pershing tanks joined the fleet. They weighed 41 tons and carried a 90-millimeter main gun. The engine produced 500 horsepower, the capacity to push a two-ton muscle car 200 miles-per-hour. However, it could propel the Pershing only 25 miles per hour.

By the end of summer 1945, with World War II over, twelve million veterans were returning home, including over 800,000 black veterans. After fighting for freedom and democracy abroad they came home to find it still denied to them. What they found was a wave of anti-black terror, mostly, but not limited to, southern states. Christian-based hate groups such as the Ku Klux Klan (KKK) and others, with active support from law enforcement, swung into action. The sight of returning black veterans proudly wearing their uniforms became tantamount to asserting equality. The KKK responded with violence.

In one example, Sergeant Isaac Woodard, hours after being honorably discharged from the United States Army, was attacked while in uniform by South Carolina police. On February 12, 1946, he traveled on a Greyhound bus from Camp Gordon, Georgia, to reunite with his wife in North Carolina. When the bus reached a rest stop outside of Augusta, Georgia, Woodard asked the bus driver if there was time for him to use a restroom. The driver grudgingly agreed and cursed loudly at him. Woodard later admitted in a deposition that he cursed back. The bus stopped in Batesburg, South Carolina, outside of Aiken. Though Woodard had caused no disruption, the driver contacted the local police chief, Lynwood Shull, who with his men forcibly removed Woodard from the bus. After demanding to see his discharge papers and searching his belongings, they took Woodard to a nearby alley and beat him repeatedly. Then they took him to jail and charged him with disorderly conduct, accusing him of drinking beer in the back of the bus with other soldiers. The attack left Woodard completely and permanently blind.

This event would soon spark national outrage, galvanize the civil rights movement, and draw the ire of the president of the United States. On the ABC radio show *Orson Welles Commentaries* actor and filmmaker Orson Welles petitioned for Shull and his deputies to be held accountable. In his July 28, 1946, broadcast Wells read an affidavit provided to him by the NAACP and signed by Woodard. Wells criticized the lack of action by the South Carolina government as intolerable and shameful. His continued broadcasts proved instrumental in prompting the Justice Department to take action. Due to South Carolina's refusal to pursue the case, President Truman ordered a federal investigation and subsequently Shull was indicted and went on trial in federal court in South Carolina. The all-white jury acquitted him after 30 minutes of deliberation. These common-place miscarriages of justice by state governments compelled civil rights initiatives at the federal level.

By 1947, as the Cold War with the Soviet Union intensified and America became increasingly anticommunist and intolerant, Truman shocked everyone. He suddenly supported civil rights. The killings and bludgeoning of dozens of returning black veterans outraged Truman, who had once held strong racial biases. Prior to that incident he used the word "nigger" freely in his lingo. Now he would make civil rights a national issue by authorizing a committee on civil rights to recommend new legislation to protect Americans from discrimination. Speaking from the steps of the Lincoln Memorial, Truman became the first president of the United States to address the NAACP and promised that the federal government would act to end racial violence.

Truman pointed out to Congress that America's Jim Crow policies were being used by Soviet propagandists in the Cold War to sway the rest of the world against America. The southerners retorted that the civil rights movement was supported by communists. President Truman began examining the issue of desegregating the military in earnest with the appointed President's Committee on Civil Rights. By January 1948 it became obvious that he would issue an executive order that would include a Committee on Equality of Treatment and Opportunity in the Armed Services, known as the Fahy Committee. However, it was not until the delegates at the 1948 Democratic National Convention called for a liberal civil rights agenda that included desegregating the armed forces that Truman felt the confidence to issue the order. On July 26, 1948, he released it: "It is hereby declared to be the policy of the President that there shall be equality of treatment and opportunity for all persons in the armed services without regard to race, color, religion, or national origin" (Executive Order 9981).[1]

South Carolina governor Strom Thurmond, an 82nd Airborne Division veteran of World War II, led a group of southern delegates in storming out of the Democratic National Convention when the civil rights platform passed. Thurmond and his segregationist ilk formed the States Rights Party and became known as "Dixiecrats." A reporter asked Thurmond why he had bolted from the Democratic Party when President Truman had not done anything substantially different from his predecessor, Franklin D. Roosevelt. Thurmond instantly replied, "Yes, but Truman really means it!"[2] Truman's stance on civil rights won him the black vote in 1948 but lost him the

southern vote. By all indications Truman would lose the presidential election. Then on November 3, 1948, the day after the election, the front-page headline of the *Chicago Tribune* proclaimed, "Dewey Defeats Truman." In reality, Truman ended up scoring a surprise victory over his opponent, New York governor Thomas Dewey.

Heavy resistance to Executive Order 9981 followed. The military leadership from all branches protested integration, but they would be dragged kicking and moaning into the modern age. However, there were rare exceptions. One notable one was Major General James Gavin, the commanding officer of the 82nd Airborne Division. Upon triumphantly returning from war in Europe, and prior to Executive Order 9981, Gavin displayed an uncommon type of bravery. Gavin, unlike the upper-middle/ upper-caste army officer, was an adopted orphan. He had also served as an enlisted man and entered West Point on merit rather than influence. Thus he had differing experiences and views on race relations. "The first black man I ever saw was a Pullman porter who allowed me to go through his car selling newspapers when the train stopped in Mount Carmel, [Pennsylvania]. He was very kind and helpful to me," Major General Gavin recalled. "[After West Point] I served with the all-black 25th Infantry on the Mexican border near Douglas, Arizona. I enjoyed my service with this hard-driving well trained regiment. Its members often talked about the histories of black units in the Spanish-American War that made clear their effectiveness in combat, providing they were well-trained, well-armed, and well-led. The NCOs knew their business and of course with long service, we had a Sgt. Bilko or two, who knew how to take every advantage of the system."[3]

Fort Bragg had an area set aside for blacks, a segregated section called Spring Lake just outside of Spring Lake village. That's where black artillery and support units along with the world's first black airborne unit, the 555th Parachute Infantry Battalion ("Triple Nickels"), were located. They had their own stores, clubs, theater, and the lake to swim in. They were billeted in old tarpaper-covered shacks. Despite this the black soldiers took pride in their area and equipment with a sense of esprit de corps, knowing that a large number of convenient empty barracks where white soldiers lived were available. When Major General Gavin saw the Spring Lake area he proclaimed it a swamp and began integrating Fort Bragg by starting with merging the "Triple Nickels" into the all-white 505th Parachute Infantry Regiment. Although they became a segregated battalion (3rd Battalion) in the 505th, it was a start and soon other army infantry regiments followed. The 2nd Infantry Division's 9th Regiment and the 3rd Infantry Division's 15th Regiment set aside 3rd Battalion. This opened the way for other units to follow. Major General Gavin commented:

> Recalling my own personal experience with black troops, I knew the 555th had to be integrated into the 82nd. This was a serious problem, not to be taken lightly, for our Army had been a two-colored Army for a long time, just as was our own society. I was concerned that if I asked for a

Opposite: **"Joseph E. Wilson, left, Platoon Sergeant, accompanied by his tank driver. Co A. 758 Tank Battalion—A14, the fastest tank on the lot. February 1947. M-26 Tank Ft. Knox" (courtesy First Sergeant Joseph E. Wilson, Sr., USA-Ret-Dec).**

letter of authority to integrate the triple nickels into the 82nd there certainly would be opposition. Tradition in the Armed Forces is very strong and I was certain to get a rejection. So I decided to grab the issue and go directly to the department of the army staff. I called on the Chief of Plans and Operations in the War Department at the Pentagon. I was aware that the 82nd was going to be part of the Army's strategic reserve [ASR] and that if the 555th was integrated into the 82nd Airborne Division it would become part of the ASR and that meant the 555th would be superbly trained and equipped and have the highest priority for the newest equipment and weapons.... The S-3, Lieutenant General Hull had but one question, "General, do you intend to give all those fourrageres and medals that the 82nd won in Europe to the 555th?" "Yes General" I replied, "I will and they will earn them. I'll see to that." There was no further discussion. I returned to Fort Bragg and the integration order followed.[4]

On January 15, 1948, also prior to Executive Order 9981, the 758th Tank Battalion relocated to Fort Bragg, North Carolina, and was accepted into the 82nd Airborne Division. No other unit wanted them. The army decided that each infantry and airborne division required a tank battalion. The battalion's training mission entailed driving through enemy lines and linking up with paratroopers already deep in enemy territory, training that would serve them well in the future.

President Harry S. Truman in the Rose Garden with integrated soldiers of the 82nd Airborne Division during their tour of the nation's capital, February 26–27, 1951. On the president's left (viewer's right) is Secretary of the Army Frank Pace, Jr. (National Archives and Records Administration).

3rd Battalion, 505th Paratroopers, are hitching a ride on a 758th tank during an advance against the aggressor force during Operation Tar Heel, at Camp Mackall, a subcamp of Fort Bragg, North Carolina, May 12, 1949 (National Archives and Records Administration).

On November 3, 1949, the 758th Tank Battalion was redesignated the 64th Heavy Tank Battalion and assigned to the 2nd Armored Division at Camp Hood, Texas. Camp Hood became Fort Hood in April 1950.

On June 25, 1950, North Korean communists, spearheaded by Soviet T34 tanks, overran the 38th Parallel into South Korea and rolled over the South Korean forces. Latitude 38 degrees north on the world map roughly divided Korea into north and south. This arbitrary line chosen by simple-minded military planners at the Potsdam Conference in July 1945 delineated where Soviet and American forces would accept Japan's surrender in Korea. The line was intended as a temporary division of the country, but the world would have hell to pay for this rushed decision.

The South Koreans withdrew in the face of this onslaught but the United States reacted quickly. President Truman directed General Douglas MacArthur, commander of U.S. Occupation Forces in Japan, to stem the communist tide. On July 5 American Task Force Smith, a makeshift infantry battalion of the 24th Infantry Division, flew to Korea on C-54 transports and the remainder of the division followed by water.

They made contact with the enemy and fought a delaying action until they were overrun. The Soviet T34 tanks had armor too thick for American bazookas to penetrate. Other American and international forces entered the war shortly thereafter. In July 1950 the 64th Tank Battalion received orders for deployment to Korea and was assigned to the 3rd Infantry Division. They trained in Japan with the new M46 tank, the best-armored and armed vehicle in the Far East. The old M26 Pershing tanks had been rebuilt with an improved 840 horsepower Continental engine and renamed the M46 Patton tank.

The overtly racist Edward Almond reared his ugly head again. Now a three-star general, he got promoted despite his poor performance in World War II. His short stature along with his blond hair and blue eyes made him an endearing pet. In Korea, Almond served as General Douglas MacArthur's personal assistant and chief of staff. Almond also commanded the X Corps, a large, multinational unit. He was suspicious of his nonwhite troops and denigrated them constantly. The same disasters that afflicted the 92nd Infantry Division followed: "In the end, the Army paid a high price for promoting Almond" (military historian Shelby Stanton).[5]

Five months into the Korean War, in November 1950, the 64th Heavy Tank Battalion performed an assault landing on Wonsan, North Korea, where it relieved elements of the 1st Marine Division, the "Frozen Chosin." Together they withdrew under the onslaught of a massive Chinese intervention while assisting in the evacuation of Korean civilians by holding the final line of resistance. Behind that line 105,000 troops, 100,000 civilians, and 17,500 vehicles were evacuated in the largest beachhead evacuation in U.S. Military history.

Sergeant First Class Silus Devine (left) and Private Albert Troth, 758th Heavy Tank Battalion, on a field problem, Operation Tar Heel, Camp Mackall, a subcamp of Fort Bragg, North Carolina, April 29, 1949 (National Archives and Records Administration).

Top: **64th Tank Battalion HQ, Camp Hood, Texas, 1949–50, photo by Sergeant "Kid" Love (courtesy Robert Hyde).** *Bottom:* **Sergeant Love's tank crew, Korea 1951, photo by Sergeant "Kid" Love (courtesy Robert Hyde).**

South Korean troops advancing with the 64th Heavy Tank Battalion, Korea, winter 1951/52, photo by Sergeant "Kid" Love (courtesy Robert Hyde).

64th Heavy Tank Battalion, vicinity of Chorwon, Korea, 1951/52, photo by Sergeant "Kid" Love (courtesy Robert Hyde).

In early 1951, the battalion joined Task Force Bartlett to clear a path for the 25th Infantry Division. They inflicted heavy enemy casualties and accomplished their mission in five days, giving the Allies a needed boost to their confidence. In March the 64th Heavy Tank Battalion participated in Operation Tomahawk. Mindful of their training with the 82nd Airborne Division, they raced north with the 3rd Infantry Division and linked up with the 2nd and 4th Ranger companies and the 187th Airborne Regimental Combat Team ("RAKKASANS"), who had parachuted behind enemy lines. Together they caught the enemy in a crushing vise and continued pushing north. On March 29 the 64th was among the first American units to cross the 38th parallel in the current Eighth Army advance.

In late April 1951 the Chinese launched another major offensive in support of North Korea, this time a two-army attack against the United Nations' front. The 64th Heavy Tank Battalion covered the 3rd Infantry Division's withdrawal to the Seoul area, where the line of resistance stabilized at the 38th Parallel. From May 1951 to July 1953 the battalion held and defended positions around the 38th Parallel while it underwent a historic change with the integration of white soldiers into its ranks.

The United States of America got embarrassed in front of the entire world for sending a segregated military to fight in the name of Democracy, and the Communist propagandists took full advantage. No longer could the American racist generals drag their feet; integration had to commence with or without them. It started with the infamous 3rd Infantry battalions about a month into the war. One such unit, the 3rd Battalion, 9th Infantry Regiment ("Manchu"), 2nd Infantry Division, landed in Korea on July 30, 1950, and went immediately into combat. When they returned from the line, to their amazement the white soldiers from the other battalions cheered them on. Clearly it was time to integrate. A few weeks later white soldiers took up ranks in the 3rd Battalion and black soldiers took up ranks in the 1st and 2nd battalions. The U.S. Army went to Korea segregated and returned integrated.

In the 64th's final action of the Korean War they repelled an enemy penetration into South Korean lines. In the fierce fighting that ensued, Company A drove into an enemy regimental assembly area, where they fought at point-blank range. Finally, they had to call artillery on themselves—short-fused air bursts. When the smoke cleared, 300 enemy soldiers lay dead. For this action, they received the Distinguished Unit Citation.

Chinese soldiers captured by elements of the U.S. 3rd Infantry Division, 1951, photo by Sergeant "Kid" Love (courtesy Robert Hyde).

Taking aim at a Communist position, Korea, 1951, photo by Sergeant "Kid" Love (courtesy Robert Hyde).

In November 1954 the 64th Heavy Tank Battalion departed Korea as heroes after earning the Distinguished Unit Citation and two Korean Presidential Unit Citations. They returned to the United States and remained with the 3rd Infantry Division at Fort Benning, Georgia. Four years later the battalion was deactivated again.

In 1954 the Supreme Court delivered the unanimous ruling in the landmark Civil Rights case *Brown vs. Board of Education of Topeka, Kansas.* It decreed that state-sanctioned segregation of public schools was a violation of the 14th Amendment and therefore unconstitutional. This historic decision marked the end of the "separate but equal" precedent set by the Supreme Court in the 1896 ruling of *Plessy vs. Ferguson.* American society marched one step behind its military.

In June 1963 the 64th Armored Regiment, a parent regiment under the Combined Arms Regimental System with three battalions, was activated in Germany, thus perpetuating the lineage of the 758th Tank Battalion. In 1966 a fourth battalion was activated and assigned to the 3rd Infantry Division in Wurzburg, Germany. That same year, Secretary of Defense Robert McNamara issued Directive 5120. This slowly set into motion the ending of segregation and discrimination in the communities surrounding military installations. The directive empowered commanding officers to use economic power to influence local businesses by declaring them off limits to military personnel under their command. After obtaining the approval of the secretary of defense, commanding officers could declare an area off limits to military personnel, such as segregated housing, dining, and recreational facilities. The first nonmilitary establishment to be declared off limits was in 1967. Bureaucratic inefficiency followed until 1970 when the requirement that commanding officers first obtain permission from the secretary of defense was lifted.

The 2/64th and 3/64th took part in the Cold War defending the Federal Republic of Germany in accordance with the North Atlantic Treaty Organization (NATO),

Sergeant "Kid" Love in an integrated 64th Tank Battalion platoon foot inspection (courtesy Robert Hyde).

while stationed at Schweinfurt. They operated with the M1 Abrams tank and performed numerous REFORGER (Return of Forces to Germany), Winter Warrior, border missions, and Peace Keeper operations until their deactivation in the mid-1990s. With their deactivation the 758th Tank Battalion was down to two surviving descendants, the 1/64th "Desert Rogues" and the 4/64th "Tuskers." In 1983, the 4/64th deployed from Germany to Fort Stewart, Georgia, and joined the 24th Infantry Division. The 1/64th joined them there in 1987.

Exercise REFORGER was an annual exercise conducted during the Cold War by NATO intended to ensure that NATO had the ability to quickly deploy forces to West Germany in the event of a conflict with the Soviet Union. Second Lieutenant Matt Hewett, 1/64th Armored Regiment, gives some insight:

> When I was a young Platoon Leader, I saw these quotes on a sign in the S-3 (battalion staff office for planning and operations). They gave me great comfort when we did our training, especially maneuvers like REFORGER:
> "The reason that the American army does so well in wartime, is that war is chaos, and the American army practices chaos on a daily basis" (German Army General of WWII).
> "One of the serious problems in planning against American doctrine is that the Americans do not read their manuals nor do they feel any obligations to follow their doctrine" (Unknown Soviet Document).
> "If we don't know what we're doing, the enemy certainly can't anticipate our future actions" (Anonymous).
> I love maneuver better than gunnery. It's what I signed up for. Unlike Soviet maneuver training, which was rehearsed and outcomes guaranteed, REFORGER is a true free for all. Commanders at all levels are expected to make mistakes and then learn from them. Better to screw up in training. REFORGERs are supposed to be as realistic as possible.
> A lot of it was a pain—example—before we went out in the field, platoon leaders were given fifty large maps (3' × 3' each—1:50,000 scale) of the area where we'd be maneuvering. It took a lot of [S]cotch tape and a large living room floor to assemble all of those together. And then they had to be folded into a waterproof map case so you could make grease pencil marks for the graphics. Of course, the map never slipped inside the case.
> When possible, we'd be given formal OPORDS (Operation Orders) by our company commander and then do the same for our platoons. In a tank unit, many of our orders where on the fly, i.e.: FRAGOS (Fragmented Orders), with new orders given over the radio. This was perfect training for the real thing. We often had no idea what was going on. In war you have no idea what's going on.
> I remember passing the exact same road intersection four times. My platoon was sent west, then east. "Oops, change of mission, back west, and then head north—Oops, nevermind, head back east." There was an old German man sitting there watching. Why not, he had nothing better to do, and it's pretty cool watching armor units fly by, at least I think so. The first time I went by him, we both waved. The second time, we exchanged small waves. The third time I didn't look at him, I was embarrassed.
> German kids would line up on the side of road begging for food or candy—not that they were hungry like in WWII, but for bragging rights, trading stuff, or getting candy for free. GI's are still suckers in that way, we'd toss them some of our rations. If we came to a stop in a field, kids would ride up to our positions and offer to get us sodas. We'd give them money and damned if they didn't come back. American kids would have taken the money and run. Maybe they thought you don't mess around with someone riding in a 63 ton tank.
> We were supposed to avoid "maneuver damage." The US government would pay the German citizens for anything we tore up, broke, or damaged. Fields, walls, trees were common casualties, especially when muddy. There was one time it rained so much we were forced to

hunker down in a wood line and wait it out. No maneuvers, not even on the road. We made hooches with our tank tarps to keep us as dry as possible. We were there for several days, eating, sleeping, and staying dry. Nice duty if you could get it.

It was good training, especially for the higher ups. They got to practice moving large units around, command-and-control on the radio, seeing how logistics impacts the battle. The M-1 tank was brand new in the early 1980s. It had bugs that needed to be worked out, that meant broken tanks all over the place, had to use heavy armored recovery vehicles (M-88's) to get them out of the mud or drag them back for repair.

"The fog of war" was certainly driven home by REFORGER exercises. Just being a pawn, a small piece of hundreds of thousands of troops moving about in mock battle, not knowing what was going on. A small taste of war—dirt, fatigue, getting lost, chow being late, vehicles breaking down, and getting killed in a mock battle. They put you out of action for a while and then you were allowed to go back in. Watching out for "enemy" choppers or attack planes. Realizing how quickly they could kill you without you ever seeing them.

One last story—my platoon of four tanks got separated from the company. We find out where the company is and move to link up with them. We're taught to use cover & conceal-ment when possible and the shortest distance between two places, right? So, off we go—four tanks through a wood line and a hill. As we crest the hill, a captain comes running out yelling at us to: "Stop, Stop, Stop!" He demands to know who's in charge. We all are wearing our rain gear which does not have name tags or rank on them. I'm not going to volunteer anything to this man who outranks me and is obviously pissed at something. I shrug. He goes to the next tank. The tank commander shrugs. The captain gives up. He yells at me— "Do you know what you just did? Do you?" No, I didn't. "Your tanks just ran over the Divi-sion COMMO [communications] unit cables! We just spent all day digging the COMMO lines in and your tanks ripped them up."

I looked over my shoulder and saw all kinds of COMMO lines in our sprockets. Ah, shit, I thought—that's going to be a bitch getting that out. More yelling at me "this area is off lim-its to maneuver units, isn't that on your map?" I felt like telling him very little being that my map was most certainly outdated. I said: "No Sir!"

The captain, giving up, waved at us to move along. So we did, continuing right past the rest of his COMMO unit, finishing our job of ripping up his COMMO lines. I think I heard him yelling at us to go back the way we came, but I'm not sure of that. After all, our destination was right in front of us. And we were Tankers, by God—not some REMF COMMO pukes."[6]

On August 6, 1990, the 1/64th and 4/64th were alerted for duty in the Persian Gulf. They deployed on August 27 to Saudi Arabia with the 24th Infantry Division, where they joined Operation Desert Shield and trained with the new M1-A1 Abrams tank.

On January 27, 1991, the start of Operation Desert Storm, the 1/64th and 4/64th jumped off and began routing Iraqis from Kuwait. On February 19 they began cross-border operations into Iraq and spearheaded the 24th Infantry Division through a sandstorm with less than 100-meter visibility. They destroyed dug-in elements of Iraq's 26th Republican Guard Hammurabi Division and cut lines of communications to Baghdad. On March 9 the 1/64th and 4/64th went back to Saudi Arabia and pre-pared for redeployment to the United States. Later that month, they arrived at Fort Stewart, Georgia, and received a hero's welcome.

In October 1993 elements of 1/64th deployed to Somalia for Operation Continue Hope on the continent of Africa, where they responded to the shooting down of

American Black Hawk helicopters in Mogadishu. They deployed an immediate reaction force in support of the 10th Mountain Division and conducted security missions for six months before returning all soldiers home safely in March 1994. During this time other elements of 1/64th deployed to Bosnia.

Meanwhile, on January 13, 1997, President Bill Clinton declared, "History has

January 13, 1997, Vernon J. Baker receives his long awaited Medal of Honor at the White House (courtesy William Jefferson Clinton Presidential Library).

been made whole."[7] After a hard-fought victory to restore honor, a long-awaited investiture took place at the White House. This became a rare "Dream No Longer Deferred."[8] Seven World War II veterans, only one of whom remained alive that day, became the first African Americans of that war to receive the Medal of Honor. President Clinton continued: "Fifty years earlier President Harry Truman presented the nation's highest military award in the largest-ever ceremony, but no blacks were involved. Today we fill the gaps in that picture.... In the tradition of African-Americans who have fought for our nation as far back as Bunker Hill, they were prepared to sacrifice everything for freedom, even though freedom's fullness was denied them." At the end of the somber remarks, the president turned to the sole surviving recipient: "God bless you, Vernon Baker, and God bless America."[9]

To Joe Wilson, Jr.
Best Wishes,
Bill Clinton

The author at the Medal of Honor Investiture, January 13, 1997 (White House photograph courtesy Edward A. Carter, Jr. Family).

June 21, 2000, Senator Daniel K. Inouye (D–HI) is all smiles as he receives his long awaited Medal of Honor at the White House (courtesy William Jefferson Clinton Presidential Library).

Then the president presented the seven Medals of Honor, first to Second Lieutenant Vernon Baker for action near Viareggio, Italy, on April 5 and 6, 1945, then to a family representative of each deceased recipient: Edward Carter III, son of Staff Sergeant Edward Carter, Jr., for action near Speyer, Germany; Arlene Fox, widow of First Lieutenant John Fox, for action near Sommocolonia, Italy, December 26, 1944; Valencia James, widow of Private First Class Willy James, Jr., for action near Lippoldsberg, Germany, on April 7, 1945; Grace Rivers-Woodfork, sister of Staff Sergeant Ruben Rivers, for action near Guebling, France, November 16–19, 1944; Sandra Johnson, niece of First Lieutenant Charles Thomas, for action near Climbach, France, on December 14, 1944; and Sergeant Major of the Army Eugene McKinney accepting for Private George Watson, who had no known relative, for action near Porloch Harbor, New Guinea. After the ceremony, Vernon Baker recounted his service in the 92nd Infantry Division: "As a black soldier I fought a war on two sides. I was an angry young man, and all of my soldiers that were with me were angry ... but we had a job to do."[10] "We've all been vindicated. Those that are not here with me, thank you fellas, well done and I'll always remember you."[11]

In 1998, 4/64th returned to Kuwait for Operation Desert Fox to defend against possible Iraqi aggression. The "Tuskers" served as a ground deterrence force. Then in 2000 they deployed to Bosnia. The "Tuskers" and "Desert Rogues" provided security at Eagle Base Tuzla, performing a key role in ensuring stability of Bosnia-Herzegovina.

On June 21, 2000, President Bill Clinton awarded the Medal of Honor to twenty-two Asian-Pacific Americans. This stemmed from 1996 when Congress directed the secretary of the army to conduct a review of all African Americans who were awarded the Distinguished Service Cross in World War II to determine if the award should be upgraded to the Medal of Honor. This opened the door for Japanese Americans and Pacific Islanders to be considered. Senator Daniel Inouye of the 442nd Regimental Combat Team was one of the twenty-two recipients. Senator Inouye served in the U.S. Senate from 1963 until he departed this world in 2012. "People have asked me how I want to be remembered and I say very simply that I represented the people honestly and to the best of my abilities. I think I did okay," he said.[12]

After the September 11, 2001 terrorist attack the 64th began preparations for deploying soldiers and tanks to Afghanistan. The role of the "Tuskers" and the "Desert Rogues" in the war on terror came the following year when they deployed with the 3rd Infantry Division to Kuwait. After five months of preparations and training, both battalions were among the first in the division to cross the border into Iraq. For the next three weeks of Operation Iraqi Freedom, both battalions battled in the outskirts of Baghdad. They swept through and destroyed the Medina Division of the Iraqi Republican Guard south of Baghdad. On April 7, 2003, they fought up into Baghdad and seized high-profile targets. Their daring assault into the city helped force the regime's collapse. After two months in Baghdad, the battalions moved their operations to Habbaniya, Iraq, between Fallujah and al Ramadi, and stabilized a dangerous and unsettled region.

Both tank battalions were reassigned to various elements of the 3rd Infantry Division in 2004 in respect to transforming to the new modular brigade concept. They redeployed and deployed several times and served in Iraq until 2008. The seemingly endless Iraq mission ended in December 2011 as a fulfillment of an election promise President Barack Obama made to the American people.

Now, looking back, the 5th Tank Group, which produced the 758th, 761st and 784th Tank Battalions for a segregated army in World War II, fell from the army's roster. Falling with them were their 761st and 784th Tank Battalions. However, the ancestral 758th Tank Battalion's lineage lives on through their descendant 64th Armored Regiment. The 64th Tank Battalion, which entered the Korean War segregated, emerged integrated as a result of President Truman's first critical step at achieving equality. He issued unpopular executive orders and endured the pain that followed. "Harry Truman, although he was brought up as a racist, became such a great champion of Civil Rights," said Ken Hechler, Truman's speech writer.[13]

Prejudice comes from having one's mind washed, conditioned, and rewashed in fear, ignorance, and hatred. It is nearly impossible to remove "dye in the wool" but not impossible. We just observed how it was removed from the mind of the thirty-third president of the United States. Prejudiced individuals are often ignorant of their own prejudice and very comfortable with it. To them, racism is the truth—their comforting truth. They go through life angry and empty-spirited, never admitting their prejudice. They feel that their prejudices are simply well-founded opinions. When confronted

Fifth Annual Salute to Buffalo Soldiers, May 1–4, 1997, at Fort Huachuca, Sierra Vista, Arizona. Medal of Honor recipient Vernon Baker and Stephany Wilson take time out to pose for picture (author's photograph).

Top: An M-1 Abrams tank of the 1st Battalion, 64th Armor Regiment "Desert Rogues," 2nd Armored Brigade Combat Team, 3rd Infantry Division, Fort Stewart, Georgia (June 18, 2014), photo by Staff Sergeant Richard Wrigley (courtesy U.S. Army Office of Public Affairs). *Bottom:* Centenarian William H. Smith and his daughter Delores Williams at the World War II Memorial in Washington, D.C., meet with the author (right) on September 20, 2016. The Honor Flight Network made this meeting possible (author's photograph).

with logic and fair play, they feel attacked. They are simply accustomed to privilege and any mention of equality feels like oppression to them. Therefore, the simple terms prejudice, racism, and bigotry are socially and politically incorrect and society refuses to address these problems.

As we look back on these historic developments and look forward to the future of the 64th Armored Regiment, it is clear that "prejudice was and is an emotional commitment to ignorance."[14] What finally defeated that ignorance was the uncommon courage of leaders who first conquered their own ignorance. This well-entrenched pattern of racist thinking received support from several presidents. President Woodrow Wilson once said, "The colored people of this nation have no right to expect special treatment. It is my policy that no individual of color should expect a free ride." Wilson, who received a majority of the black vote when he was elected president, knew what he had to say to get reelected. President Teddy Roosevelt once stated, "Colored soldiers will not fight. It is just a fact of life that they are yellow hearted and will not fight in battle." Ignoring the fact that Roosevelt became a hero at San Juan Hill largely due to black Buffalo Soldiers, he cowardly said what he believed would

3rd Bn., 9th Inf. Regiment on parade, Ft. Lewis, Wash. 2nd Inf. Div. Squad Leader, First Squad, First Platoon, Co. K, 9th Inf. Just before embarking on the USNS *Morton* for 12-day voyage to Korea (1949–1950) (courtesy First Sergeant Joseph E. Wilson, Sr., USA [Ret.]).

compel him to the presidency. He evaded the inevitable question: "You aren't really a nigger-lover, then, are you?"[15]

With freedom at stake both abroad and at home during World War II, an estimated 1.2 million African Americans set out to defend this freedom with devotion to a country where people of color were not free. By doing so they slowly exposed the extreme futility of the institution of discrimination, segregation, and racism. Out of the ashes of World War II came a renewed, proud, and assertive race of people who would henceforth demand their equal share of the American dream. Obviously, "all lives matter," but this book focuses on black lives because they were left out of the history. When you hear "black lives matter" and it is controversial to your way of thinking, it is clear that you have not conquered your own "emotional commitment to ignorance."

This book's purpose is to remind America of the courage and sacrifice made by all Americans, and in this particular case, African Americans. Afflicted with negative characterizations, their contributions seemed to have been left out of history. President Lyndon B. Johnson put it best: "If you can convince the lowest white man that he's better than the best colored man, he won't notice you're picking his pocket." Nonetheless, this accusation of ignorance does not apply to you, the reader, because obviously you could not have read this far—your prejudice would not have allowed it.

The time has come to take leave of the 758th Tank Battalion, even if I am disinclined to do so. My hope is that you benefitted from and enjoyed reading this as much

Dr. James Baldwin visits American Legion Post 96 in Brunswick, Maryland, on August 20, 2016. Left to right: 1st Vice Commander David House, Adjutant Curtis Leonard, Corporal James Baldwin (HQ/784th), and Captain Matt Hewett (1/64th).

Veterans Day 2015. Dr. James Baldwin and Senator Bob Dole lay a wreath at the World War II Memorial in Washington, D.C., in front of the inscription: "Here We Mark the Price of Freedom." They are in front of 4,048 "Gold Stars"; each star signifies one hundred American military deaths. Over 400,000 soldiers, sailors, marines, airmen, and military personnel lost their lives or remain missing in action. Of sixteen million men and women in military service during World War II, that represents one death out of every forty individuals. When an American went off to war the family often displayed in their window a flag bearing a blue star. If one of those dreaded telegrams arrived informing them of their family member's death, they would replace the blue star with a gold star.

as I did writing it. This labor of love completes the trilogy of the 5th Tank Group, in essence, the 758th, 761st, and 784th Tank battalions. Most of the brave warriors who served within have departed this world and I miss them dearly. Together we ask future generations to learn from their deeds. They were the first African Americans to serve in armor but not the last. Their valiant struggle established that courage is an act of refusing to give up, and by that refusal they paved a way for us to serve in a better military and live in a better country.

In a final thought: On September 20, 2016, Ms. Delores Williams escorted her father, Mr. William H. Smith, to Washington, D.C., on a tour sponsored by the Honor Flight (Conyers) Network. This tour is a "last hurrah"— the last time her 100-year-old father will be recognized for his wartime contributions. In describing the magnitude of World War II, President John F. Kennedy said, "In the long history of the world, only a few generations have been granted the role of defending freedom in its hour of maximum danger." This was the deadliest military conflict in world history, in which over 60 million people perished, including 407,300 Americans, and we honor those who fought and died for freedom during our nation's "hour of maximum danger." The 758th Tank Battalion, in which Mr. Smith served, and other units like it, fought under the "Double V," which called for victory abroad against the forces of global domination. They also faced an additional enemy. They had to fight at home for the right to fight. It is no longer a secret how African Americans lived and were treated throughout World War II and how they defended a way of life that didn't include full partnership. The wounds received in that battle were as deep as any honored by a Purple Heart.

These Honor Flights, paid for entirely by citizen donations, provide honor and closure for these veterans. This special day served as a distinct token of gratitude from a grateful nation. Mr. Smith's daughter, Delores Williams, will have the final word:

I was long from being born when my father served in World War II, but the conversations I've had while sitting at my father's feet will carry me throughout the rest of my life. He wasn't always treated kindly, but still maintained his dignity and respect for this country. When you're treated unfairly, God has a way of returning you to whole. Now seeing and experiencing strangers approach my Dad to thank him for his service, take pictures with him, and apologize for the mistreatment he endured, showed me that there is a desire to be together as one. If there is ever an honor to be experienced, it's the honor of realizing a parent's contribution of service, sacrifice, and reverence through a child's eye (even though the child is nearly 60 years old). Moreover, when that contribution is historic and affects the lives of mankind, it moves you at the soul level. Thank you does not begin to express my gratitude to the Honor Flight Conyers for the opportunity to be a part of this journey and to Mr. Joe Wilson, Jr. for taking twenty-four years of his life to tell the stories of these heroic World War II soldiers.[16]

Afterword

by First Sergeant Joseph E. Wilson, Sr.,
USA (Ret.), 1925–2003

The United States Army has come a long way since its inception in 1775, making it the nation's senior service. Drifting on a memory, I recall being inside an American tank called the General Sherman. We, as tankers, knew it as the M-4A1, and a later model, the M-4A3-E8. Those of you who have never experienced combat in a Sherman tank, listen to this: The interior is painted a cold, non-color white, but what gets your attention immediately is the frigid atmosphere. It's cold, cold as a winter night on the Lincoln Sea. I think this is what my son had in mind with the working title to this book *Wrapped in Cold Steel*.

Later in the war two new tanks were issued to us: the M-24 light tank, the Chaffee and the M-26 medium tank, the General Pershing. These two new tanks introduced welcomed improvements, but the single improvement that pleased us all was that they had heaters.

Some leopards are chosen by nature to lose their spots and turn black in their mother's wombs. Why Mother Nature does this remains a mystery that can be explained by some. But what is not a mystery is the fact that a black panther is a source of intimidation, whether by hearing the words, seeing the beast, or knowing it is in the vicinity of your comfort zone. Realizing that the black panther is the most efficient and ferocious of the predators, the U.S. Army seized upon this principle during World War II and sent the 761st Medium Tank Battalion to fight and support white infantry units in the European Theater. This separate battalion fought with distinction, earning a reputation that lives today but is unknown to black youth who will be proud of their forebears once they learn of the 761st. To that end, this literary effort is dedicated to the memory of those brave black men who helped win the war by piercing enemy lines with the ferocity of a pouncing black panther.

"Come Out Fighting" was the call to battle that energized the 761st Tanker to a high-level of intensity that enabled him to perform in an above-average manner.

Despite his heroism, he was denied his rightful place in history. It seems that if he was walking on water, they would say, "See, he can't swim."

Before coming to the 761st I was a member of the 2nd Gun Section, Battery C, 686th Field Artillery Battalion, and had not yet developed into a mature, job-sophisticated cannoneer. There were times when my mouth was agape as I watched older black artillery men perform their duties with an unimaginable sophistication in handling this 155 millimeter howitzer. This medium artillery piece threw a 95-pound explosive shell nine miles, and when it hit, white American infantrymen would jump and shout: "Fickle Charlie is adjusting!" Fickle was the code name for the 686th Field Artillery Battalion, and Charlie stood for Battery C, and its four guns. My section chief was a heavyset black man who answered to the name of Joe Willie, and when he told me to jump, my only response was: "How high, Sarge?" When I first heard this name, I assumed it was a sobriquet, but later I learned that he was so mean, his friends were afraid to give him a nickname. Joe Willie was his real name. He was from Oklahoma.

These were African American soldiers who did their utmost to accomplish their mission. They were dedicated and loyal despite the rigors imposed by white supremacy and segregation, which were more pronounced in those days. Today "Jim Crow" has taken on a subtlety designed to perpetuate its existence.

Looking back in history, we find many whites who swore that the races must be kept apart. Look at the late, great General George Smith Patton, Jr., who often said that the Negro soldier couldn't think fast enough to fight in armor. How ridiculous, especially for an educated man in a high leadership position. However, this deep-seated nescience was canceled prior to his untimely death in Room 101, 130th Station Hospital in Heidelberg, Germany, in 1945. Before he died, Patton recognized the 761st Tank Battalion in glowing terms. There were other generals who held the Negro back until they too were compelled to revise their thinking. What a waste of time and humanity.

Many of these generals were educated at the United States Military Academy at West Point, New York, an institution where racism was practiced as a matter of routine. I agonize over the treatment black cadets received at this institution. When I read of the abuse meted out to Cadet Henry O. Flipper, graduating class of 1877, my pain was similar but could never equal his. Later, other cadets suffered the same fate. There was Charles Young and others but the one

First Sergeant Joseph E. Wilson, Sr., 1954, at age 29.

who stands out in my lifetime is Lt. General (Retired) Benjamin O. Davis, Jr., U.S. Air Force, class of 1936. Cadet Davis, like black cadets before him, was given the silent treatment—no one spoke to him for four years. On Sundays, Cadet Davis was forced to go to each dinner table and ask permission to be seated. During the week he ate at a separate table using disposable plates and utensils. What inhumane treatment.

Despite living through this painful period, blacks had to fight for the right to fight, and we fought without the accolades bestowed upon others, even though deserving such recognition. During World War II, not one African American was awarded the nation's highest medal for bravery, even though commanders submitted the proper and necessary recommendations.

World War II, the war that saved humanity from the greatest menace imaginable, found black America fully involved in our national effort. The 686th Field Artillery Battalion landed at Southampton, England, on a foggy morning in October, 1944. From there we embarked on trains and disembarked at Pontypool, Wales. Here we occupied Quonset huts on the Polo Grounds. During the day and often at night, we made ready for combat. Our off-duty hours were spent doing the same thing, but there was time for socializing with the citizens of Pontypool. In fraternizing, we were astounded to learn of some of the beliefs of these British subjects, such as: "Do you colored blokes have tails?"

It was January 19, 1945, early in the a.m., a day so dismal that the sun threatened to take the day off, the 686th loaded its weapons and equipment on amphibious vessels and set sail from Weymouth, England, for Le Havre, France, located on the opposite shore of the English Channel. From Le Harve, our battalion joined with other American units in a line of vehicles, a convoy stretching over the horizon.

During this introduction into the combat phase of the ground war, the shock that I believed would never happen to me happened. Two Stuka dive-bombers strafed our section of the column in the vicinity of Nancy, France. One of our men, Private Fingers, was killed. This casualty, one of ours, created an atmosphere of sadness and gloom that fell over us and hardened us to face the daily air attacks that followed.

I always thought that a dogfight referred to the snarling, biting entanglement of two canines. Later I learned of another definition listed in the lingo of fighter pilots. Combat artillery men sought protection in slit trenches while the infantry dug foxholes, which lowered the body below the surface of the ground while being strafed by German fighter planes such as the ME-262, the first jet fighter plane. I recall bullets from a strafing German plane striking the front edge of my slit trench, then the other edge without hitting me in the middle. Thanks and thanks again, Father God. While trying to find a level lower than the bottom of my slit trench, I noticed that the strafing had ceased but the sound of gunfire had not. Climbing out of our slit trenches we looked skyward and saw the source of the continued firing, American planes had arrived on the scene. Up to this point we had only seen P-47 Thunderbolts and P-38 Lightnings, but here was an American fighter plane that we were completely unfamiliar with. It was the P-51 Mustang, a new plane. We watched in spellbound fascination as a single P-51 knocked two German fighters out of the sky. The remaining Luftwaffe pilots fled in terror. While watching this deadly display of aerial combat, we were oblivious to the bullets falling to the ground around our feet. This, we learned, was the other definition of a dogfight.

Oftentimes, those with an anti–Jewish slant deny that the Holocaust ever happened. Well, Dachau unfolded before my eyes after our guns blew away the gates and permitted the infantry to enter this concentration camp. Here was one of Hitler's most notorious death factories where the extermination of human life was carried out in assembly-line fashion. During these days in combat, the American Red Cross would give each of us a small bar of chocolate, a bar of soap, and a four-pack of cigarettes. Not being much of smoker, I saved the Red Cross gifts and when we entered Dachau, the death camp, I had a barracks bag full of these goodies. We were so moved by what we saw that we began to hand out chocolate and cigarettes to these emaciated survivors until a sharp command filled the air: "Don't give them candy! It will kill them!" This was easily understood but we gave them cigarettes. Over the years I have been jolted back to the days of Dachau, which happens every time I see a thin Caucasian.

Getting back to the convoy, even though we had come under attack and suffered fatalities, we were not officially in combat—this I learned half a century later because of my son's research into this literary effort, but the 686th Field Artillery Battalion was a part of a vast armada that would bring death and suffering to the German Army, the force that would apply the coup de grâce.

In this area of France, the staging area camps set up were named after American cigarettes. Our camp was named "20 Grand," a cigarette that has gone the way of others like Old Gold, Wings, and a number of other brands. Cigarettes were part of the soldiering experience and some brands will forever be associated with World War II. (Lucky Strike adopted the slogan "Lucky Strike has gone to war" and changed its green package for the white uniform it still wears today.)

I can remember that after we crossed the English Channel, I was missing my gas mask. This disturbed me so much that my only concern was to find the bastard who stole my mask. My father was in Germany during World War I and it is common knowledge that poison gas was used as a weapon against them. The thought of going into combat without a mask terrified me so much that I strolled through an empty pyramidal tent and picked up a mask that belonged to someone else. I have confessed this sin and have been forgiven, but this transgression hung over my head, though my comrades and I agreed that a good soldier never loses in this man's Army. Days later, our battalion entered combat inflicting full-fledged devastation on the *Wehrmacht*.

What has the foregoing to do with the 761st Tank Battalion? Well, there were many other black fighting units that were ignored and are absent from recorded history. Why? Because they were manned by African Americans. There was the 92nd Infantry Division in Italy; the 93rd Infantry Division in Bougainville, South Pacific; there was the 349th Field Artillery Battalion—a sister battalion to the 686th; there was the 969th and the 999th Field Artillery Battalions; the 614th, the 679th Tank

Destroyer Battalions; there was the 758th and the 784th Tank Battalions; and there were the volunteer infantry replacements. There were all kinds of Negro (as we were called then) combats units in the war, engineers, transportation units, quartermaster battalions. I could go on and on, but I am especially proud of the 99th Pursuit Squadron, commanded by Lt. Colonel Benjamin O. Davis, Jr. His father, B. O. Davis, Sr., was the first black to attain the rank of brigadier general in the U.S. Army. The 99th Pursuit Squadron became the 332nd Fighter Group when it added other squadrons, and their claim to fame is that they never lost a bomber while escorting American heavy bombers.

It was the fear of death that gave combat a special fascination to me. To listen to a man who says that death doesn't get his spellbound attention is to listen to a liar. This was pronounced as we made tactical moves in advancing on the enemy. Daily we would see dead German soldiers lying all around and in ditches along the road. This we took in stride but to see American infantrymen lying dead among them was quite another experience and we handled it badly. There were occasions when rigor mortis put on morbid and unnerving demonstrations. One that refuses to relinquish a spot in my memory is when we turned over the body of a lieutenant who had been killed as he crawled out of a ditch. His legs were frozen in a grotesque configuration.

I can remember my Battery taking up firing positions in an apple orchard, which provided concealment from the air. There were German dead lying all about, which was to be expected, but to see German women from nearby homes come out without fear, remove these corpses, and scowl at us as though we were the American infantrymen who killed them was unforgettable. Our feelings were soothed somewhat when darkness fell and these same females returned and offered us sex.

The war was rapidly approaching its end and the weather was the worst one could expect. Those days were complete misery, but the events of other days more than compensated, such as the food we combat soldiers ate. A-rations was the normal food prepared by our cooks, B-rations was a small can of meat or cheese with crackers that were the strongest form of bread that I have ever known. C-rations had a more favorable acceptance than B-rations. D-rations was a solid bar of dark chocolate that was difficult to bite or cut and if you ate too much of it, liquid consumed later would cause your stomach to swell to an uncomfortable degree. Because of our disgust with field rations, we would scrounge the villages for food. Top on our lists were live chickens, potatoes, and eggs. The feasts that followed were often interrupted by Stukas and ME-109s, who found many of us in one place, providing a tempting strafing target. Despite this, our morale remained high.

Army officers enjoyed a privilege that we enlisted men (peons) were denied. We watched with envy as officers enjoyed what is known Army-wide as: "Rank Has Its Privileges." This was a whiskey ration for each officer. "Alcohol and enlisted men don't mix and must be avoided" was the widespread belief, but it is common knowledge that the men will get alcohol, especially when it's available in the destroyed villages we passed through. One day when there was a lull, a long break in firing missions, I wandered off to a nearby house that had been destroyed by artillery fire. With my carbine slung over my right shoulder, I entered the basement of this house and received one of the greatest shocks of my life: four fully armed Germans, who surrendered to me. They could have killed me easily, but decided the hands-up posture was the wisest, a "Hobson's Choice."

Thinking back on this incident, I now understand why it turned out this way. In one of my mother's letters she told me not to worry about dying because as she put it: "You're not going to get killed, because I won't let God let you die." My mother was the prayingest woman I have ever known before and since.

The end of World War II approached ahead of schedule. The German Army was defeated, the Jews were freed, and the world celebrated. We in the field also celebrated by firing our weapons in the air, only to have eight men killed as these same bullets came crashing to the ground. What goes up must come down, gravity demands it.

So, my son, that is how I spent my days during World War II. Following the cessation of hostilities in Europe, the 686th Field Artillery Battalion sent many of its men to units that had to be brought up to full strength because of their missions. I became a tanker in Company B, 761st Tank Battalion, located in Siegsdorf, Germany, not far from the Bavarian city of Traunstein. Later I joined Headquarters Company in Teisendorf, Germany. From there I rotated to the States in March 1946.

Thanks for the privilege of telling my story, which gives vent to the pent-up emotions that have weighed heavily on my mind and shoulders all these years. I am elated to see that by accomplishing this rare literary task, you have helped all who peruse these words to face the future with a greater understanding of what really happened.

Requiem of the Buffalo Soldier
by Debra Donald Goree*

The battlefield may be different
The uniforms may have changed—
But one thing that's certain,
Our fight is still the same.

Your cavalry freed our people,
Your tanks and bombers helped end a war.
Vietnam taught us a lesson—
Pride and dignity is worth so much more.

Bravery and courage were the trademarks of,
A history left unwritten—
Of all the battles that were won, and all
The truths that were hidden.

But, we know you as our heroes,
Your sacrifices cannot be erased.
Although, the battlefront may be different,
Our fight is still the same.

*Debra Donald Goree is the daughter of former Sergeant Edward Donald, Co. B. 761st Tank Battalion. Poem used by permission.

Appendix:
Tank Specifications

by Matt Hewett

Tank	M3 Stuart	M5 Stuart	M4 Early Prod.	M4 A2 (late Prod.)	M4 A3 (76) HVSS	M26E2 Pershing	M46A1 Patton	M60A1	M-1 Abrams	M-1A1 Abrams
Length (ft)	16.5	15.8	19.3	19.4	20.6	20.3	20.8	22.8	25.9	25.9
Width (ft)	8.3	6.7	8.6	8.6	9.8	11.5	11.5	11.9	12.0	12.0
Height (ft)	8.4	8.9	9.0	9.0	9.8	9.1	10.4	10.7	9.5	9.5
Weight (tons)	16.2	16.8	334.5	35.1	37.1	47.0	48.5	52.5	60.0	65.0
Crew	4	4	5	5	5	5	5	4	4	4
Main gun (mm)	37	37	75	75	75	90	90	105	105	120
Main gun rounds carried	174	147	97	97	71	70	70	63	55	40
Machine guns	3 × .30 cal	3 × .30 cal	2 × .30 cal, 1 × .50 cal	2 × .30 cal, 1 × .50 cal	2 × .30 cal, 1 × .50 cal	2 × .30 cal, 1 × .50 cal	2 × .30 cal, 1 × .50 cal	1 × 7.62mm, 1 × .50 cal	2 × 7.62mm, 1 × .50 cal	2 × 7.62mm, 1 × .50 cal
Engine horsepower	250	296	400	375	500	500	810	740	1500	1500
Armor (max turret)	38	44	75	97	62	100	102	284	*	*
Speed (mph)	31	36	26	25	26	25	30	30	45	41.5
Range (miles)	135	100	100	150	100	175	80	300	275	289

*Welded assembly of rolled homogeneous steel armor with special armor arrays

Note:
M-1A1 saw introduction of 120mm cannon; M-1A2 had digital upgrades for the fire control system, driver, gunner and tank commander; 1/64 Armor transitioned from M60A1 to M-1 in 1982, then M1-A1s in 1987.

Sources:
R.P. Hunnicutt, *Abrams: A History of the American Main Battle Tank* (Novato, CA: Presidio, 1990).
Patton: A History of the American Main Battle Tank (Novato, CA: Presidio, 1984.
Pershing: A History of the Medium Tank T20 Series (Novato, CA: Presidio, 1999).
Sherman: A History of the American Medium Tank (Novato, CA: Presidio, 1978).
Stuart: A History of the American Light Tank, Vol. 1 (Novato, CA: Presidio, 1992).

Chapter Notes

Chapter 1

1. wikipedia.org/wiki/Gran_Sasso_raid.
2. www.historynet.com/rage-over-the-rapido. htm.
3. *Ibid.*
4. www.historynet.com/rage-over-the-rapido. htm.
5. www.redbubble.com/people/warwolf/writing/ 3571203-nightmare-at-rapido-river.

Chapter 2

1. Topps, Willie, interview, 01/19/2014.
2. Mann, T.J., interview, 12/08/2008.
3. Weston, John, interview, 07/09/2014.
4. Smith, William, interview, 08/28/2016.
5. *Courier Journal* (AP), 12/09/1991, "Army Got a Shock but Still Honored Black Soldier in All White Unit."
6. *Ibid.*
7. U.S. Armored Research Library, Fort Knox, Kentucky, 12/22/1941.
8. *Ibid.*
9. *Ibid.*
10. T.J. Mann interview.
11. *Courier Journal*, "Army Got a Shock."
12. Truman K. Gibson, Jr., *Knocking Down Barriers*, 2005.

Chapter 3

1. Ollie Stewart, *Afro-American Weekly*, 01/24/ 1942.
2. *Ibid.*
3. *Ibid.*
4. *Ibid.*
5. *Ibid.*
6. Joseph H. Hairston, Segment 4, National WWII Museum Interview, ww2online.org.
7. Stewart, *Afro-American*, 01/24/1942.
8. Topps, Willie, interview, 09/30/2008.
9. Stewart, *Afro-American*.

10. Mann, T.J., interview, 12/08/2008.
11. Truman Gibson, *Knocking Down Barriers*, 2005.
12. *Ibid.*
13. *Ibid.*
14. *Ibid.*
15. *Ibid.*

Chapter 4

1. Weston, John, interview, 7/09/2014.
2. Mann, T.J., interview, 12/08/2008.
3. Topps, Willie, interview, 09/30/2008.
4. *Life*, "Negroes at War," 06/15/1942.
5. Topps, Willie, interview, 09/30/2008.
6. Weston, John, interview, 7/09/2014.
7. Topps, Willie, interview, 09/30/2008.
8. Maggi Morehouse, *Fighting in the Jim Crow Army*, 2000.
9. Weston, John, interview, 7/09/2014.
10. Mann, T.J., interview, 12/08/2008.
11. Frazier, Claude, interview, 12/05/2008.
12. Baldwin, James, interview.
13. Frazier, Claude, interview, 12/05/2008.
14. *Ibid.*
15. Mann, T.J., interview, 12/08/2008.
16. Morehouse, *Fighting in the Jim Crow Army*.

Chapter 5

1. Topps, Willie, interview, 07/29/2008.
2. Weston, John, interview, 07/09/2014.
3. Topps, Willie, interview, 7/29/2008.
4. Motley, *Invisible Soldier*, 1987.
5. Topps, Willie, interview.
6. Bates, Paul L., letter to author, 03/04/1994.
7. Frazier, Claude, interview, 09/09/2008.
8. Motley, *Invisible Soldier*.

Chapter 6

1. Topps, Willie, interview, 09/30/2008.
2. *Ibid.*

3. Weston, John, interview, 07/09/2014.
4. Wikipedia.org, 10th Cavalry Regiment, no date; Globalsecurity.org, 7th & 10th Cavalry, no date.
5. Topps, Willie, interview, 9/30/2008.
6. Smith, Lloyd D., interview, J. Hairston for AfriGeneas, 08/27/2003.
7. Mann, T.J., interview, 12/08/2008.
8. *Ibid.*

Chapter 7

1. Mann, T.J., interview, 12/08/2008.
2. Duplessis, Harry, in *Invisible Soldier*, 1987.
3. *Ibid.*
4. Bates, Paul L., interview, 03/04/1994.
5. *Ibid.*
6. Evans, Horace, in *Invisible Soldier*, 1987.
7. Weston, John, interview, 7/29/2008.
8. Topps, Willie, interview, 09/30/2008.
9. Weston, John, interview, 07/29/2008.
10. Duplessis, in *Invisible Soldier.*

Chapter 8

1. Duplessis, in *The Invisible Soldier*, 1987.
2. Brissey, Eugene L., "What Did You Do in the War, Daddy?" www.517prct.org.
3. Coleman, Randolph, "Meet the Troops: The Battling Buzzards," www.517prct.org.
4. Morehouse, *Fighting in the Jim Crow Army*, 2000.
5. National Archives Reports, 758th Tank Battalion, 11/30/1944.
6. Duplessis, in *Invisible Soldier.*
7. Weston, John, interview, 07/09/2014.
8. Topps, Willie, interview, 09/30/2008.
9. Morehouse, *Fighting in the Jim Crow Army.*

Chapter 9

1. Topps, Willie, telephone interview, 07/29/2008.
2. Weston, John, telephone interview, 07/09/2014.
3. *Ibid.*
4. Motley, *Invisible Soldier*, 1987.

Chapter 10

1. Motley, *Invisible Soldier*, 1987.
2. Lloyd D. Smith, "WWII Buffalo Division in Italy"; Joseph Hairston interview, AfriGeneas, 8/27/2003.
3. Motley, *Invisible Soldier.*
4. Weston, John, telephone interview, 7/9/2014.
5. NARA, Report After Action, 12–1945.
6. Ulysses Lee,, *Employment of Negro Troops*, 1966.
7. Smith, H.W., *One More River*, 1946.

8. Thomas Saint John Arnold, *Buffalo Soldiers*, 1990.
9. Truman Gibson, *Knocking Down Barriers*, 2005.
10. *Ibid.*
11. *Ibid.*

Chapter 11

1. Weston, John, interview, 07/09/2014.
2. *Ibid.*
3. Russell, Harold, Jr., I/366th Infantry, 2008.
4. *Ibid.*
5. Smith, William, interview, 08/28/2016.

Chapter 12

1. After Action Report, 758th Tank Battalion, 03/02/1945.
2. Thomas St. John Arnold, *Buffalo Soldiers*, 1990.
3. *Ibid.*
4. Mary Motley, *The Invisible Soldier*, 1987.
5. Weston, John, telephone interview, 7/09/2014.
6. Hightower, Jefferson, telephone interview, 8/25/1996.
7. Motley, *Invisible Soldier.*
8. Arnold, *Buffalo Soldiers.*
9. Motley, *Invisible Soldier.*
10. Joseph H. Hairston, Segment 4, National WWII Museum, interview, ww2online.org.
11. Arnold, *Buffalo Soldiers.*
12. *Ibid.*
13. *Ibid.*
14. Truman K. Gibson, Jr., *Knocking Down Barriers*, 2005.
15. *Ibid.*
16. *Ibid.*
17. *Ibid.*
18. *Ibid.*

Chapter 13

1. Motley, *The Invisible Soldier*, 1987.
2. *Ibid.*
3. Russell, Harold E., Jr., *Company I, 366th Infantry*, 2008.
4. Topps, Willie, interview, 2008.
5. Weston, John, interview, 2014.

Chapter 14

1. Weston, John, interview, November 7, 2015.
2. Weston, John, interview, July 9, 2014.
3. Black Jack Pershing, in *AZ Quotes*, no date.
4. Topps, Willie, interview, July 29, 2008.
5. Weston, John, 11/7/2015.
6. *Ibid.*

7. Motley, *The Invisible Soldier*, 1987.
8. Weston, John, interview, November 7, 2015.
9. Daniel K. Inouye Institute, *Quotes* (1967).

Chapter 15

1. Weston, John, interview, 7/9/2014.
2. Topps, Willie, interview, 7/29/2008.
3. Weston, John, interview, 7/9/2014.
4. Weston, John, f interview, 11/7/2015.
5. Smith, William, interview, 08/28/2016, 09/10/2016.
6. *Ibid.*
7. Weston, John, interview, 11/7/2015.
8. Topps, Willie, interview, 7/9/2008.

Chapter 16

1. Trezzvant Anderson, *Come Out Fighting*, 1945.
2. Houle, Bill, telephone interview, 2015.
3. Anderson, *Come Out Fighting*.
4. *Ibid.*
5. Bruno Ehlich, "Born on the Wrong Side of Fence," 2004.

Chapter 17

1. Garrido, Franklin, interview, 09/14/1994.
2. Gallagher, Wes, *Los Angeles Times*, April 1945.
3. Hamilton, James, interview, 01/28/2005.
4. Faubus, Orval Eugene, *In This Faraway Land*, 1971.
5. Frazier, Claude, interview, 09/02/2008.

6. Garrido, Franklin, interview, 9/19/94.
7. *Ibid.*
8. Wes Gallagher, *Los Angeles Times*, April 1945.
9. Hughes, Bill, e-mail to the author, 01/16/2012.

Chapter 18

1. Harry S. Truman Presidential Library, "This Day in Truman History."
2. Richard Wormer, "Harry S. Truman Supports Civil Rights," 2002.
3. Gerald Astor, *The Right to Fight*, 1998.
4. *Ibid.*
5. Smith, Lloyd D., "WWII 92nd 'Buffalo' Division in Italy," 08/27/2003.
6. Hewett, Matt, e-mail to the author 09/06/2016.
7. Scott Foster, "Writer Recalls Truman's Risky Order to Integrate Military," NBCnews.com, Aug. 7, 2008.
8. Associated Press, "Filling History's Gaps," *Washington Times*, January 14, 1997.
9. "A Dream No Longer Deferred," *Los Angeles Times*, January 15, 1997.
10. Fremson, Ruth, "7 Black WWII Vets Awarded Medal of Honor," *USA Today*, January 14, 1997.
11. Foster, "Writer Recalls Truman's Risky Order to Integrate Military," NBCnews.com, Aug. 7, 2008.
12. Daniel K. Inouye Institute, *Quotes*, 2012.
13. Ken Hechler, "Civil Rights in the Truman Administration," 2011.
14. Jane Elliot, *Why Color Matters*, 2011.
15. Harper Lee, *To Kill a Mockingbird*, screen adaptation quote, 1962.
16. Williams, Delores, e-mail to the author, 09/22/2016.

Bibliography

Anderson, Rich. *Manpower, Replacements, and the Segregated Army.* Tysons, VA: Dupuy Institute, 1998.

Anderson, Trezzvant. *Come Out Fighting.* Teisendorf, Germany: 761st Tank Battalion, 1945.

Arnold, Thomas St. John. *Buffalo Soldiers.* Manhattan, KS: Sunflower University Press, 1990.

Associated Press. "Army Got a Shock but Still Honored Black Soldier in 'All-white' Unit." *Courier Journal*, 1998.

_____. "Filling History's Gaps." *Washington Times*, 14 January 1997.

Astor, Gerald. *The Right to Fight.* Boston: Da Capo, 2005.

Atkinson, Cecil, and Kathy Tilley. *Camp Claiborne.* Forest Hill, LA: Ack Hill, 1990.

Atkinson, Thomas S. Interview with Sgt. Randolph Coleman. Admiral Nimitz Museum, 1993.

Baker, Vernon J. Interview, 4 May 1997.

Baldwin, James W. Interviews with the author, 2004–2016.

Biava, Marcello. E-mails to the author, 2014–2016.

Bibolotti, Italo. E-mails to the author, 2014–2016.

Brissey, Eugene L. "A Devil in Baggy Pants: Wartime Autobiography." 517prct.org. 23 April 2014.

Brown, Brian. "Vernon Baker." indianamilitary.org. 13 July 2007.

Brown, Joel. E-mails to the author, 2014–2016.

Buffalo Soldiers National Museum. buffalosoldier musem.com.

Bundesarchiv. Atlantikwall, Batterie Todt Bild 146-1986-104-10A. German Federal Archive.

Burton, John. *World War II Maneuvers and Other Activities in Tennessee.* TMCA News Archives, 2005.

Cameron, Robert S. *Mobility, Shock, and Firepower.* Washington, D.C.: Center of Military History, United States Army, 2008.

Carlisle, David K. "Black Combat Units in Korean War Action." americanwarlibrary.com. 1998.

Carnevale, Harry. "Tennessee Maneuvers." campfor rest.com. 1983.

Cenla, Alex. "Alex Cenla's Rants and Ravings." alex cenla.wordpress.com. 2006.

Chen, Peter. "Battle of Garfagnana." ww2db.com. 1993.

Compton, Etta. Letter to the author, 1 May 2012.

"Congressional Medal of Honor Recipients." encyclo pedia.densho.org. 2016.

Cook, Roy. "Plains Indian View of the 'Buffalo Soldier.'" americanindiansource.com. 2000.

Craig, Naomi. *Minorities and Women During World War II.* Providence, RI: Brown University, 1987.

Cunseen, Charles. "And Now God's Chillun." *Yank: The Army Newspaper*, August 1942.

Curtis-Wheatly, Frieda. "Fort Knox Parade Ground Named in 1941 for Scott County Soldier." *Kentucky Explorer*, 1992.

Davis, Stanford L. "Buffalo Soldiers and Indian Wars." buffalosoldiers.net. 28 July 2008.

"A Dream No Longer Deferred." *Los Angeles Times*, 15 January 1997.

Durham, Caldwell. "Tennessee Maneuvers of 1943 Letters Written Home by PFC Mitchell Dabrowski." ancestrywww. July 2009.

Ehlich, Bruno. *Born on the Wrong Side of the Fence.* Sydney, Australia: N.p., 2009.

Elliot, Jane. "Why Color Matters." *Boise Weekly*, March 2011.

Foster, Scott. "Writer Recalls Truman's Risky Order to Integrate Military." *NBC News*, 7 August 2008.

4/64th Armored Regiment. *History of the 758th/ 64th Armored.* VHS Video. United States Army, 1992.

Frazier, Claude. Interview with the author, 5 December 2008.

Fremson, Ruth. "Seven Black WWII Vets Awarded Medal of Honor." *USA Today*, 14 January 1997.

Gibson, Truman K., Jr. *Knocking Down Barriers.* Evanston, IL: Northwestern University Press, 2005.

Giorgi, Giorgio Augusto. E-mails to the author, 2014–2016.

Gonzalez, Kris. "Triple Nickels Recall Days of Segregated Army." army.mil. 18 February 2010.

Goodman, Paul. *A Fragment of Victory in Italy.* Nashville: Battery, 1945.

"The Great Depression." RandomHistory.com. 9 December 1991.

Hechler, Ken. "Civil Rights in the Truman Administration." C-SPAN, 2011.

Hewett, Matthew. E-mails to the author, 2010–2016.

Hodges, Robert, Jr. "Buffalo Soldiers." *World War II*, July 2000.

_____. "Buffalo Soldiers Assault the Gothic Line." historynet.com. February 1999.

Holley, Bill. E-mails to the author, 7 June 2014.

Hoyt, Edwin P. *Closing the Circle: War in the Pacific, 1945.* Craley, PA: HG, 1982.

Inouye, Daniel. "Quotes." danielkinouyeinstitute.org/quotes. 1967.

Janega, James. "Lasting Bond Were Their Spoils of War." *Chicago Tribune*, May 2006.

Kennedy, Adam P. "Chronicling Greatness Interview (Vernon Baker)." youtube.com. 2 July 2016.

_____. "Interview with Lieutenant Vernon J. Baker." Arlington, VA: International Urban Exchange Center, 2014.

Kolakawski, Chris. E-mails to the author, 2014.

Kurson, Robert. *Shadow Divers.* New York: Random House, 2005.

Lee, Harper. *To Kill a Mockingbird.* Screen adaption. Los Angeles: Universal Pictures, 1962.

Lee, Ulysses. *The Employment of Negro Troops.* Washington, D.C.: Office of the Chief of Military History, 1966.

Luche, Beppe Dalle. E-mails to the author, 2014–2016.

Mann, Thomas James, "TJ." Interview with the author, 7 April 2015.

Matheny, Michael R. *History of the Sixty-Fourth Armor.* Carlisle Barracks, PA: U.S. Army War College, 2015.

Matthews, Ralph. "Lee Street Riot." *Afro-American*, 24 January 1942.

McBride, Alex. "*Plessy vs. Ferguson* (1896)." PBS, 22 November 2013.

McQuire, Phillip. *Taps for a Jim Crow Army.* Lexington: University Press of Kentucky, 2013.

Montgomery, Lymm. E-mails to the author, 2016.

Morehouse, Maggie M. *Fighting in the Jim Crow Army.* Lanham, MD: Rowman & Littlefield, 2011.

Motley Penick, Mary. *The Invisible Soldier.* Detroit: Wayne State University Press, 1974 (1987).

Mountcastle, John W. "Po Valley, 1945." history.army.mil. 3 October 2003.

"Negroes Kept in Camp After Louisiana Riot." *New York Times*, 1942.

Nix, Elizabeth. "The Truman-Dewey Election 65 years ago." history.com. 2013.

Novak, Bruce. E-mails to the author, 2010–2016.

Oberman, Laurie, Ted Talbert, Emery C. King, Coleman A. Young, and John Conyers. *Buffalo Soldiers Wrapped in Steel.* VHS video. WDIV-TV. Detroit: Post Newsweek Stations Michigan, 1989.

Ocampo, Cecilia. E-mails to the author, 2016.

"Olde Tanker." E-mails to the author, 2014.

Opolony, Jim. E-mails to the author, 2016.

Perry, Mark. "Louisiana Maneuvers (1940–41)." historynet.com 2002.

Pershing, John J. "John J. Pershing Quotes." azquotes.com.

Pike, Brett. "Discrimination Against African American Soldiers in World War II." Johns Hopkins University, HIS 4936 Prof. Benowitz. 11 April 2011.

Potter, Lou, William Miles, and Nina Rosenblum. *Liberators.* San Diego: Harcourt, Brace & Jovanovich, 1992.

Powers, Rod. *Basic Training for Dummies.* Hoboken, NJ: John Wiley and Sons, 2011.

Pyor, Mike. "Sixty Years After Integration." *Defense News*, U.S. Department of Defense, 28 July 2008.

"Race During the Great Depression." Library of Congress, 2016.

Ramsberger, Jack F. *Battle History: 473rd United States Infantry, World War II, Italy, 1945.* Ann Arbor: University of Michigan Press, 1945.

Reardon, John. "Nightmare at Rapido River." red bubble.com. January 1995.

Rector, Matthew. E-mails to the author, 2007–2016.

Reichelt, Walter E. *The Ninth Armored Regiment (Remagen) Division, 1942–1945.* Novato, CA: Presidio, 1987.

Reid, Joy-Ann. "Harry Truman and the Desegregation of the Military." *theGrio*, September 2002.

Rubens, Paola. E-mails to the author, 2014–2016.

Russell, Harold E., Jr. *Company I, 366th Infantry.* Pittsburgh: Rose Dog, 2008.

Rutstein, Nathan. "Jane Elliot Speaks on the Psychology of Racism." youtube.com. 15 July 2016.

Schmidt, Vern N. Letters to the author, 2005–2016.

Schultz, Duane. "Rage Over the Rapido." historynet.com. 29 August 2012.

758th Tank Battalion. *After Action Reports and Journals.* College Park, MD: National Archives & Records Administration, 1945.

760th Tank Battalion. *After Action Reports and Journals.* College Park, MD: National Archives & Records Administration, 1945.

Shirey, Orville C. *Americans: The Story of the 442d Combat Team.* Washington, D.C.: Infantry Journal, 1946.

Simpson, William A. "A Tale Untold: The Alexandria, La., Lee Street Riot of Jan. 10, 1942." *Louisiana History* (Spring 1994).

"64th Armor Lineage and Honors." Mihalko-family.com. 17 October 2014.

Smith, H.W. *One More River: The Story of the Eighth Indian Division.* New Delhi: War Department, Government of India, n.d.

Smith, Lloyd D. "WWII: 92nd 'Buffalo' Division in Italy." AfriGeneas Military Research Forum Archive. 27 August 2003.

Smith, Steven D. *The African American Soldier at Fort Huachuca, Arizona, 1892–1946.* Columbia: University of South Carolina Press, 2007.

Special Services. *Welcome Home: Camp Patrick Henry, Va., Hampton Roads Port of Embarkation.* Washington, D.C.: War Department, Army Service Forces, 1944.

Speer, Steve. "Tennessee Maneuvers." CampForrest.com. 12 January 1942.

Spence, Gerry. *How to Argue and Win Every Time.* New York: St. Martin's, 1995.

Stanton, Shelby L. *World War II: Order of Battle.* Bel Air, CA: Galahad, 1984.

Stone, Bob. Interview with Jackie Robinson. *Yank,* 1945.

Stone, M.P.W. "Introduction: A Brief History of the U.S. Army in World War II." Washington, D.C.: Center of Military History, 2003.

SWABS. http://swabuffalosoldiers.org. Fort Huachuca, AZ: South West Association of Buffalo Soldiers, n.d.

Sylvester, Tony. "'Would Rather Be Broke': G.I. SFC Booker Beckwith, Ex-Battler." Fort Knox, KY: Inside the Turret, 1999.

Tanaka, Chester. *Po Valley Campaign.* Novato, CA: Presidio, 1997.

Taylor, Quintard. "A View of the Buffalo Soldiers Through Indigenous Eyes." *The Raven Chronicles,* 1997.

Tennessee Historical Society. *Tennessee Maneuvers.* Knoxville: University of Tennessee Press, 1998.

Thompson, Ben. "Daniel Inouye." badassoftheweek.com. 2009.

_____. "Vernon Baker." badassoftheweek.com. 2009.

Topps, Willie. Interview with the author, 2008, 2009.

Trostorf, Albert and Sheila. Emails to the author, 2006-2008.

Truman, Harry S. *This Day in Truman History.* Harry S. Truman Library & Museum NARA. 25 November 2008.

Truman Presidential Library. *Negro Troops, Italy.* White House File. College Park, MD: National Archives and Records Administration, 1945.

United States Fifth Army. *Race to the Alps: Fifth Army History.* Historical Section, Headquarters Fifth Army. October 1947.

Viviano, Frank. "Almost-Forgotten Heroes." SFGATE.com.

Wales, Jimmy. "Camp Patrick Henry." Wikipedia.

_____. "Directive 5120.36 (1963)." Wikipedia.

_____. "Gothic Line." Wikipedia.

_____. "Gran Sasso Raid." Wikipedia.

_____. "Issac Woodard." Wikipedia.

_____. "Italian Campaign (WWII)." Wikipedia.

_____. "James M. Gavin." Wikipedia.

_____. "Landing Craft Infantry." Wikipedia.

_____. "Landing Craft Tank." Wikipedia.

_____. "Louisiana Maneuvers." Wikipedia.

_____. "Military History of Italy During WWII." Wikipedia.

_____. "Operation Barbarossa." Wikipedia.

_____. "SS *John W. Brown.*" Wikipedia.

Wallace, Robert. *"Buffalo Soldier, 92nd Division: WWII and Korean War."* Madison: Wisconsin Veterans Museum Research Center, 2007.

Weigand, Brandon T. "Index to the General Orders, 92nd Infantry Division." Worthopedia. 2009.

West, Melinda. *Camp Claiborne and Segregation: The Mystery or Not of the Lee Street Riots.* Shreveport: Louisiana State University Press, 2010.

Weston, John S. Recorded conversations with the author, 2008.

White, Larmar, Jr. "Lee Street Riot and the Mystery of the 364th." CenLamar.wordpress.com. 2008–2016.

Wilcox, Elliott. "Quotations for Trial Lawyers." TrialTheater.com. 2005.

Williams, David J., II. *Hit Hard.* New York: Bantam, 1983.

Williams-Smith, Delores. E-mail to the author, 2016.

Wilson, Dale E. "Recipe for Failure." *Journal of Military History* (June 1992).

_____. "758th Was First Black Tank Battalion in WWII." *Inside the Turret,* 29 May 2006.

Wilson, Joe, Jr. *761st Black Panther Tank Battalion in WWII.* Jefferson, NC: McFarland, 1999.

"World War II at Fort Huachuca, 1940–1949." *Huachuca Illustrated,* May 2012.

Wormser, Richard. "Harry S. Truman Supports Civil Rights (1947–1948)." Public Broadcasting Service, February 1999.

Yeide, Harry. *Steel Victory.* New York: Ballantine, 2003.

Index

Index